LOOPTAIL

LOOPTAIL

WHY COMMUNITY, CULTURE, AND KARMA MATTER IN BUSINESS

—◦◦—

BRUCE POON TIP

FOUNDER OF G ADVENTURES

Collins

Published by Collins, an imprint of HarperCollins Publishers Ltd

First published in Canada by Collins in a hardcover edition: 2013
This trade paperback edition: 2014

HarperCollins Publishers Ltd
2 Bloor Street East, 20th Floor
Toronto, Ontario, Canada
M4W 1A8

www.harpercollins.ca

Library and Archives Canada Cataloguing in Publication
information is available upon request.

ISBN 978-1-44342-027-3

Printed and bound in the United States
RRD 9 8 7 6 5 4 3 2

This book is dedicated to everyone who ever wanted to follow their passion or struggled to find their purpose. To the people who didn't fit in because they think differently. To the people who know that freedom lies in being bold and that the secret to happiness is freedom. This is a story of what we are all capable of if we listen to our hearts and follow our destiny. Believe it or not, that's something they didn't teach you in school, but it's inextricably linked to your business and your life.

Contents

Foreword from His Holiness the Dalai Lama   ix

PART I: Influence

Chapter 1:   Happy Birthday to Chi   3

Chapter 2:   Be Something or Be Nothing   19

PART II: Innovation

Chapter 3:   It's How You Get Up That Matters   39

Chapter 4:   All-In   56

Chapter 5:   Pay It Forward   66

PART III: Community

Chapter 6:   Success Doesn't Happen by Accident   99

Chapter 7:   My ESPN Turning Point: 2007   108

PART IV: Culture

Chapter 8:   Leaving Las Vegas   135

Chapter 9:   The Death of HR   154

Chapter 10:   Your Culture Is Your Brand   170

Chapter 11:   If You Don't Love Your Customers, Someone Else Will   192

PART V: Karma

Chapter 12:   Defining the Looptail   219

Chapter 13:   People, Planet, Profit, Passion, and Purpose   228

PART VI: The Looptail

Chapter 14:   The End of the World as We Know It   251

Chapter 15:   The Infinite Loop   262

Appendix   273

Acknowledgments   277

Index   279

THE DALAI LAMA

FOREWORD

The growing gap between the rich and poor is one of our planet's biggest challenges. Successful business people can make a contribution to solving this by creating opportunities for the poor to improve their lot. None of us exists in isolation, we depend on others not only for our success but for our very survival. Therefore it is in our interest to help our fellow human beings and to protect this planet that is our only home in whatever ways we can. In so doing we will not only make this world a better place for ourselves, but ensure that it remains a happy place for our children too.

This book by Bruce Poon Tip encourages me. I met Bruce in May this year. In today's materialistic world where people risk becoming slaves to money, Bruce seems to be one of those entrepreneurs who understand that human dignity, freedom, and genuine well-being are more important than the mere accumulation of wealth. Wealth should serve humanity, and not vice versa. The stark economic inequality between rich and poor is not only morally wrong, but is the source of many practical problems, including war, sectarian violence, and the social tensions created by large-scale economic migration.

When it comes to creating wealth and thereby improving people's material conditions, capitalism is without doubt very effective, but we need to adopt an approach to economic justice which respects the dynamism of capitalism while combining it with a concern for everyone involved. On the one hand we must do all we can to end poverty, on the other, the sooner we accept that riches alone do not bring happiness, and the sooner we learn to live with a sense of modesty, the better off we will be.

Not only in his business, but also in this account of his adventures, Bruce Poon Tip is making an active contribution to creating a more peaceful and happier world, while at the same time creating a model from which others can learn.

July 29, 2013

PART I
INFLUENCE

CHAPTER 1

Happy Birthday to Chi

MARCH 14, 1997. TATOPANI, NEPAL.

Water fell on my face, bringing me back to consciousness. In one sudden movement, I sat straight up, gasping for air. My face was numb. It was so dark, I wasn't sure whether my eyes were open, what time it was, or even where I was. I was disoriented. I heard snoring around me.

My mind quickly came back to reality. I had been sleeping in an overstuffed, down-filled winter jacket I had rented days before. In our hotel, there was no heat and no electricity; I assumed that the moisture on my face that woke me was made up of my own breath freezing in the air. I was in a room with different travelers, some of whom were my friends; the rest were strangers. The darkness surrounding me was absolute; I couldn't see the gigantic fire-engine-red jacket I was wearing, which was so bulky, I couldn't even lie down flat in it.

We were in a hotel along a mountain pass that led through Nepal and into China. It was colder than seasonally normal, and the small town was covered in snow and ice. During the day, we

3

played Yahtzee to pass the time while we waited for our Chinese visas to arrive. The cold front had frozen the roads, making it hard to drive. On the way to Tatopani, our van had slid off the road a few times. We had to get out and push the van, which was ill-suited for the frigid weather, back onto the frozen path. It had seemed funny at times, but that may have just been the high altitude affecting our moods. I didn't realize when planning the trip that we'd be at some of the highest altitudes you can drive in, and for long periods of time. I remember eating lots of candy bars because you lose your appetite when you're in those altitudes, and I'm a bad eater at the best of times. So I was devouring all these Mars and Snickers bars I had brought along in addition to a diet of mostly noodles, and frankly, I thought I was going a bit mental.

The winding roads had become thinner as we went deeper into the unforgiving Himalayan mountain range, and our youthful humor gave way to a more intense concern that we might not make it. By "make it," I don't mean staying alive—I mean making it into Tibet and completing a major personal goal of mine: to have visited one hundred countries before my thirtieth birthday.

But what should have been a time of celebration was overshadowed by worry because of the critical situation that awaited me when I returned home. Over the last year, the Canadian dollar had fallen to all-time lows against the greenback, and the British pound was gaining strength with every passing day. For companies like ours that pay in foreign currency for services such as hotel stays and equipment rentals, a weak Canadian dollar meant that our costs were skyrocketing on a daily basis. We didn't have systems in place to react quickly enough, and in a frighteningly short period of time, our liabilities would surpass our assets—technically we were bankrupt. Unless we found a way to get back on our feet, we'd lose our tour operator license after the next reporting period. I knew when I went home, I'd have to deal with it.

Sitting in my room at night, with the Tibetan border within

reach, I should have enjoyed the feeling of being on the verge of achieving my wildest dreams. Instead, I was playing out different scenarios in my head of what might happen when the trip was over. I was tired. It had been quite a fight to keep the company afloat during the past year; after all our success and growth in previous years, everything had screeched to a halt.

I lay back, realizing I needed to get up and head to the roof to take a pee. (Before we went to bed, the owner of the hotel had informed us that the doors to the outhouse were frozen. If we need to go during the night, she had suggested, we should make our way to the roof to do our business, and aim over the side of the building. I don't remember thinking this was unusual.)

A minute later, I stood on the roof of our hotel, doing my thing while looking out across the Tibetan plateau. Even though it was dark, the stars stretched out in front of me. I had never seen so many of them in my life. It was impossibly quiet, terrifically cold, and breathtakingly beautiful. I was completely alone. I will never forget that night—under the frozen blanket of stars, my life flashed before my eyes, and my mind whirled with thoughts of what felt like the end of my dream. I was exploring and doing what I loved. But I couldn't explode with happiness—my eyes welled up and my head rang with the words of everyone who said the company would never work, that I couldn't do it. I had to acknowledge that maybe they were right. Maybe I really couldn't do it. I was coming to grips with the possibility that this was the end.

I managed to return my focus to the excitement of entering Tibet the next day. The sensation was overwhelming. I had felt a strong connection with the people of Tibet since I was ten. That was when I asked my teacher where Tibet was on the map.

If you're of a certain age, you'll remember those long encyclopedia sets that schools used to have in their libraries. One day a salesman going door to door showed up on our family's doorstep offering one of those magnificent sets of books, housed in a tall wooden bookcase. There was no way as a family we could afford those books, but I believe my mom was riddled with guilt over having to work full time while raising seven children. In a moment of weakness, she agreed to invest in a set and pay for it in installments, thinking that it would be our key to getting good grades. I have no idea where she found the money.

I spent many nights looking up entries about various far-flung places and being amazed at how other people lived. I was particularly fascinated by the story of Tibet and its spiritual leader, who was in exile. The country was under arrest in a way. At school the next day, looking at the map that was right in the middle of the wall in the front of my class, I noticed that Tibet wasn't on it. I asked my teacher—where was Tibet? She told me that there was no such country, and when I tried to explain, she waved me off and told me to sit down.

Nearly twenty years later, here I was on the verge of seeing Tibet up close. The triumphant feeling I craved was clouded with sadness and a sense of failure. I quietly crept into the communal room and lay back on the hard surface where my sleeping bag was. My mind continued to flash back on my life and the events that got me here. Even though I was only twenty-nine, I had launched three businesses before I turned sixteen and was now on my fourth. I had never really failed before. But this time, I thought, I may have run out of luck.

As I lay there in the cold, I wondered whether I should have just called off the trip entirely, even though I knew it wasn't really an option. The tour I was leading was a paid one, which was both bringing in revenue and which could have cost upwards of $30,000 in refunds to our passengers if I had flaked out. I couldn't just cancel it.

In fact, we didn't even have the money to cover it if I had. Just before I left, I came in the office one morning and there were somber looks on everyone's faces. Apparently, all of the paychecks had bounced. We didn't have enough money in the account to cover the handwritten checks, so the bank had frozen our account. As you might imagine, the uncertainty spread through the office like a plague, and soon we experienced our first wave of resignations. It was an emotional moment; up until that point, no one we had hired had ever left the company. We had become a family, fueled by our desire to create something different in the world of exploration, adventure, and travel. But now it seemed like the dream was over.

I knew sleep wasn't in my immediate future. I tried everything I could, including counting yaks, to distract my mind and get some sleep. The next day, which would dawn in a couple of hours, we'd be moving on in our quest to reach the Tibetan border before March 15. We didn't heed the old saying that we should beware the ides of March—we proceeded at our own risk.

The next morning, everyone was quiet. Even though it was technically spring in Tibet, it was bloody cold. As we sat in our puffy jackets, we looked like a Michelin mascot convention. We finished our breakfast, located our things, and packed up the bus to begin what would be the most difficult part of the journey, driving along winding, snow-covered roads in our final push before the border.

On the way out, I spied a bookshelf in the corner where travelers could trade in a book they no longer wanted for a new one. I had just finished *Wired*, the John Belushi biography, and was looking for something else. A book with a blue cover called *Great Ocean* stood out. It was an authorized biography of Tenzin Gyatso, the great fourteenth Dalai Lama, which covered the history of the previous thirteen incarnations of the Dalai Lama, though, according to Tibetan Buddhist beliefs, all fourteen were inhabited by the same soul. I grabbed *Great Ocean* and proceeded to the bus to get ready for the next leg of our journey.

When we started off, our bus had difficulty in the weather. We swerved back and forth up the icy path, making several attempts to gain enough speed to crest over the hill just to make it out of town. Once we got onto those mountain roads, our minds started wandering, and some of us were suffering from altitude sickness.

Along the way, I started reading *Great Ocean*. It tied together all the little bits and pieces about Tibet that I had read over the years. What fascinated me most at the time was that when the Dalai Lama was still in Tibet—he didn't flee until 1959—it was still a spiritual country run by oracles and religious leaders. Tibetans didn't have much in the way of modern technology, like cars, then. In fact, the Dalai Lama received a car as a gift from Henry Ford and reportedly used to crash it all the time on the grounds of one of his palaces because he hadn't actually learned to drive. He fled the country when he was twenty-three. (Coincidentally, that's how old I was when I started my company.) When you think about how young he was and about what was happening around the world in 1959—and yet here was this country guided by spiritual decisions—it's easy to see how a more industrialized country with modern military technology could sweep in and take it over.

Reading *Great Ocean* meant so much more to me than the research I had done before my trip. I've always been into exploring different cultures and how people lived their lives in other parts of the world, but as someone who was motivated by entrepreneurship very early, I was pretty logical and based most of my beliefs around empirical evidence.

Yet I was actually in the country now, or about to be, and felt inspired from reading about the spiritual beliefs of the Tibetan people.

Problem was, the book was something I shouldn't have been carrying with me when we got to the border crossing from Nepal into Tibet, a crossing that turned into much more of an ordeal than I had anticipated.

We approached the border during the daytime. With our group visa, we weren't supposed to be searched at all, but I hadn't counted on the reaction of the Chinese border guards when they saw that I was ethnically Chinese. While the others were allowed to go through unmolested, I was pulled to the side for in-depth questioning.

The guards wanted to know about my name and what part

of China my relatives were from, and I didn't even know! My parents were born in Trinidad, but *their* parents were born in China, which wasn't something the border guards in this not-very-heavily-touristed crossing could fathom. Our guide at the time was left to explain in Chinese that I ran a tour company and that I was there to see the region for tourism-related purposes. There was a surreal aspect to it all. I have a funny picture taken when the Chinese guards asked me to pose for a photo with them because I'm tall and they were all very short. And I remember them asking me, What did I eat? Why did I grow so big? What did my mother feed me?

If I had realized the risks, I probably wouldn't have brought the *Great Ocean* book—which, like anything else to do with the Dalai Lama or Tibetan liberation, was considered contraband there. It was even illegal to have pictures of the Dalai Lama in the country at the time, so I probably shouldn't have bought the stickers either. In Nepal, I had bought twenty round stickers with the Dalai Lama's face on them. I wanted to make sure that the people we met knew that he was still alive. Misinformation of all kinds was then being propagated, some alleging that the Dalai Lama didn't care about his people anymore.

Once they pulled me to the side, I was deathly afraid they were going to go through my bags and discover the book or the stickers. And, of course, they did go through my bags. I remember thinking that if they did find those things, I would be just another casualty and maybe just disappear. I would be arrested and seen as sympathetic to the Dalai Lama and a traitor to China.

But good fortune was with me.

The stickers were in my jacket pocket, while the book was in my day bag; the guards checked my bag but they didn't check my day bag or my jacket.

Whew.

My photo op with the Chinese army completed, we walked across the border and breathed a sigh of relief. When we got to the other side, we came across a group of monks in their

distinctive burgundy robes. As they all came up to me, one of
them said—in perfect English—"Welcome back."

"I've never been here," I replied.

"You've been here before," he said confidently. I followed up
by asking how he learned such flawless English, and he said that
he learned it abroad. That was the end of the conversation.

At the time, it just went over my head. I wasn't buying anything to do with karma or being reborn or reincarnation. "Crazy
monk," I thought to myself.

We spent the next few days traveling across the Tibetan plateau, meeting Tibetan nomadic people and seeing their way of
life. I've been to many countries where people with very little
achieve great happiness. I wouldn't describe what I felt from
the people in Tibet as happiness; they were so oppressed. They
were suspicious and guarded. Some of the younger people even
seemed ashamed of certain aspects of their own culture because
they'd seen so much violence. But the spirituality in the way the
Tibetans carried themselves had a huge impact on me. In the
shacks in the little villages where we stayed, the people would
come out and give us yak butter tea. We witnessed a Tibetan
burial; they don't bury the corpse—they put the body out for
vultures to eat because they believe that the body is just a shell.
There was such a history of living spiritually there, and I don't
think anyone in the modern world understands what that means.

The highlight, for me, was touring the Potala Palace, including the summer palace from which the Dalai Lama fled in 1959.
Having read *Great Ocean* along the way, and seeing where he
had sat and meditated overlooking the palace, it was truly most
meaningful to me.

As I looked around, I saw an old man walking around the
grounds. He was very small, just walking outside near a group
of dilapidated buildings that looked like barns. The man disappeared into one of them, and I followed him. He had a kind face,
but it was worn and hardened like leather, and very dirty; he
had been living in the barn. I found out that he was actually the

stableman who had prepared the horses for the Dalai Lama the night he escaped and went into exile in 1959. He had been living in the barn ever since, waiting for the Dalai Lama to come home. I'll never forget the moment when I reached into my pocket and gave this man one of the stickers. When the stableman saw that the Dalai Lama, who had fled at age twenty-three, was now this old man in the picture, he exploded with emotion, and his tears left streams in the dirt on his face.

I used to say jokingly that the only time I remember myself crying was when I watched *E.T.* But in that moment, as he grabbed my hand, dropped to his knees, and put his forehead against it, I broke down too. For Tibetans like that stableman, their singular passion for life, and the commitment to their beliefs, is on a whole other level. After all the violence and pain these people had witnessed over the years, to still hang onto what they believed in was, for me, an object lesson in what passion really means. People like to tell me I'm so passionate about the work that I do, but compared to people like that, I'm a light-weight. Through our translator, I peppered the stableman with questions about where he slept and what he did while he waited for the Dalai Lama to return. We took a picture together; generally, Tibetans were shy about letting me take their picture, since many believed that taking pictures took away part of their soul. But once I made personal connections with them, they would gradually become more open.

Looking back, I recognize that encountering that stableman was one of those turning points when you meet someone in your life who inspires you so much, yet that person doesn't even realize it. It was a magical experience that just opened my mind.

Before we left Asia, when I would have to go back and figure out a solution for the company, we visited Bhutan.

There's a monastery there called Taktsang on the top of a mountain in Paro. People come from all over the world to make a pilgrimage to the top. Seeing the pilgrims making their way to

Taktsang, I said to my friends, "I want to make this pilgrimage for myself." Others didn't want to hike up there, because once you get up there, you can't actually go into the monastery.

Regardless, I still wanted to go. So, some of us went up. It was a boiling hot day and a tough uphill climb. The trails were unfinished, the terrain was rough, and we had to climb over numerous large rocks. But it was the perfect hike to clear my head.

While we were struggling up the mountain, we would sometimes pause and look back at the pilgrims going to Taktsang. Rather than walk like us, they would prostrate themselves, raising their arms above their heads and falling to the ground, then rising up again and repeating the process, moving forward slowly as they did it. They were much older than us—in fact, most were quite elderly.

After a very long walk, we arrived at the top of the mountain. When we got up there, we started taking pictures, standing outside the big gate. All of a sudden, the door opened, and this young monk stuck his head out and waved us into the monastery. Our guide—whose name was Karma, incidentally—freaked out at this; he was bowing and bowing. It was an honor for him as well. Tentatively, we went inside. I remember feeling like such outsiders, wearing our regular hiking shoes and t-shirts and shorts, and sweating.

Inside, I asked a young monk whether I could take his picture. He said, "If you take a picture of me, it won't come out."

"Ummm, OK," I replied. Crazy monk. "...but can I take the picture?"

And he said sure, so I took a few and went on my way.

Funny. When I returned to Toronto and had my slides developed, I was taken aback. In my photos, you can see his outline, but he is faded; you can't see him.

I couldn't believe that the pictures didn't come out. I hesitate to write about this for fear that people will say I'm crazy. My logical side says that didn't happen. But I've got the pictures. My critical side says that people will think the images were

Photoshopped. So for the record, they are slides, and you can't Photoshop a slide.

Upon my return to Canada, I knew I faced a major crisis with the company. We were bankrupt and demoralized and on the verge of shutting down. Right then, I just knew I had to get help. We didn't have a problem with growth. We just had to get our operations right, in terms of charging the right amount in the various global currencies, employing hedging strategies, and other things successful businesses did that we didn't.

Back then, I was out in the field setting up our sales network and scouting trips, and I didn't know enough about our day-to-day operations. Once I started to investigate them, I quickly realized that I would have to get rid of most of the people who were presently running things and to start employing new people. Everything was a mess, and it was up to me to pick up the pieces of a side of the business I really didn't even know.

But letting people go is extremely painful. To say some people didn't take it well is a major understatement—when I closed down some of our remote offices, I actually started getting death threats. Yet these cuts had to be done if the company had any chance of succeeding. And, yes, it was rough.

After I cleaned house and invested in a few good people whom I brought to Toronto to help me dig us out, we spent months frantically juggling payments and calling operators to ask them to extend terms. It was a tough time for everyone, but the new group was committed to making things right, and those who had left made room for others who were ready for our challenges.

I had recommitted to the business, but I also knew that something had changed in me. In one sense, what I had experienced in Tibet and Bhutan were the same feelings I would have in Africa, or when I attended a religious ceremony in Borneo. But as I reflected on what I had seen, I started to understand that we have a purpose and that everyone has a place in the universe; you have to find what that place is. And I really believe that what

I'm doing—running this company—is my place. This is where I was meant to be.

When I started this company in 1990 with a couple of credit cards, I was living in a garage apartment and had a vision. I never thought it would become what it has. I wasn't given the tools from my upbringing to think that big.

Our revenue has grown by an average of 30 percent every year since 1990, and in most years our growth rate has been closer to 40 or 50 percent. During the post-financial-crisis recession in 2008, G Adventures grew by 42 percent while our competitors downsized by as much as 40 percent. And in over twenty years since its start, G Adventures is now the envy of other businesses, large and small, that want to know the secret to our success. Schools like Harvard, Oxford, and the London School of Economics regularly ask me to speak. So do companies like Apple and Google. They've both asked me to speak to their employees, but never about travel—rather, it's about how we transcend our product, in terms of giving the best customer service and changing people's lives. Some firms have been so impressed by our business model that they have made spectacular offers for the company. It's our brand and unorthodox business model—one that has raised eyebrows around the world—they want, not just another travel company. We get frequent requests from individuals and groups to visit Base Camp, our head office in Toronto, and people can come and take a tour.

Some people scoff at the idea that what worked for us can work for other companies because we're an adventure travel company. But our challenges aren't unique to the travel industry. In the early 1990s, as we were realizing the limitations of just being a North American company and began thinking about exporting our services to customers in other countries, I recognized that we had to put together a compelling brand promise if we were going to get someone in Denmark to book an African safari with a Canadian company. We had to be unique and innovative because there were a thousand travel companies in Germany that sold African safaris. Our culture would have to become our brand, and we'd have to be much more than just a travel company. At the time, that wasn't something that happened every day; but in the globalized marketplace of 2013, transcending cultural barriers is a necessity for any brand, whether they sell travel or breakfast cereal.

Today, 70 percent of our business comes from outside of North America, which is extraordinary, but it only works because we built a brand promise that was strong enough to withstand challenges from local, conventional-travel competitors. Our original mandate was to create innovative ways of showing people the world. We did that by building what we call a *sustainable* or *responsible* tourism model, with tours that didn't just exploit the communities and the resources of the countries where we ran our trips. But even that, over time, would evolve into what we have become today, as we transcended our industry and began to engage our customers to a higher purpose. There is a social revolution taking place, and I know that the only brands that will matter in the future are the ones that will make people's lives better.

When I started G Adventures, tour operators were doing everything in their power to give travelers the comforts of home by creating as close to a typical Western environment as possible. From day one, my belief was that if you want the comforts of home, you should stay home! It appeared to me that the entire tourism industry in 1990 was off-kilter. There seemed to be a race in the cruise industry to see who could build the biggest ship. Resorts had become walled-in compounds where they were going to give you everything on the grounds, so you would never consider wandering outside the walls. They even made it difficult for you to find the exit! Ten years ago, one in five people taking a package holiday chose all-inclusives; today it's 75 percent—and growing. According to the United Nations Environment Programme (UNEP), out of every hundred dollars spent on vacation by a tourist from a developed country, only five dollars stays in the destination's economy. This is a huge problem, but it was my opportunity.

I just didn't get the appeal of these kinds of trips, so as G Adventures began, I decided to do things differently from the status quo of the time. Soon, we were reimagining what a tour could be and how it could interact with the country we were sending people to—using services provided by community members, using modest-size hotels and making sure they were locally owned. Today these seem like obvious things for a company like ours to be interested in, but when we started in 1990 the idea of sustainable or responsible travel wasn't really something people talked about.

Over the years as we became more invested in our community projects, I began to realize that what I was doing was more of a calling than a job; now I realized that what we needed to become was a *movement*.

That movement, which I describe as the Looptail, centers around one of the teachings of the Dalai Lama: "Our purpose in life is achieving happiness." He wasn't referring to a momentary kind of pleasure, but a deeper sense of happiness. In my view, what keeps many of us from achieving that happiness is the flawed, outdated way we try to keep our work separate from our lives.

Work has always been about survival. From the dawn of civilization, when we worked the land for food and resources to keep us and our families alive, to the industrial revolution when families would be torn apart by members relocating wherever the work was. But today we have more choices than our ancestors did, and what I've observed is that the things that matter to us about our work and the things that we care about in our lives are often much more similar than you might realize.

I'm not saying that we should all become workaholics and give up our lives outside the office, but treating work as a place where we merely show up at from nine to five, and our time away from the office as our real life where we pursue our dreams, is never going to deliver sustained happiness. We need to integrate our work lives and our real, inner lives, and focus ourselves toward a higher purpose. The term *integration* is linked to integrity and having all sections of our lives integrated into one common purpose.

When I talk about engaging your people and transcending your product, it's not just something that will help your business. The only way to really transcend your product or what you do is to recognize that work has to be about more than work—it has to be about something greater. By transcending the idea of work being just the daily grind, and by engaging the community around you—both customers and employees—to pursue a higher purpose, the Looptail can truly work.

In sum, I believe that if businesses want to be both sustainable and successful, they have to infuse their organizations with *passion* and *purpose*, as a way to engage the people *inside* the business, which will in turn engage people outside of it. Today, our customers are as amazed by our business model and what we stand for as they are by the quality of our tours. These goals should be at the heart of every business model and are relevant to every industry.

It's about "paying it forward"—by finding your purpose, and infusing your work and your life with it, you create the conditions for your own success. When you pay it forward with the Looptail, it comes back to you in the form of happiness.

People always ask entrepreneurs why we do what we do, and few of us are shy about sharing our theories. Most of the time, you'll hear canned answers like "do what you love" or "follow your passion," and I always wonder whether they help anyone.

I'm happy to discuss my company and my work, but when it comes to telling my own story, I'm just not interested. The thought of writing a business book would come to me in random places like standing in a customs line or an elevator somewhere, and I would always shake my head at the prospect of having to write about myself. But as I started to put pen to paper, I realized I do have something to say.

It took me a long time to come around to writing about myself because I dreaded the thought, and it was a process to get to this point. This is not a biography. That said, G Adventures' history is, up to a certain point, my history. This book is about how a company's business model and company culture can change the world and change people's lives. My only motivation is to inspire people, and I hope through my experiences to impact how people look at traditional business and to show how they can become part of the modern social revolution. Though it took me a while to realize that what I had to say was relevant—and to stop seeing myself through the eyes of an immigrant kid who never had the chance to dream—after much debate I thought it was time to share my vision of how sustainability can be linked to a business becoming a force for good in our world, how it can grow more successful by redefining and expanding our spectrum of how we view success. I'll try to keep it interesting, too.

CHAPTER 2

Be Something or Be Nothing

I wasn't meant to be anything.

Imagine for a minute if you grew up with every teacher looking at you with a gaze that said you were never going to amount to anything. If you got through life staying out of trouble, that would be a good outcome.

My parents moved our family from Trinidad to Calgary on a wing and a prayer—we were a family of nine. My folks were ill-prepared for what lay ahead of them; they had never lived in a place where they experienced racism. We had very little and struggled to make a life in a new country that never let us forget we were foreigners. I don't think my parents had really researched where they were going either, because it was hard enough moving from an island located on the equator to a country with a harsh, frigid climate. My dad always claimed that he hadn't even owned a pair of long pants until he attended his first funeral.

I was always struck by my mother's sheer will and determination; she fought to give her children the opportunity to be anything we wanted to be. But the pressure of the financial and cultural burdens on such a large family, under such conditions, is enormous. Many families disintegrate into the social welfare system, buckling under the pressure, with the kids ending up in foster care. That stigma was on my shoulders, and I always felt that I was held to a lower standard because of my "situation."

The kids were merciless, of course. Living in Calgary in the late sixties, there wasn't a single other nonwhite kid on my street. I remember being chased and hearing slurs that were normally saved for First Nations people. My parents, who were always trying to improve our lives, moved us into a new neighborhood in a better part of town. To me, "better" just meant there were fewer visible minorities and that I'd stand out even more. In my first week in the fourth grade, I was jumped from behind by a group of boys who had been calling me names throughout the day. My short walk home became a fight for survival. We tumbled along the school soccer field as I gasped, "Leave me alone." I remember being held down by two boys and looking up to see the growing crowd of kids pumping their fists in the air, chanting for me to go home. This would happen two more times before the first year in our "better" neighborhood ended. By the third time, I got tougher and actually fought back. I was beating the crap out of the kid who jumped me until his friends joined in. I was nine years old.

Some teachers were more on the sympathetic side—they would treat you like you had special needs, or nominate you as the class refugee and would make a point of telling other kids to be easy on you because you had "struggles at home." They used to do that whether you had troubles or not—for all they knew, we were as happy as the Partridge family. I can still see and feel the looks on teachers' faces as they did as little as possible to help: They figured you were just moments away from becoming a statistic, one of the many immigrant families that would just implode and disappear under the pressure of integration. They would snicker at the fact that there are seven kids in our family, and they would make disparaging comments about what our religion must be and that my parents must not have believed in birth control.

Sure, there were teachers who were different and who, I remember, shaped my young mind at the time. But for the majority of my early life, I sat in the back of the classroom, simply ignored.

One fateful day in the sixth grade, I put my hand up to ask my teacher a question. When the answer didn't resolve my confusion, I put my hand up again to ask her to clarify, because I still didn't get it. The teacher appeared angry and said, "Bruce, can I see you outside in the hallway, please?"

When we stepped out of the classroom, she asked, "Bruce, where are you from?"

"Well, I was born in Trinidad," I replied, "but I am from here now."

Looking at me with a perplexed expression, she said, "Well, what language do you speak at home?"

"Uummm, English," I told her, feeling taken off guard by the question.

"It must be difficult for you that you cannot communicate with your parents, isn't it?"

I was shocked. As I stood there pondering my reply, she cut me off.

"Listen, Bruce, I cannot have you in my class distracting everyone because you can't understand and learn at the same speed as everyone else. I think we need to speak to the guidance counselor about getting you help."

I was still taken aback at what I was hearing. She continued. "I think you should go down to the office and sit and wait for me there. After class, I will come down and we will get you some special testing to see if we can get you some help."

After all that, I had to speak up. "I don't think I am that much of a distraction, I was just asking a few questions," I pleaded. "Actually, I never ask questions, but lately I have been trying to speak up because Mr. Mason told me that I have to use my voice more if I don't understand. I really don't think I was distracting anyone."

She put her hand on my head and replied, "Of course you don't see it. I will see you after class," and with that, she turned on her heel, opened the door, and went back into class, leaving me standing in the hallway alone.

I was crushed. I didn't know what to do. I was embarrassed at the thought of going to the office because I didn't know what to tell them about why I was there. I remember walking past the office four or five times, pretending I was just passing by to go to get a drink of water. At one point, I went into the boys' locker room near the gym, sat on a bench with my face in hands, and just cried.

After a while, the assistant principal discovered me in there and said that they were expecting me in the office. "I was just going to the washroom first," I said, looking forward and trying to not let him see the fact that my eyes were red. "I will be there in a minute," I told him.

"So, Bruce," the assistant principal began as we sat in his office, "do you want to tell me what happened today?"

My voice cracked as I blurted, "I just thought I was asking a question because I didn't understand, and she said I was being a distraction."

"Well, you must have done more than that. You are obviously upset and you wouldn't have been sent to see me if you just asked a question."

At that point, I was mumbling so much, the assistant principal had to ask me to repeat myself. I sat there and began to visibly shake; I crossed my arms over my chest as I fought to hold myself still.

"Bruce, are you going to answer me?" he asked several times.

Finally, I remember thinking that I was tired of being invisible. I took a deep breath and spoke. "My teacher doesn't think I speak English. She told me that I don't speak English and that it must be difficult for me because I cannot communicate with my parents at home. She said that because I can't speak English,

I can't learn as fast as everyone else in the class and that I was holding the class back with my questions."

By then, I was in a rage.

"But I do speak English! My parents speak English. It's the only language we know. We come from Trinidad and the only language that is spoken there is English. I do not know another language. I don't know what I did wrong. I never ask questions in class and I am not a distraction. I'm not! Mr. Mason told me that I have to use my voice and that I have to speak up and that is all that I did. I don't know why I am here. I didn't do anything!"

Soon after, my teacher requested that our guidance counselors give me special needs tests, which they did. But I was never moved out of my regular classes. I never heard the results of the tests, and nothing untoward ever happened. I was terrified that it would, though. For the rest of the school year, I lived in fear that, at any time, without warning, a teacher would pull me aside and tell me I was leaving. Every time I was in class and another teacher or the principal would walk in, my heart would expand in my chest, and I would think they were coming to get me. Whenever I would make eye contact with a teacher, I would think, "Did they see my results?" It was a daily source of terror.

From a very early age, my siblings and I knew that our parents came to Canada so we could have the chance to be something. It was my choice; I could either get into trouble, disappear into society, or I could change the world. I know it sounds a bit extreme, but that's how I thought and how I still think today. My parents could only give me the playing field; it was up to me to win the game.

I was a persistent kid (some might say stubborn), but that drive served me well when I embarked on my first adventures as an entrepreneur. From the age of ten, I wanted my own paper route so badly. I thought it was the coolest job and did everything I could to get it, but no luck—the rule was, you had to be twelve to become a paperboy. That two-year wait was downright painful. I cultivated relationships with older kids who had routes; if they were sick or on holiday, I'd happily take over, even though they'd only pay me five dollars for roughly two hours of seriously hard labor. At the time I thought five dollars was an enormous sum and that the job was easy money.

Finally, the longest wait ended. I turned twelve and landed my first route. Of course, within days, I had a new plan. I found out the boundaries of the distribution districts that area managers divided the city into and applied for routes in different districts. I ended up with two routes and later would add a third. Next, I contracted out the delivery to kids who—like me a few weeks back—couldn't get their own route until they turned twelve. The opportunity seemed clear as day to me. In fact, I just assumed everyone was doing it.

My first business worked out remarkably well. The kids delivered the papers; I collected payment from the houses, attended the area manager meetings, and paid the delivery kids a third of the money I made from their routes. I supplied a quality service with my paper routes that made both my customers and my workers happy, though the Canadian government probably wouldn't have been thrilled with my flouting their child labor laws. (Though, is it illegal for a child to hire another child?)

Still, it was a great little business, and in retrospect, I learned a lot. It was my first time making ledgers and balance sheets. I also had to manage people, making sure the papers were delivered on time and that kids weren't walking across people's lawns or throwing their papers on the ground. I remember one kid was three quarters of the way through his route when he realized he was going to be late for dinner, so he just dumped the remaining third of his newspapers in a trash bin and went home. It was the first time I ever had to fire someone. There were many late nights in the middle of winter when, after getting a call from the newspaper, I would trudge up people's walkways at around 9 p.m. to deliver the missing papers and apologize to the angry customers inside each house.

The lessons I learned are still true: You're only as good as the people around you; sometimes you need to make tough decisions; and when you're in business, you need to take responsibility and be accountable.

My next business was a bit more complicated. (As I look back, I am starting to agree with popular opinion—I really was a strange child.) I was a bit of a loner growing up. I often felt like an island unto myself because I never really fit in, and as a result, I often identified with animals. I've always loved animals and have even campaigned against the training of animals for entertainment purposes such as in circuses and at places like SeaWorld.

I used to dream of having my own pet one day, but I knew it wasn't an option. We were a family of nine living in a small house, and we had only just moved into that house after having spent our first seven years in Canada in a place that was even more cramped, so the idea of having any kind of pet was a fantasy that I kept to myself, for the most part. Every weekend when I got a spare copy of the newspaper, I would take the classified section and comb through the pet section, reading rows of ads by people selling everything from exotic lizards to hairless cats. Sometimes I would call the phone numbers and ask questions about what the animals were like. I was pretending to be a potential buyer, but really I was only living vicariously through these people who actually raised animals. I also used to browse through books about how to care for animals when I would go to pet stores, and was generally interested in how someone would care for their pets if they were lucky enough to have one. Looking back, it was a passion of mine and it was the first time I would try to figure out a way to turn my passion into a way of making money.

I noticed through this process that kids liked to keep rabbits as pets, but that they would always grow too big and the kids would have to get rid of them. The cute, fluffy bunnies they brought home from the pet store eventually grew up to be fat, ugly, double-chinned creatures that looked more like livestock. Then one day I read an article about a new breed of rabbit called the Dutch Dwarf. Because the adult Dutch Dwarves remained small, they solved the big-bunny problem. I hadn't seen them in any pet stores in Calgary yet. That was my window of opportunity.

Later on, I read another newspaper story about a woman named Ms. Swan who had just caused a bit of a sensation when she showed a Dutch Dwarf at a local show put on by 4-H, a community organization that gives farmers the opportunity to show off and compete with the livestock they raise. Straight away, I set out to find this Ms. Swan. I decided to call the 4-H club to try and get any information I could. Bingo. After they told me she lived in Priddis, a farm community twenty-five miles south of Calgary, within the hour I had Ms. Swan on the phone telling me about her prize animals. I told her about my interest in the Dutch Dwarf and spoke to her numerous times on the phone over the next couple of weeks as we became very friendly. She agreed to meet me if I could get out to Priddis to see her. As Calgary has grown larger, Priddis doesn't seem so far away, but at the time it might as well have been another country.

I was planning to ride my bike out there and camp out overnight, but I still had to get past my parents with some story. Eventually I broke down and told my mom about my real plan, and seeing the passion in my eyes, she told me in a sullen voice that she would take me. I know her first thought was how much it would cost to cover the gasoline.

So, the next weekend, we piled into the car and set off for Priddis. By this point I had become quite friendly with Ms. Swan over the phone, so when we pulled up to her house, I think we were both quite alarmed at what each of us looked like in person. But after the initial shock, we bonded immediately and she took me back to the farm to show me her rabbits.

The farm itself was a junkyard. But regardless, I fell in love with the Dutch Dwarf rabbits right away and began chatting with Ms. Swan about where they came from. I had started to negotiate how I could get a pair, even though I didn't have permission to bring a pet into our already-crowded home. Next, I started to give my mom the hard sell, as I showed her that rabbits could live outdoors all year long. The breeding cages were small, and I would only need to put two in our backyard. I'm sure I put my mom on the spot, but after I outlined my idea of being able to start a business selling them to pet stores, she relented.

Before we left, Ms. Swan agreed to arrange to import two Dutch Dwarf rabbits and to sell me two outdoor cages that sat on stilts so the rabbits could handle our severe winters. They weren't cheap, either. It cost me most of the money I had earned from my paper routes. In fact, I had to take over the paper route myself again to earn more money while I waited the eight weeks before the rabbits arrived.

I immediately began making my first business contacts with pet stores and drug stores (which also used to sell pets in those days). Learning how to market this unknown product made me realize how storytelling is an important part of entrepreneurship. I was introducing something that the buyers at these stores would not have seen, so it was important to create a narrative. Some of the greatest leaders in the world are also the greatest storytellers, and that's not a coincidence. I learned early how important this was when introducing a new, different idea.

Fortunately, all of them were keen to sell this new breed of miniature rabbit. My two rabbits arrived, and they were beautiful. I had a black-and-white one I named Tipper, and a brown-and-white female I named Daisy. And, from there, my second business was born.

In all honesty, I had only limited success with the rabbit business. But while it wasn't a huge enterprise, it was the first time I made contact with resellers, e.g., the pet stores. I was limited in the space I had—my parents' backyard—so the company wasn't really scalable, but the experience was fantastic and kept stoking my interest in business at an early age.

Funny story: I have never been into Facebook. But one day my marketing team was doing a promotion and registered my name on Facebook for the purposes of the contest. Within an hour, I received a handful of "likes" from various people who had sat behind me in math class or played soccer on a team with me when I was ten. Then a message came through saying, "Do you remember me? You sold me a rabbit that turned out to be full of piss and vinegar. It was the worst pet ever!" Suffice it to say that I don't have a Facebook profile anymore.

The opportunity to start my third business came when I was accepted by Junior Achievement (JA) into their Company Program, in which kids would start their own businesses with the help of teachers and local businessmen.

At that age, I was seen as a bit of a misfit, because I wanted to start a business. That's not a normal kid-thing to do. Other kids were going to ponds and catching frogs, or going fishing, while I was breeding rabbits and subcontracting newspaper delivery. Still, I hesitated over the decision. I was intimidated.

When I eventually decided to join JA, it didn't take long for me to realize I had made the right choice. It was the first time I met what I thought were real entrepreneurs, and to me, they were celebrities—I could hardly believe that people who started businesses would actually spend time with us and tell us about their experiences. In reality, none of them were actually entrepreneurs; they had jobs like being bank managers and accountants. But I was still in awe. It was the first time that I talked to people who saw things the same way that I did.

Once the program got started, I began to notice that I was being accepted, and even commended, for my thinking. My ideas were considered relevant. After a while, it seemed I had even been singled out as a leader. It was the first time in my life that I wasn't seen as the kid who was afraid to speak up or draw attention to himself. I had become vocal and even opinionated. This was a new world for me.

After a lot of researching, I decided that my JA company was going to make weather worms. The weather worm is a knitted bookmark made of temperature-sensitive yarn that turned pink when it was hot and blue when it was cold. Thanks to my rabbit business, I already had contacts at local drugstores to whom I could go and pitch my new product. I remember how amazed the JA volunteer mentors were that I was able to walk into the stores, talk to the owners, and come back with a deal to sell the weather worm on their cashiers' counters. While other students were making products to sell in our schools to other students and their families, I thought that was too limiting. I wanted to start a *real* business, and now I had my chance to do it. It felt right. I ran with it.

Pretty soon, the weather worm was a huge success, and I had many more orders than I could fill. They were sold on drugstore counters for $1; I had kids in the neighborhood knitting them for 25 cents each and I sold them to the drugstore for 60 cents each. I had some hard lessons to learn, though.

My first and most important lesson was in supply and demand. I hadn't done enough research on how long it would take to make a single weather worm. As I quickly found out, it took about half an hour, which meant my workers could only make 50 cents an hour. I had a hard time attracting labor—in those days babysitting was $1 per hour. I either had to find a faster way to get my products made or raise prices. I know, it sounds like the early stages of a sweatshop, but remember—I was only fifteen!

Ultimately, I couldn't keep making the weather worm, but I still wanted to hang onto the retail space, so I had to find something else—quickly. So I decided to start making just regular bookmarks on thick construction paper. I went back to our wonderful encyclopedia set, looked up a few motivational quotes and stenciled them onto the bookmarks. It took ages to make one at first, until I found a stamp set that would let you arrange letters in a clamp and then stamp as many copies as you wanted.

Remembering my earlier lesson about storytelling, I also changed the marketing angle on the containers on the drugstore countertops. This time I decided to sell the fact that by buying one of these you were supporting a youth entrepreneurial project. I mentioned that they were handmade and still sold them for a dollar. To my surprise, with the new product and repositioning, sales actually went *up*. This was my first experience with transcending my product and engaging customers to a higher purpose. My customers were now engaging with a purpose to support youth enterprise, and it would trigger an emotional response because you were giving back to your community, whether you needed a bookmark or not.

I sold about five thousand bookmarks and won an award from Junior Achievement. More importantly, I knew what I wanted to do, though it would take a couple of brushes with the world of working for somebody else before I got up the courage to strike out on my own.

Many years later, I was asking why our sales out of the United Kingdom were looking soft, and I was told that many people there weren't traveling because it was the queen of England's Diamond Jubilee that year (2012). It had been sixty years since Her Majesty Queen Elizabeth II's ascension to the throne, and people across England (and the world) were celebrating all year. To honor the occasion, a small number of special Queen's Jubilee medals of honor were issued to recognize people for their positive impact on the world. In order to find the most worthy recipients, these medals were to be given out by various organizations who had had positive impact in their communities. I was humbled and surprised to be contacted by Junior Achievement (JA), the same organization that took an eager fourteen-year-old all those years ago and showed him that his thoughts and ideas really mattered. The president of JA had nominated me and wanted to present me with one of Her Majesty's medals along with a certificate signed by Queen Elizabeth II herself. I was touched beyond words and felt especially proud to accept the honor from an organization that took a chance on me at an early age.

At sixteen, I got a summer job at Denny's working the night shift. I was excited to get my first real job, not to mention that it paid more than I had ever earned before. I was hoping to impress them with my work ethic so that I would get better hours and be able to continue working while going to school. I think I may have even lied about my age, because I can't imagine they would have let a sixteen-year-old work the graveyard shift at a diner.

On the night shift, I got to meet a whole new group of people that I had never encountered before: drunks. It was a major eye opener. I had never seen either of my parents drink alcohol, yet there I was being yelled at by intoxicated beasts demanding to be fed, if they hadn't already passed out on the table. There was also a group of people who would regularly try to leave without paying—dine-and-dash.

Anyway, at around 4 a.m., after the crowd had left and the place died down, we were supposed to scrub the restaurant from top to bottom. That was the role of the night shift, to clean everything for the breakfast rush in the morning. I had been given my list of duties, and I was eager to do them.

In my second week, I met Stephanie. Stephanie was a hardened veteran at Denny's. She had been there for more than a decade and was the kind of server that the rough night crowd enjoyed having around—tough, sassy, and farm-girl attractive. The night I was introduced to Stephanie, she came up to me after the crowd left and gave me her list of duties, telling me to let her know when I was done so she could come by and check my work. I wasn't sure at first what she was getting at. As her busboy, she said, I was supposed to cover her duties or I would not be given my share of the evening's tips.

I argued back, saying that this was my second week and had been tipped even though I didn't do anyone else's work during my first week and that I had my own list of duties to do.

I will never forget her exact words.

"Listen, Chink, I have been here a lot longer than you and know how things work around here. So if you want to be here for a *third* week, you'd better get moving."

"You are not my boss," I replied, though I was shaking. I was hired by Jason; he had given me specific instructions on what I was supposed to do, and that is what I was going to do.

"You obviously don't want to work here anymore," she shot back.

"I am doing a good job here, and I have been doing fine with the other waiters," I said.

Then she said what I had heard before as a kid growing up, but this time it just hit me harder. "What are you anyway, a wagon burner or a chink? I can't tell. Either way, you won't be here tomorrow."

"Fuck you," I said as I turned, took a deep breath, and walked off to earn my $5 an hour. I was shaking for the rest of the night, watching in terror as Stephanie made her way around to the various staff as well as the regulars, talking about me and pointing and laughing. I kept quiet; I just wanted the night to be over.

The next day at work, as I walked to the staff area behind the kitchen, I was met at the door by Stephanie and Jason.

Jason asked me to apologize to Stephanie for my comments. I couldn't do that, I told him, and said that I would like to talk to him privately about the events of last night. He said I would have to apologize or else I was fired; I replied that I felt I was owed an apology as I had done only what he told me to do.

"Well then," Jason said, looking me in the eye, "you're fired." At first, I stood there shell-shocked, but then I had to gather my things and leave. With the eyes of the whole restaurant silently judging me, I walked out, feeling so angry I could have broken a window. When I think back, it was a mixture of being ashamed and embarrassed, with a healthy serving of shock. Because of how I was brought up, I was more concerned about embarrassing my family, and I knew I couldn't bring myself to tell them what happened.

Instead, I went into the McDonald's across the street, trying to think about what I was going to tell my family. While I was there passing time, I asked for a job application and filled it out on the spot. By chance, the team leader happened to be there and said I could come back the next day for an interview. I did, and got the job. Problem solved.

I was in training for the first two days. On the second day, things went sideways. My trainer was a bully and called me a "Paki" while I was trying to learn the ropes. That's fine with me, I thought; I just want to work. I can handle kids like this. Not a problem.

Later that same day, the trainer asked me to wear a hairnet. I knew that the training manual said hair had to be certain length to wear a hairnet, and my hair wasn't that long, and furthermore we were not training in the restaurant so I didn't need one. I asked him why I should wear it.

"Just put it on, Paki," he said, laughing as if he was just saying it jokingly. To him, this had become my nickname. I wasn't sure if he thought he was saying anything offensive. The way he laughed caused the other people in training to laugh, too, so I accepted it.

"Why aren't you wearing one? Obviously, your hair is longer than mine," I replied.

I don't really remember what happened from there or the exact words that were exchanged—all I know is, the next day I was called by the manager and was fired. I was asked to stay home and not come in again. They would send me a check for the pay that I was owed for the two days I was in training.

I was gutted. I remember feeling like I was a failure and that I had to work harder and shut my mouth. That was always my way—I have to work harder.

I was also embarrassed and kept the shame to myself. My parents would never understand, I thought; I already stood out among their seven children as being the strange one. They didn't know what to do with me, really. There was always so much going on in the house, what with seven children under foot, that I don't even remember whether my folks knew what happened. At times like those, I would just go quiet and disappear.

Those two work experiences in two weeks taught me lessons

I have applied to my business life today. I would learn to accept intolerance or prejudice as a part of life. I would do the opposite and celebrate uniqueness, but it also taught me to recognize the value of individuals who might be individually different but collectively could achieve extraordinary things.

As a family, we couldn't afford to travel a lot. As I sat at home on many nights, reading our encyclopedia set, my mind would wander and I would imagine what it would be like to visit foreign lands. I knew if I ever wanted to do that, I would have to make it happen, so one day I hatched a plan. I would take the money I had saved from my businesses and fly myself and my brother to Jamaica to visit our family there. I decided I would ask to bring my brother along because I thought the chances of my mom letting me go would be better if I wasn't going to travel alone. Because it would be so much better for a fourteen-year-old to travel without an adult if his eleven-year-old brother came along with him, right?

I laid out the plan to my mom. I would pay for the trip, I said, and I had found in the course of my research that the airline had a service called Lovebird Care that would monitor us on the flight. I told her all this in a certain way that said I was going, and my mom just looked up and said, "Yes." So off I went to Jamaica on my first solo trip—well, with my brother in tow, but I considered it my first solo trip—and it was sweet. The feeling of heading off into the unknown, the excitement and the adventure of it, convinced me that I had found my next passion. Everything else that was happening around me was left behind as I jetted away to freedom. I worked hard and made it happen for myself, on my own terms.

I started high school that year, and one of the first orders of business was to see the guidance counselor. After taking a bunch of tests and questionnaires, I sat down with the counselor himself, and I will never forget what he told me. Because I loved animals and was "outdoorsy," he said that I should become a forest ranger. Seriously! At the time I even thought that would be a cool idea.

When I finished high school, I chose to start taking business courses at college. But not long after the first two courses, I knew that business school wasn't the right fit for me. I didn't relate to any of the thinking. At the time, they were just teaching me to get a job with IBM, and I didn't want that. I thought school was about how I was going to free my mind; instead, they were teaching me how to conform and to go work for someone else. Remember, my only experiences working for someone else up to that point hadn't been great.

To be fair, business programs have changed a lot since the eighties. The whole Silicon Valley and dot-com millionaires movement hadn't happened yet. There were no twentysomething billionaires like Facebook's Mark Zuckerberg. You were heavily recruited by huge firms like Procter & Gamble and Nabisco, and if you landed a job at one of those companies, you were a success. Personally, I couldn't imagine anything more horrible. So I switched to a college that had a tourism program, and in short order decided "This is it, this is what I want to do." I dreamed again of being free and seeing foreign lands. Maybe one day I'd even get a chance to see Tibet.

PART II
INNOVATION

CHAPTER 3

It's How You Get Up
That Matters

After working my way through school as a waiter and bartender, and graduating with honors, I felt that it was time to map out my first real adventure. I decided to go traveling around Asia for a few weeks. It was 1989; there was no internet to research travel destinations on. You either bought guidebooks, went to the library, or approached a travel agent who would try to sell you a cruise, resort, or coach-tour holiday.

As I began to scrutinize the travel industry through the eyes of a tourism-program graduate, I observed that there were really only two options for prospective travelers: packaged bus tours that took tourists from their Western-owned hotels to see the sights in air-conditioned buses, or backpacking, which wasn't really for me. For one thing, it takes a lot of time to back-pack; you have to devote months and months to do it right. I remember friends trying to convince me to join them on these coming-of-age backpacking trips through Europe, but I always thought that I just couldn't spare all that time. The clock was ticking—I needed to get on with my life.

My objection to generic tours, meanwhile, became a political one. The idea that Western tourists would come to developing countries only to spend their time in a swank bus, with a Western tour guide, staying in Western-owned hotels, and driving around to "see the country" offended me. These operators were doing everything in their power to create a Western environment, which to me defeats the entire purpose of going to another country in the first place.

Worst of all, when these travelers would come back and tell their friends that they had seen Thailand or experienced Peru, that just made me crazy. They didn't see anything! And by saying they did, they were insulting the one thing that makes any country great—that country's people.

It seemed to me that the entire tourism industry was just ass-backwards. The resorts back then were getting bigger and more "inclusive." These resorts were also developing shopping plazas on the grounds, so you didn't have to even interact with local citizens to do some shopping and contribute something to the local economy. Some resorts even made it difficult for you to find an exit, warning, in effect, that the "natives were restless." Being from the Caribbean and having a different perspective than the average tourist, I could see why the natives might be a little restless: local people weren't benefiting in any way from tourists being there. Instead, the locals watched foreign companies use up massive amounts of natural resources to build their fortresses, while the people living on the other side of the walls in some areas had no access to clean drinking water—not to mention their own coastal beaches.

Now, I don't want to come down too hard on these parts of the travel industry or those who enjoy traveling this way. I understand the desire to recharge, to take a quick trip to the beach and to just sleep and have everything done for you. What troubles me is how ingrained this philosophy has become in our society—how your yearly holiday to the Caribbean has become a status symbol. Many of us are brought up to view this as a sign of success. We are all born with a natural curiosity to be explorers or travelers, but society pressures us to be tourists. Tourists are made, not born.

My trip to Asia confirmed what I had already started thinking—that there was room in the industry for a travel company offering package tours using local services—giving visitors a chance to experience a real flavor of their destination, rather than to just stroll around a few notable landmarks. Who wants to see, say, the ancient temples of Angkor Wat in Cambodia without interacting with actual flesh-and-blood Cambodians or seeing how they live today? There was a gap in the market between the mainstream traveler and the backpacker. Realizing this was my "Eureka!" moment. I saw that group travel had the stigma of being restrictive and overscheduled. I started to think that group travel could be far less restrictive and that we could market that type of travel: touring with like-minded people and with a leader could provide the freedom of independent travel with the security of a group.

Asia changed my life in so many ways. Everything about it was an assault on the senses. It was so colorful and so rich with culture. Some aspects of the trip were harsh; seeing extreme poverty, prostitution, and pollution was very sobering. But the overall impact of the trip was still magical to me. In many ways, I was still a wide-eyed kid from Calgary, and being taken so far out of my comfort zone forced me to appreciate who I was and where I came from, as well as giving me a greater understanding of my life at home.

I loved Asia so much, that trip became the spark that inspired me to move to a new city to chase my dream. As time went by, I eagerly awaited my chance to return, and just over a year later I would get my chance. I made my second journey to Asia; that time, I was a bit more comfortable and was hungry to experience as much as I could in the short visit I had allotted myself.

After spending time staying with minority hill tribes and

hiking through the mountains, I ended up in Chiang Rai, a remote city in northern Thailand. Chiang Rai sits on the banks of the Mekong River and is one of the points of the famous Golden Triangle between Thailand, Burma, and Laos. At the time, visitors were not allowed into Burma. There was a physical gate separating Burma and Thailand, and on either side lay the hustle and bustle of local markets. The gate was lightly guarded. Even though Burma was a closed country at that time, Thai nationals were allowed to flow back and forth between the two nations and shop in the markets on either side. Thai and Burmese people were bouncing back and forth, creating a lively scene in what was otherwise a quiet border town. Observing this, I had one of my now-infamous brilliant ideas.

For the entire time I was in Thailand, people would mistake me for being Thai. When I was with a group of travelers, people selling stuff on the street would often speak Thai to me, thinking that I was a local guide. I had pretty much gotten used to it. I decided this would be the time to take advantage of my ethnically ambiguous look. My local guide agreed to switch clothes with me, so that I could walk freely through the unguarded gates into Burma, disguised as a Thai national.

So, wearing Thai fisherman's pants and a hat covering my eyes, I walked over the border with ease and spent the day in Burma. Truth be told, it wasn't so different from the Thai side of the border, but for some reason I guess I'm just attracted to the forbidden. I spent a wonderful day in Burma and, after taking some amazing photos, started to head back into Thailand.

On my way back to the gate, I noticed that a few more guards were standing around than there had been before. But since I didn't see anything formal or unusual, I just put my head down and made my way toward the gate. As I was walking, I suddenly felt someone tap my shoulder and say something to me in Thai. I glanced up and then quickly down and kept walking. I tried to move sideways into a group of people to confuse the guard, but then I felt a second tap on my shoulder—this time, he kind of grabbed my arm.

From that moment, everything seemed to move in slow motion. I looked at the guard and back at the gate. The guard was now aggressively asking me for something, which I assumed was for some kind of identification. In a flash, I took off toward the gate. I was within fifteen feet of safety when, from out of the crowd, two other guards appeared and tackled me to the ground. I struggled and even gained another three feet before I was stopped and handcuffed. I had been arrested. *In Burma.*

I was taken into a border prison which was right next to the market. They quickly discovered my camera, which was illegal in Burma at the time. (Oh yeah, and the camera was stashed down my pants. *That* didn't look suspicious.) My guide, who was still with me at this point, translated what they were saying for me. They looked at me and wanted to know where I was from; apparently, they were convinced that I could speak their language and that I was just refusing to communicate.

My guide held up my passport, screaming that I should be set free immediately. One of the officers smacked the passport out of his hands and it flew over my head as I sat in a chair with my hands cuffed behind my back. They accused me of being a spy because of the camera, and after a bit of roughing me up in order to try and make me talk, they put me in a cell and left to call their superiors. Later that night, another man arrived. He seemed to hold a position of authority. This man told me, through my guide, that I would be transferred to Rangoon and sentenced to seven years in prison. There wasn't a lot I could do.

That night, I didn't sleep. My mental wheels were turning and I was in my "what would MacGyver do" mode. I was determined not be transferred to Rangoon. If I was, I was convinced that I would just disappear. I surveyed the area all night long, looking for some kind of opportunity to get away. All of the guards were half my size, and I had vowed that, as soon as they opened the

door in the morning, I was going to bust out of there or die trying. After everyone (including my guide) left for the night, I was
alone in the one-room border jail with the night guard. He spoke
a bit of English, so I started talking about family and tried to get
familiar, but it wasn't working.

I tried another tack. Burma is one of the poorest countries on
the planet, and I knew that I had about $2,000 in travelers checks
in my confiscated belongings. We began to talk about money,
and after I drew on all of my powers of persuasion, soon we had
worked out a deal. I would bribe him to contact the colleague
who would be transferring me to forge my release documents
and to let me go at another border. I would sign over the $2,000
in travelers checks that I had with me and return to Chiang Rai
one week later with an additional $2,000 to be split between him
and his partner. This would be more money than they would
otherwise most likely earn in their lifetime.

The next morning, I woke after a short rest. The guard
showed up for my transfer and escorted me out the building and
into a van. We drove a short distance and suddenly the van doors
opened. As the sunlight poured into the van it blinded me, and
as my eyes focused all I could see was him giving me the international hand signal for "hurry up." He uncuffed me and pointed
toward the border. I ran like a bat out of hell, whispering thank
you, thank you, thank you under my breath. Who was I thanking?
At that point I wasn't sure; I was just thankful.

Then I traveled to Kanchanaburi to arrange for money to be
wired to me, so that I could return to Chiang Rai and live up to
my promise one week later. It was truly a cloak-and-dagger scene
out of a James Bond movie. We met again in the crowded market
on the Thai side and did a clandestine drop. I handed off a bag
full of cash to conclude our agreement. With a wink, I thanked
them for giving me my freedom, and I then walked away through
a crowd of people and didn't look back.

In many ways, it was one of the best things that ever happened to me, as it made me truly appreciate what freedom was.

In the Western world, we take freedom for granted every day; we don't understand it until we lose it, even if only for a fleeting moment.

Not long after I got back home from that first, eye-opening trip to Asia, I packed up everything and announced to my parents that I was moving to Toronto. I didn't know anyone there; there was no real reason for me to go to Toronto. Part of me thought that I might go back and try business school when I got there, or at least take a few classes; that was my stated plan.

My parents thought I had joined a cult. "What's there?" they asked me, and "Why are you doing this?" I explained my perspective. My uncle had once told me, "Whatever you do, you don't want to be a big fish in a small pond. You always want to make sure you're working with the best and beating the best." At the time, Calgary was a much smaller place than it is today, with a less developed business community, and I viewed Toronto as being the biggest pond.

So I bought a one-way plane ticket, packed my stuff, and landed in Toronto with eight hundred bucks in my pocket. I was there to change the world.

But before I could set out to change the world, I needed a job. And a place to live. Sure enough, shortly after I arrived, I found a garage apartment in a low-income part of the city.

And for employment, I took a contract at a travel company that sold active, nature-based travel. I saw it as a continuation of my tourism studies, learning the ropes of the industry from the inside. In school, I had done a project based on the idea of developing a tourism company that would bridge the gap between mainstream travel and backpacking. My trip to Asia, as well as my experience working in the mainstream travel industry, confirmed in my mind that there was a space in the market. One thing I learned backpacking through Asia is that a lot of people like me were trapped in limbo: young professionals with some disposable income who didn't want to take a pointless coach tour, cruise, or resort holiday. They wanted to meet like-minded people and preferred small groups, but because they wanted something different, they were forced to grab a guidebook and go backpacking. That was my window.

I wanted to reimagine group travel. I wanted to strip it down and look at everything, no matter how basic. Imagine how much more enriching a holiday you'd have, I thought, if you were willing to open your eyes and really see the world and its people?

My thoughts were a mix between a political stance and a business strategy, what today we call disruptive innovation. I knew that if I was going to enter the crowded travel industry as an entrepreneur, I could only do it in a way that altered the existing model of what a tour was. The two main components that I would have to remake, I thought to myself, were accommodation and transportation—where people stay and how they get there. Those are the things that people take for granted, expecting to have their Western creature comforts everywhere they went.

I took the question of where people would stay very seriously. The accommodations would have to be locally operated and family owned. I wanted to be creative by having passengers stay in bed-and-breakfasts, farms, monasteries, anything that would capture the flavor of the area—not just the continent or the country, but the actual area you were visiting.

And, if getting there is half the fun, I was going to make it one of the highlights of your tour. While most tour companies treated the trip between destinations as downtime, my passengers would travel on trains, canoes, rickshaws—anything that would offer variety, excitement, and capture real local color.

Like I said, the people are what make any country truly great. Tourist attractions are fine, but they are only one aspect of a visit, not necessarily the highlight. I wanted travelers to have a cultural exchange, to get people from around the world in touch with one another.

I always talk about the "CNN factor." Before the internet, the ubiquity of CNN made the world seem smaller and more familiar. It was everywhere you went, and it gave people a common view of what was going on across the planet. CNN removed people's often poorly informed perception of foreign lands and presented them as they are, in vivid color, right there in your living room. If Africa was once the "dark continent," CNN gave it lights and a camera to show people what life there really looked like. People are curious to meet and understand their fellow global citizens. I was banking on it.

These were big plans for a guy who was living in a garage. Regardless, I decided my business would bridge the gap between mainstream tourism and the backpacker. That's where our original name, G.A.P Adventures, came from; it was also an acronym for the Great Adventure People.

Toward the end of my first year in Toronto, I went to my boss at the travel company where I was working and told him I wanted to start my own travel company. Maybe I was naïve, but I figured I would be honest with him; I told him that I hoped we could work together to get my idea off the ground. You can guess what happened next: He fired me. He told me to leave immediately and gave me five minutes to clear my desk. He smirked and yelled to everyone across the office jokingly that I thought I could start my own travel company and that I was fired, turning my exit into a walk of shame.

As I was leaving, one of my coworkers told me she liked my idea and wanted to come with me. She later quit and joined me. It was the start of my next business adventure and now I was free to do it on my terms. Thinking back on it, I can now say jokingly, "I had youth on my side."

My big ideas and plans quickly hit a big stumbling block—finding someone to finance my idea. It was 1990, in the middle of the Gulf War. I went to every bank in the country to sell my idea and my business plan but got blank looks from across every table. No one seemed to understand the concept or the market, or they just refused to even listen.

One day, on my way out of yet another fruitless bank meeting, a brochure on the rack about a government summer job program caught my eye. The flyer said that if you came up with the capital to start a business for your summer job, this program would match your contribution dollar for dollar, to a maximum of $15,000. It was really intended for people to set up typical summer businesses like house painting, lawn care, or bike repair. But I figured it was worth a try, so I filled out the paperwork and tailored my business plan to read as though the idea was just to take people on vacations over the summer holidays. After an interview and a careful review process, we got approved. They would check our bank accounts at noon on a specific day and if everything was in order, that they would add the matching funds based on what was in the account at that time.

The next question was, where was I going to get $15,000 right away? I went to the only people who I thought might believe in me—my family and friends. I asked everyone I knew whether they would give me a loan. Finally, one of my sisters agreed that she would lend me the money, on the condition that she would get it back after a short period of time. I was all set; I really started to believe this was going to happen.

The night before my account was to be checked, however, I called my sister to arrange to wire the money and got some bad news—my sister and her husband suddenly got cold feet and had changed their minds. They said they didn't believe in me or what I was doing and that they wouldn't loan me the money. I pleaded with them, but it was no use.

My world came crashing down. I was alone in my garage apartment, and I felt as though everything I had worked hard for up until that point had been destroyed. I didn't sleep at all that night. The good (as well as bad) news was that I had fifteen hours to come up with the money.

First, I withdrew every penny I had in my bank account from my businesses and from my savings, and maxed out the cash advances on both of my credit cards. I also managed to borrow about $2,000 dollars from a friend. That got me up to about $9,000. Then I called my other sister, who had been saving her money to go on a round-the-world trip and to teach English in Asia. My voice choking with desperation, I asked her to lend me the remaining $6,000, promising that I would replace it before she left on her trip a month later. Even though this sister had little money to spare and no means to really help, she believed in me enough to give me a chance. The next day, all the stars aligned as the bank checked to find $15,000 in our account and, like magic, another $15,000 appeared!

Empowered by this stroke of good fortune, we started by putting together a couple of tours. Most hotels didn't even have fax machines back then, so we had to book them by sending checks through the mail. But our motto was "Changing travel through fearless innovation," and we were fearless in forging ahead. I put the first concepts out there; it was agreed that my new partner would handle the administrative side of the business while I did all the sales and marketing. Then, I basically just hit the streets. I spoke anywhere and anytime someone would have me—at colleges, universities, bookstores, outdoor stores, and even at private parties when people would let me come into their houses and speak to their guests. I had something to say, and I was very passionate about it.

I started getting regular appearance offers. I would speak every Wednesday night at an outdoor clothing store and another night every week at a bookstore. The local college allowed me to speak to their travel classes every semester. I would stand on a corner at street festivals and hand out flyers to my various talks. I just did whatever I could to get the word out and to create some local buzz about a new concept in travel. I was never shy about claiming my idea was revolutionary, and I was happy to speak to anyone about what I was doing.

We went step by tiny step. I started to buy small advertisements and ran a toll-free line that covered Canada and the US, including Alaska and Hawaii. I traveled to give talks anywhere where I could afford to go. The word *ecotourism* wasn't out there yet, and the concept of sustainable tourism was even further off in the distance. But I was convinced that there was a market for what we were offering.

Soon enough, I had my first tours up and running, with eager, wide-eyed explorers who didn't know what they were getting themselves into. The initial groups were small, with only about six people, but they enjoyed themselves. After our first trips we gathered photos and material to show what we were actually doing and what our tours were like. It was no longer just a theory or an idea.

It was an exciting time, and even though I still couldn't always afford to pay my rent, I knew that I was doing what I was meant to do. There are few things in life I've ever been so sure about.

By 1992, I had run into my first real business problem: Most North Americans only get two weeks of holiday time, while the British have four weeks of holidays, Germans have five weeks, the French have as much as six weeks holidays, and who even knows *when* Australians work? I think they just work between holidays. I realized that if we only appealed to North Americans, our customer base would be limited. Somehow, I needed to find a way to export our tourism product beyond the reach of our North American base.

The ideas began bouncing around my head the day I saw my first fax machine. In the first couple of years of my working life, any communication we did with the developing world was through telex, which was slow and expensive, or by mail. But when fax machines gained popularity in the late eighties and reduced the cost of exchanging documents and messages internationally, it really was my window to the world. I was speechless when I first got my hands on an actual fax machine. I just could not stop thinking of the potential and how my ambitions of exporting services and tourism would be enabled by this thermal-paper-spitting beast.

My challenge was to get someone in a foreign country to book their tour with a Canadian company, rather than with their own local operators. Part of the way I sold our tours was by focusing on how we specialized in taking people to see other cultures, how our trips gave people a chance to interact with the real people who lived in the communities we were going to visit. But another part of my vision was that it would be incredible if the group itself was made up five or six cultures. You'd be getting a bunch of people from Japan and Australia and New Zealand and America and Scandinavia to get to know one another *and* to experience one another's culture while they're discovering a new country. It's almost like a holiday inside a holiday, a vacation inside a vacation. The thought of different nationalities interacting with one another in a foreign country was an exciting idea and almost by accident it would later end up being one of the company's strongest selling points. Within the last year, people from more than 160 countries have booked trips with us and are excited to travel with other people from around the world experiencing a new country for the first time.

So, to kick-start my international business, in 1992 I set out to the biggest travel conference in the world, the World Travel Market, in London. I used my entire marketing budget for the year to fly over and stayed in a dorm room in a hostel alongside a contingent of Nepalese sherpas and operators. They accepted me because they thought I looked Nepalese; in fact, in the end I didn't even have to spend any money on food, because each night around the back of the hostel, they would fire up a camp stove and make lentils with rice, which they were happy to share with me.

Walking into the massive exhibition hall where the conference was being held, I can remember my sheer awe at the football fields' worth of exhibitors and the various national tourist boards with their grand, multilevel displays. I spent my time getting in front of as many wholesalers and tour operators as possible, and spoke to anyone who would grant me an audience. My excitement was palpable, and pretty quickly, I could tell that what I was doing was indeed different enough from the status quo that they were interested. In short, the trip was worth it—I came back with a list of companies that were interested in selling my product to their customers overseas. All I would have to do was deliver brochures in the various different currencies where these companies operated, in time for the 1993 season.

I had orders for fifty thousand brochures. This was both good news and bad news—it would cost about $70,000 to print and ship them. I didn't know how I was going to do it, but just like any time in my past when I was up against the wall, I was determined to figure it out. I made all the arrangements, promising that I would have brochures delivered within four months.

I left London on a high, thinking to myself that if I could pull this off, it would be our defining moment. As an entrepreneur, situations like these teach you that you can never give into your fear. Fear is a made-up emotion; it doesn't really exist. I would learn throughout my career that fear is never an option.

The most successful people don't view problems as walls stopping them. These solution-based thinkers just see obstacles that are temporarily in their way. My life has shown me that it's not how you handle defeat or adversity, it's how you get up that matters.

Back in Toronto, I hit the pavement, meeting with every printer in the city to try and arrange the terms I needed in order to print the fifty thousand brochures spread across five different currencies—Canadian dollars, US dollars, Australian dollars, New Zealand dollars, and British pounds. At this point, I was prepared to promise anything to get them done. True, I had no money for a deposit—or, in fact, anything other than a promise that I would pay it back from the business I would generate. But I knew I would only get one shot at this opportunity—that the whole business hinged on it. Even with all the energy I could muster, I was turned down by everyone—and laughed at by most.

Call it youthful exuberance or call it crazy, but even in the face of rejection from every printer I approached, I never doubted I was going to get it done. I made contact with a big printer over the border in Ithaca, New York. He agreed to meet with me if I would make the trip out to see him, so I packed up my presentation and headed out onto the highway for the five-hour drive to Ithaca.

I arrived and set up in the company's boardroom. After the owner and a few other senior managers came in, I gave it my best shot, with everything I had learned in a year of mastering the art of the pitch and telling a story. At the end of the meeting, they looked up and the owner said, "Well, we wish we could help you, but we just can't at this time." It was another rejection, but I thanked them anyway for listening to my presentation and started packing up.

I had everything in the lobby of the building when a woman came up and commented on the kids in one of my mounted posters. She asked where they were from and inquired as to what I was doing. I was exhausted, so I kept it short and briefly explained that I was there to convince this company to help me out with my dream, but that it didn't work out. Then she introduced herself as Mrs. Franz. She was the owner's wife.

I launched into my spiel again, and, knowing that she liked the cute pictures, I focused a bit harder on the community development aspect of what we were doing. This time, I really nailed it. She looked at me and asked me if I would wait around for her to speak to her husband, and then later asked if I would like to join her and Mr. Franz for dinner at the pub next door that night. "Hmm, let me check my schedule." YES!

To say it was an interesting dinner would be quite an understatement. I just kept quiet and let it all unfold, as I had done so many times in the past. As Mrs. Franz began to nag more and more, Mr. Franz just ordered himself one drink after another. The only pitch I really made was when I turned to Mr. Franz at one point, looked him in the eyes, and said, "I don't care what I have to do, I promise you I will pay you every cent of this money back, even if my company goes under." Before I even had a chance to say anything else, Mr. Franz told me to send over the artwork and he would print our brochures. I like to think it was my persuasive skill, but really I think at that point he would have done anything to get Mrs. Franz to stop bugging him!

This is when my story touches on the spiritual, demonstrating another one of those times when I knew I was doing what I was supposed to be doing. The universe was speaking to me.

The brochures were printed and delivered. Days later, the printing company closed, and they went out of business—they never invoiced me for those brochures. I contacted Mr. Franz and told him that our deal was still good between us and that I would pay him back every cent. He replied, "I know you will, Bruce."

Years later, I kept my word and contacted them again. Mr. Franz told me that he had been following what we were doing and that he had felt "great joy" in watching our success. When I told him that I was ready to start making those payments, he said, "You know what? Me and Mrs. Franz wanted to take a trip to Africa," and that would be good enough. He said that he was happy to know that it all worked out for me. After one other phone call, I lost touch with Mr. and Mrs. Franz. They never called me back, and they never took that trip to Africa.

I will never forget what Mr. and Mrs. Franz did—I have never met a more generous couple. And bear this in mind: Companies don't go out of business overnight. When he agreed to print our brochures, I believe he knew that his business was ending and that he used the resources and the paper he had in stock to help out a good cause. This was my first lesson in paying it forward. I was being given a rare gift, and I knew that I could never take it for granted. It almost seemed as though the generosity I received was something out of a parallel universe, or that I was on borrowed time; that these events were out of my control. I felt like everything aligned and I was given this one moment in time, and had I slept in that day we might no longer exist, or maybe we shouldn't exist? As I drove back I thought to myself that maybe it wasn't mine anymore. It was one of many times in my life when I have felt as though I was being guided. I was on a path to understanding even more about what paying it forward really meant and how it was relevant to the sometimes hard-hearted world of business.

I have always said I would never take for granted what Mr. and Mrs. Franz did for me.

Over the course of the next eight years, a lot of my focus was on developing the strength of our brand. While that was going on, we were growing, but not enough to make anyone rich and famous. I even took a part-time job at a deli to keep the lights on at home. I also made sure everyone else at my company got paid before I did. I didn't take a salary until 1996, and even then it was below minimum wage; it was just to supplement the jobs I had on the weekends. I ate Doritos for four years. Also, there was a guy on the corner who sold falafels for a dollar; I think I ate a falafel every day for almost three years. Three years. I'm not kidding—people think that I'm exaggerating, but I'm not.

Those years were tough and far from glamorous. My parents were horrified the whole time. They thought I should get a real job and didn't understand exactly what I was doing, even though the business was growing.

The funny thing is, I was totally happy. The camaraderie and the sense that we were following our dream made it all worthwhile.

I thought, this was it, I'd made it. I'd hit the big time. *I was free.*

CHAPTER 4

All-In

Everything had been going great, right up until the collapse of the Canadian dollar, which threw the business into turmoil and sent me on my soul-searching journey to Tibet and Bhutan in 1997. When I came back to Toronto, I knew I faced a company that was in disarray. But I was inspired and wanted to guide the company into becoming the movement I had started to envision during my journey. Still, things got much worse before they got better, and in those first days after I returned, we were spending most of our energy just trying to stay afloat. As fired up as I was from my travels in Tibet and Bhutan, going to the office was grim.

But then, almost miraculously, I got a break.

To my total surprise, one of the letters that was waiting for me when I got home was from *Profit*, a magazine aimed at entrepreneurs, informing me that we had been nominated for a feature spotlighting "Canada's 100 Fastest Growing Companies." Had the issue been about our overall numbers, it would have been a different story, given how much financial trouble we were in at the time. But I guess I shouldn't have been surprised by the letter, since in seven years, we'd gone from being financed by my credit cards to capturing $6 million in annual revenue. Yet, with all the debt hanging over our heads, it seemed almost surreal. Looking back, we still hadn't even hit bottom at that point.

This was also the dot-com boom era, so with all the press that the so-called hot tech companies were getting, I assumed our travel company was way down on the list, somewhere around ninety-eight or ninety-nine. Nonetheless, when I responded to the letter, they asked me not only for an interview but also for a photo shoot, and to bring a couple of changes of clothes. I knew I didn't want to take a boring office shot, so I suggested another location and deliberately didn't bring a suit.

I showed up at the site, a leafy part of the bank of the Don River that runs through Toronto, with a few different outfits. One of them was a t-shirt that said "Free Tibet" on the front. I met the photographer, and noticed immediately that his head was shaved. As it turns out, he was a practicing Buddhist. I told him I wanted to wear the "Free Tibet" shirt, and he loved it. We agreed to do a few shots with the shirt on; since the magazine people told me to follow the photographer's instructions, I didn't think anything of it.

Not long after the shoot, the magazine's art director called and berated me for making what she called a "political state-ment." She was quite angry, lecturing me about how expensive it was to do a photo shoot and that they could easily find someone who appreciated the exposure. I didn't really know what to say; ultimately I did what I was told and simply followed the instruc-tions of the photographer. She threatened not to run a photo of me at all and briskly hung up the phone.

Regardless, I was invited to a gala event for the premiere of the issue, and when I showed up—again, not thinking we'd be prominently featured—I very quickly felt out of place. While the other people from the various tech companies that made up the rest of the *Profit* 100 were dressed in suits, I was wearing a brown suede jacket and looked way too cool for school. (I was hobo hip before hobo was hip.) There were reporters all over the place, and I didn't expect to get a lot of attention from them. Also, I'm generally not good in crowds, so I headed for the free snacks. I was still on a steady diet of falafel and Doritos, so any break from that was a treat.

Then Rick Spence, who was then the editor and publisher of *Profit* and who remains a friend today, appeared on stage in front of a massive sign covered by a curtain. He started talking about the power and importance of the fastest growing companies and explained that there were companies that had achieved in excess of 5,000 percent growth in the five-year period that the magazine had tracked in order to compile the issue. As Rick finished speaking, a curtain on the stage dropped to reveal a giant blow-up photo of the *Profit* 100 issue's cover—*with me on it*.

My jaw dropped, and I froze. I didn't know what to say. The cover had my head shot coming through some trees, but when you opened the inside, you saw the whole shot, with "Free Tibet" on my shirt as I'm emerging out of the bushes. (I look like I'm twelve years old in that picture.) Forget ninety-eight or ninety-nine on the list; we were the fourth fastest growing company. I was absolutely blown away.

I went up to the mike to give a totally impromptu speech to the assembled press and told them I was just so shocked because I'd almost never had anyone make a big deal out of anything that I'd ever done. I told them, "I've always felt like I was on the outside of the business community looking in. I've approached every bank in this country to help me over the course of the last seven years, and my ass is still sore from where the door hit me." The next day, people went crazy reporting that line (or at least a family-friendly version of it) in the papers; I still haven't lived it down.

After going to the same bank every day for seven years to make my deposit, when I walked in the next day, the bank manager came out and said, "Hello, Bruce"—I was like, "What?"—and the teller whispered, "Congratulations!" as I walked up to the counter. It was a nice feeling, though it didn't change the fact that we still were having major problems.

* * *

That period was when we started getting quite a lot of praise for the way we were changing the travel industry, and while I would never have admitted it to the people who were giving us these awards—they thought we were on top of the world—there was a side of me that felt like I didn't deserve the recognition. Before that point, I actually refused a lot of opportunities to do interviews. If I did do one, I used to ask the interviewer, "Can we just talk about our tours? Don't put me ahead of the trips. I'm here to put butts in seats." I still hadn't done everything I wanted to do, both in terms of bringing the business through this rough patch and in becoming a movement.

I didn't know it when the company began, but when I started meeting other entrepreneurs and executives, it began to dawn on me how unique my thinking about business was. At that point, people were attracted to the significance of what we were doing and what we stood for, on the sustainable side of our business, what had by this time been dubbed ecotourism. I wanted to open a dialogue with people, to use technology like the internet to respond to them, and to create relationships based on our brand promise. I wanted to reimagine the way we communicated and spoke to our travelers: how we wrote, and what we wrote, and how we viewed travel.

First and foremost, though, I had to get us out of the financial mess we were in. I had been so busy traveling around and setting up our sales channels, I hadn't built up the operational side of the business, and it was time to buckle down. By 1998 we were pulling in $7 million in sales, but because of the steep decline of the Canadian dollar, our debt was growing rapidly as well, going from about $400,000 up to $550,000 in just six months. (The irony of all the attention being lavished on us for our uniqueness as a company while we were struggling to pay the bills wasn't lost on us.) I had to make a decision about how to move us forward, not least because my business partner—the woman who had come with me after I was fired from my first job—wanted to exit the company. She no longer wanted to share the burden of figuring out how we would survive and was scared of the mounting debt and pressure. I had no choice. I had to either take over all of the debt and let my partner move on or shut down the whole thing. On paper we were bankrupt, and our days were consumed with juggling payments and avoiding calls from bill collectors. It was a dark time that was also stressful as people started to leave.

But after my epiphany in Tibet, I returned stronger than before. I knew this was what I was meant to do, so I signed an agreement to assume her share of the debt, paid her a nominal fee, and let her walk away with zero responsibility. At the time, our balance sheet showed we had no value, and now I was all-in.

I had spent most of my time up until this point traveling around the world, setting up our international network, and chasing our dream to export tourism, and suddenly everything was my responsibility alone. The operations side of the business really didn't know me personally, and I knew very little about what everyone did. But I would have to learn fast—*real* fast.

After looking at what was going on in the field, I knew every-thing and everyone had to change. The people in this area of the company didn't work for me at this point, and they were going to fight for their commission schemes and kickbacks. They didn't care what I had to say; they started building e-mail groups rallying people together to reinforce the belief that I couldn't exist with-out them. Every day, I received anonymous e-mails threatening my life and promising to destroy the company if I didn't do as they said. I had to build a new team with people who understood my growing philosophy, but many people I approached were scared to go against popular opinion within the company.

I moved quickly to make drastic changes to the business, both in terms of the operations and the staff. In short order, we had a whole new team. That period really taught me how important the recruiting process is. I was careful to bring on staff who could recruit people themselves and who understood that what we were doing wasn't just a job but a calling. I wanted to meet every single person who was hired and to prepare them for what was expected of them. Being absolutely clear at the beginning is a critical part of recruiting in general, but it was particularly crucial given the struggle we were facing—it was the only way we could start the rebuilding process.

At that point, I still couldn't afford to pay myself. I had to sell my car and move into the attic of the office. It was infested with mice, but that didn't really bother me. All I knew was that I had to turn the ship around. But I also knew that I was learning a huge amount. Suddenly I was using leadership skills I never thought I had; instead of just leading by example, I became more like a coach or a Henry V–type figure leading people into battle. The family atmosphere we had in the beginning had morphed into more of a team environment, and realizing that I could do it was really energizing.

Inevitably, more and more of the long-serving employees started to leave. Most of them didn't share my evolving vision of the business. Before the Tibet trip, even though I hadn't yet formulated what it was I wanted the company to become, I had already started to build partnerships with nonprofits. I wanted to build community projects and create that sort of karma within my business, to tie that into the business model, because I thought that good things would happen if we did good things. It was the "pay it forward" philosophy I felt I owed to Mr. and Mrs. Franz.

This approach earned me a lot of criticism within the company. As the people leaving moved on to work for our competitors, I started hearing that I had lost it, that the accolades and the publicity we'd experienced lately was going to my head, and that I had no idea what I was doing.

Another criticism was that I had become tougher to work with. I can see how this perception emerged. Suddenly, when I was in charge of the office, people saw that I expected their work to meet a very high standard. My sense is that most people are not used to working in an environment where excellence is expected. There are still those who say that I'm difficult to work with, or even that I'm impossible to work with. But I will never apologize to anyone for holding people to excellence. I push people to achieve their potential. I want everyone to do their best work under my watch, and that's one of the driving forces behind why I do what I do. I call it the Michael Jordan effect; I demand excellence and performance from the entire team, myself included, and there's a hard side to that.

In 1996 the Chicago Bulls, led by Michael Jordan, beat a long standing record set by the Los Angeles Lakers in 1972—winning the most games in a single regular season. That particular Bulls team has many leadership lessons to teach, but it's particularly great as an example of how, under the leadership of their coach, Phil Jackson, they had everything needed to create a winning team. Individually, each player was just good—even Jordan, who was in the twilight of his career—but together, they were unstoppable. There was clear communication from the top down, and everyone knew their role. But most importantly, even though they had weaknesses—their front court was not the best—any flaws were masked by their sheer determination to win. Their culture of excellence ran like wildfire through anyone who was part of the organization, and that desire is what I try to stoke in the people who I work with, too.

I've often said that in the early years of the company, I had to make decisions based on what we could afford as opposed to what might be the best for the business. During our crisis period, I knew I couldn't recruit experienced people based on salary or job security, so I focused my search on less experienced candidates whose attitude and relationship with their work put them over the top. These were people who held themselves to a higher standard—if they believed in something, they were going to invest blood, sweat, and tears into it. I started hiring people for their passion for life and travel, thinking that skill was secondary. You can teach people how to do anything, I thought, but you can't teach passion, loyalty, and commitment. And I combed the globe, looking for people who were leaders for us out in the field and who had genuine enthusiasm for showing travelers our beautiful world.

The people I found were excited to be doing something different and, even though I couldn't pay very much, they were motivated to do great things. I was working harder than I ever had, sleeping for only a few hours a night in the attic of the office and spending as much time as possible gathering a great group of people who wanted to be part of something special, while at the same time asking our suppliers to hang in there through our transition. It was hard work, but we were having the time of our lives.

In 1999, once the financial recovery was under way and the personnel exodus had subsided, I saw pretty quickly that there was value in skills after all and that we had to professionalize the business to a higher degree if we were going to survive. We were still achieving explosive growth, and I found I couldn't retrain everyone who had been working there, many of whom had learned their jobs on the fly. There were certain times when I had to make big changes. It was all about what I felt the company needed; *it wasn't about people not working hard*.

Then, one day in the summer of 1999, I got a phone call from a big multibrand travel company; they wanted to meet with me. The voice on the phone was friendly and jovial as he explained that they had heard about what a great company we were. He wanted to know whether I would join them for lunch the next time they visited Toronto, which, incidentally, was the following week. I was flattered and agreed to meet them. Besides, at the time, I never turned down a free meal.

We met at a very formal, fancy restaurant. When I got to the table, I was taken aback by the three men sitting there in what seemed like identical navy blue pinstripe suits. Was this a coincidence or did they talk that morning to make sure they matched? They welcomed me and we started talking about the travel industry. They were all very complimentary about my company. I felt like I was having lunch with the popular kids; their kind words were so flattering. I had been so deep in the trenches; it was nice to hear from people who appreciated what we did. Soon the idle chat became more serious, and they began a presentation about their company. They explained to me about where they came from and what their brands stood for in their roster of products. Then they came out and said that they wanted to acquire my company. They told me they wanted me to join them, to continue to run the company, and that they wanted our brand to represent adventure travel. It was all very exciting, and I thought, well, there was no harm in chatting about it. So we agreed to get the bill, leave the restaurant, and stop by our office. I would show them our past few years' books, and they would give me a quick assessment of what they would consider paying for G Adventures.

I will never forget the looks on everyone's faces in the office as I walked in with the Three Amigos in their pinstripe suits and locked myself in the back room. After a long conversation, they said they would get back to me. Soon after, I got a call from the lead guy running their acquisitions. What he said then, I will never forget as long as I live because it reminded me of how different my views are about business. He proceeded to tell me that they didn't see any value in my company at the time and that they were not in the business of paying based on potential.

He then said, in a moment of what he thought was kindness (but which was actually the worst thing you could say to me), "You know, Bruce, we really don't care about your company as much as we care about you." He said that they really wanted to build our brand into the premium global adventure brand, but that it was me they were most interested in. I really think that he thought this was a compliment, but I was not impressed. He then detailed a plan: They would be willing to pay one million dollars for my company on the condition that I sign a five-year contract to build the brand and work for them, and there would be additional incentives based on growth.

I wondered whether he knew what he was saying. They didn't

care about the company; they saw this as an investment in me. Underneath it, I know they were trying to flatter me, in their own way. And a million dollars was a lot of money, considering my present reality and the fact that I was still living in the attic of the office with a bunch of mice. But one thing I have learned over the years in business is "Know your audience," and by telling me that they didn't care about the company at that time—when I was fighting so hard for this company that meant so much to so many people, not to mention all the promises that I had made in the process of trying to get through the crunch period—that I felt like taking the money would be like asking me to sell everybody out, to quit fighting. And if there's one thing that I was certain of, given all of my experiences up until this point, I am not a quitter.

So many people had been "paying it forward" in terms of extending payment deadlines and sticking with me during some rough times, I felt that I was responsible for their faith in me, and to take the money now would have been selfish. Once again, I was going to push my chips across the table and go all-in. I turned them down.

For an entrepreneur, moments like these, when you have to put your passion ahead of what many people would say is the smart decision, just become fuel for your burning desire to succeed. This was a tough, emotional period. But I was determined to make my dream real, and in the period after I came back from Tibet, I started to recognize the seeds that would grow into a crucial aspect of the next stage of the company.

Once we brought in people who could help us rise above the limitations of their predecessors, we repaired the issues with our operations and continued to grow. By 2000, our top line revenue had passed $16 million. We started to raise eyebrows and the attention was now reaching a fever pitch. I was still uncertain whether all the dramatic changes were going to work out. I was confident that only time would tell, but there just didn't seem to be enough hours in any given day.

CHAPTER 5

Pay It Forward

Though a lot of things were now clearer in my mind in terms of what the company meant to me and what my purpose was, the new focus was just building on our existing values. We had done some incredible stuff, and my plan to move forward was not about throwing out everything we had done but, instead, about harnessing it. What I would eventually define as "the Looptail" was starting to take shape.

We had already been trying to run the company in a sustainable way, along the lines I've mentioned—involving local communities and taking a low-impact approach. I'm all about moving forward, but I also know that the things you do today become the foundation for your success tomorrow. That's part of what I talk about when I use the phrase "pay it forward." When I looked at where the company was, I saw that we got there by trying to create happiness and freedom for the communities we worked with. The vision I had for the future of the company was built partly on what we had already done.

Looking back, I also saw the mistakes that we had made. If we learn from our past losses, we are unstoppable. Losses, when we learn from them, turn to wins. I know it's a bit of a cliché, but the foundation of your power is built when you internalize everything you have been through to create a more powerful version of yourself. And as you continue to learn from your mistakes and pay it forward in terms of having a positive impact, the cycle of the Looptail returns that positive impact to you, only greater than it was before.

The questions I get asked the most are about how I started G Adventures—what did I do to get it off the ground and how did I turn my idea into a company? The answer is that it was the ideas and passion we had in the early days—our original concepts that came about organically—that really set the foundation of the great company we would become. I knew that there was a lot of change ahead for us and that, to go forward, we needed to remember where we came from and to channel that learning into what we would do in the future. Freedom lies in being bold, and I couldn't take bold steps without reflecting on where we came from.

In the very first year of the company, I set out on a backpacking trip to Ecuador, Venezuela, and Belize to do research for the first tours I was planning to offer. I brought only a guidebook and very little money—less than $15 per day. In fact, partway through my tour of Belize, I found myself with only $10 to get me through five days of travel until a friend of mine was scheduled to join me.

I spent $5 on a water taxi out to Caye Caulker, a sandy island community full of backpackers, and took the cheapest room at the guesthouse, which was a windowless square box lit by a single exposed lightbulb, with a fan but no bathroom. For the next five days, I ate one 75-cent burrito per day and rationed out a large bottle of water; amazingly, it worked out okay. When you're in a traveler's town like Caye Caulker, you always meet other friendly people. I never told anyone I was out of money, but I would offer to finish off people's plates at dinner, so I'm sure they figured it out. I remember someone offered to buy me a Coke as we sat chatting on the beach one day—I thought I had won the lottery.

Eventually my friend arrived, we settled up at the guesthouse, and I got back to my research.

The first trip we planned out was to Ecuador. Ecuador is a spectacular country and one of my favorite places in the world, even today. It's an unspoiled gem that isn't on the radar of the average traveler; as a travel professional, I challenge anyone to find another country that can offer the diversity and natural assets that Ecuador has in spades. There is no other single country that can take you, in one day, from snow-capped mountain peaks to a tropical rain forest. Couple that with one of the world's most incredible wildlife spectacles—the Galápagos Islands—and it seemed to me to that Ecuador was a natural first destination for the company. Maybe if I had done an MBA and given the situation a thorough cost-benefit analysis, I might not have chosen to go to Ecuador first, since it was both infrequently toured and difficult to get to.

The program we were planning during our research trip had our tour groups traveling by local buses and trains to a number of charming stops, small villages that were unspoiled and had little-to-no tourist traffic. Once you got out of the capital of Quito, the Ecuadorian people were still relatively unaffected by the Western world. Many still dressed in their native costume throughout their daily life, which was normal for them but would be remarkable to our travelers.

The guidebook said that there was a market every Saturday in the mountain town of Otavalo, so I jumped onto the public bus and rode up to check it out. When I got there, I was amazed at the absorbing, festive environment. The native communities from the surrounding hills would come down to the market every week to display their crafts, blankets, rugs, and leather goods, which made it a real spectacle. We definitely had to include that.

Next, the guidebook suggested I explore the nearby lake district, but without a car, I would have to hitchhike. I stood out on the main highway with my thumb aloft, and in short order a car pulled over and the couple inside asked me where I was going.

I jumped in the backseat and we drove off, making conversation easily since the man spoke perfect English. He introduced himself as Diego and asked me what I was doing in his amazing country. I went into my sales pitch, explaining the concept behind the business and that I was scoping out the area as a destination for one of my first tours.

After conferring with his wife in Spanish, Diego began to tell me that his family had a farm nearby that they didn't know what to do with. He said that it had once been a monastery and that now it was run down, but that it had been in his family for generations. Would I like to go there to see it? he asked. I agreed and we drove slightly off the highway and pulled into the farm.

The structure was extraordinary, but it was in extremely bad condition. There was a large open area that had been a cobblestone courtyard, though now it was so covered in grass and shrubbery that it looked like a field. The former quarters of the priests surrounded the courtyard; the doors to each room were hanging on the hinges, leading to cold and dingy stone enclosures.

As he gave me the tour, Diego explained that the place was called Guachala and that he and his wife had thought that with the rising popularity of the Otavalo markets right nearby, perhaps they and their family could get it up and running as a working farm again. He then guided me across the field to the monastery's chapel, and, of course, it was also a disaster. The walls were covered in gigantic religious paintings that had faded and were peeling and caked with dirt, and the pews were broken and lay strewn around like firewood.

I told Diego that if he could repair six of the rooms, in eight months we would bring tour groups through. I thought the place was perfect; for me, the clincher was his claim that people had seen spirits around the grounds and that it was haunted. I loved that. Ghosts are awesome!

Diego and I bonded in that moment; I told him that I'd be back with groups and he would have to have these rooms ready.

One thing I learned early on from dealing with drugstore owners for my bookmark business, and then with pet store owners,
is how to do a deal on a handshake. It does take a certain skill,
and you have to follow your heart. When it feels right, you know
it, and you just have to run with it.

We went back and looked at the various rooms again. In some
cases, we had to shoulder-check the doors in order to open them.
I chose the rooms I thought he should refurbish, and then we
sat on the edge of the courtyard and on a piece of paper did the
math of what it was going to cost him to fix up each room versus
what we would pay him per person. I told him my plan was to
bring one group every month, and from there, we figured out his
break-even point. I told him we didn't have money to help him
with the renovations, but that we'd pay him in advance of each
group's arrival. We'd both be taking a leap of faith, but I said I
hoped to send him steady business if he could put it together.

So, on a handshake we agreed, and we said we would stay in
touch by mail. (That's what you did in those days.) In the months
following, we wrote each other letters; he would update me on
how the construction was going, and he would get updates on
how the tours were selling.

It was a serendipitous meeting that led to a business partnership that has now lasted more than twenty years. Since then, I've
stayed in Guachala many times. I've never seen ghosts, unfortunately, but we have had passengers report different things over
the years.

After we left the area around Otavalo, we went back to Quito to
repack and prepare to head into the Amazon. The last stop on
our Ecuador tour was going to be a lodge in the jungle where we
could take our passengers for three days. From Baños, we took
a bus into Tena, and then carried on to Misahuallí, which was a
dilapidated town on the edge of the Napo River, a tributary of
the mighty Amazon River.

Riding on top of the bus, as I did most of the time, I had a front-row seat to watch the streets turn into dirt roads. As we transitioned from the cool climate of the mountain region into a sticky, tropical heat, the vegetation changed dramatically. By the time we reached our destination, we were dodging vines and loose branches, holding onto the bus's roof rack with one hand and using the other to sweep away the vegetation. After a long, uncomfortable ride, we reached the small town, where we began to research lodges in the area. There was no shortage and they were actually all roughly the same—thatched-roof jungle huts with electricity, plumbing, and other basic creature comforts, which was a bit underwhelming. Though we knew that most travelers would find the experience authentic enough, we still asked around about what else was in the area.

I had always been taught that there was no room for emotion in business, that it's a strictly black-and-white world. You constantly have to make tough and often unpopular decisions, ones that at times need to be devoid of feeling. The old school traditional leader showed strength in making quick decisions that were best for the business, without worrying about how they made people feel. Tom Hanks said in *A League of Their Own* that there is no crying in baseball. I was taught to believe that there's no crying in business.

I was also taught that you were only as good as your last decision. But, as my thinking evolved, I had experiences that changed the way I thought about decision making and leadership, that made me understand that there's a compassionate side of business. People never remember the details of what you may have said, but they will always remember how you made them feel. And while there is no doubt that tough decisions need to be taken every day, there is a way to create happiness and community in everything you do.

There's a handful of amazing people and serendipitous events that I would credit for our company's success. Some of them seemed like more than mere coincidences; at times, I felt as though I was being guided. I'm a believer in the idea that, in life, we're measured by the number of meaningful connections we make and the chance meetings we have. They create every opportunity that comes before us, opening the door for us to create change in our lives. We're either in tune with them or not. Nothing happens by accident; people just have various levels on which they choose to listen. As a company, as well as on a personal level, it's our choice whether to pay attention when destiny turns on the radio.

Let me tell you a story. There was one deeply humble and serene man I would meet in the Amazon who would change the course of my existence. His name is Delfin.

As we were asking around Misahuallí, we learned about an indigenous community called the Pimpilala tribe. They speak Quechua (pronounced *ketchwa*), believe in Pachamama (Mother Earth), and live according to principles handed down by their ancestors, surviving off the riches of the lush, fruitful Amazon jungle. One of them, Delfin, was a young, spry, proud, and handsome man who lived with his family in the rain forest. He took pride in his way of life and was a strong warrior who had little interest in or exposure to the modern world.

Through Delfin, we learned that his tribe's lifestyle was being threatened. Loggers and oil companies had moved in, and although he didn't seem to understand what they were up to, he was aware that something in the environment had changed for the worse. For the first time, his tribe's kids were getting sick from the fish they caught in the nearby rivers, and their traditional medicines no longer worked. Where once the community encompassed many families and villages, their numbers were dwindling as people moved into urban centers to find jobs and gave up their lives in the rain forest.

We arranged a dialogue with the Pimpilala community and made an agreement that our very first groups would visit Delfin and stay with him and his family. Later, when we met, Delfin would tell me that he didn't understand why people wanted to come to his village. He didn't have much food, nor was there plumbing or electricity. "Why do they want to stay here?" he kept asking. We responded saying, "We just want to see your way of life, to just hang out with you and learn about life in the jungle."

Our arrangement was that we would bring our own sleeping bags and that we would just hang around. There were no expectations about exactly what our customers would be doing. We agreed on a fee, which I'm sure wasn't Delfin's motivation at the time; I believe he would have done it for free because they really didn't have any use for money, outside of making occasional trips into town to buy a knife, an axe, or fishing tackle.

At any rate, we went back with a plan to market our first tour, "Ecuador: Inland and Amazon," priced at $995 for fifteen days. Our customers would take local transportation, including canoes and trains, and would stay in small, locally owned, family-run guesthouses and farms, as well as in Diego's monastery, and, finally, in the Amazon with Delfin. Our first tour leader, Neil, was the first person to meet Delfin to iron out the details.

We've brought a group to Delfin's village every month for more than twenty-two years. He and his wife, Stella, have been outstanding partners; they have a perfect service record with us, meaning that we have never had a single complaint from a customer about them. We still offer the Ecuador: Inland and Amazon tour, and I would argue that it's one of our best. Every evaluation that comes back from customers raves about the hospitality, kindness, and generosity of Delfin and his family. We've long since upgraded the services that are offered; our passengers no longer sleep on bamboo floors in sleeping bags—the tribe have built basic cabins, put in rustic beds, electricity, and plumbing—and they have done this on their own with the money they made through hosting our groups. It was our first trip, as well as our first experience with creating a sustainable solution through tourism. To this day it still captures the spirit of the region and respects the way that Delfin wants to share his culture with us. It was the first time that I created what I eventually understood would redefine tourism into something more like a community, an idea that became the seed of how we could redefine our business through social innovation.

Delfin and I have become good friends over the years. Spiritually, we've bonded as brothers. I recently received a message from one of our people on the ground saying that Delfin would like me to visit his family again, and I plan to go soon. I'm not as young as I once was, so the trips seem tougher and it takes longer to get out there—my days of riding on top of the bus are over. I do still insist on taking the local bus to remember and pay tribute to our first serendipitous meeting. I guess I could hire a driver or a car to take me there, but it just wouldn't be the same.

Whenever I visit, Delfin and I head out to the rivers around his village, he covers me in sacred mud to cleanse my soul, and then he rubs me down with herbs to chase away the bad spirits that have accumulated since my last visit. After a short ceremony, I dive in the water and swim around with the kids of the village. At night under the stars, Delfin tells me through a translator how there are only two families left in the area. They are forced to farm their own fish now, because they're worried that the fish coming down the rivers carry dangerous chemicals they've picked up swimming by the shoreline oil camps and paper mills. With the money from hosting our groups over the years, Delfin and his family have built a school; and his kids, whom he hadn't expected to be able to read or write, are educated and now attend the university in town. In fact, his son—who had just been born when we first started working together—won a scholarship to study in Russia and has since returned home. It was our first example of closing the loop, creating a perfect 360 by bridging sustainability and tourism. I think that's amazing; our serendipitous meeting changed the course of their lives as well. And, through our meaningful connection, Delfin and his family have managed to preserve their culture. They are proud of their ability to maintain their lifestyle and stay true to their ancestors' way of life.

Delfin and I have both grown up together, but in many ways, we haven't changed. Our mutual respect for each other is absolute, and we're both thankful for how things have worked out. When we talk about each other, we get emotional because we've created a symbiotic friendship. Our meeting was meant to be, and we both know how we've helped each other succeed. We're more a tribe than a family, and we will forever be bonded in a way that is otherworldly.

The last time I visited him, I made a speech to the kids at the local school but I couldn't get the words out as I was overwhelmed with emotions. I bowed my head as tears filled my eyes and Delfin put his hand on my head and told me that we were warrior brothers bound together.

*Scan this QR code or visit Looptail.com
/delfinvideo to meet Delfin and to see the
power of a meaningful connection.*

For some reason, adventure trips to Venezuela never really caught on, which was a disappointment. So we settled on Belize as a new destination. We wanted to start a kayaking program there, as Belize has the second largest barrier reef in the world and its coast is dotted with hundreds of small, sandy islands. Some of them had settlements, but most were uninhabited. Many people have said that Belize was another odd choice for one of our first programs because, like Ecuador, it was both relatively unknown and difficult to get to. There were no direct flights into Belize, and the total population in 1990 was just under two hundred thousand people. To me, I thought it was heaven on Earth. Though Ecuador is my favorite country, I would have to say Belize is a close second. I love it there. It is a place where you can get lost and just totally unwind.

When I went down to set up our operations for the Belize kayak program, I had to find a community that would work with us to deliver on our developing brand promise. I went to visit a community in southern Belize called Placencia. After spending time to get to know pretty well everyone in the small, sleepy town, I met the mayor, Jimmy Westby, who agreed to work with us. We funded Jimmy's operation, buying them the boats and kayaks that they would pay us back for with the revenue from the program. The whole town was ultimately involved in running the business, whether that meant learning how to repair kayaks, how to manage the equipment and the support boats, or how to track supplies inventory. A lot of the teens in the town learned how to kayak so they could work on the trips, and a number of others learned how to cook so they could also take part in the operation.

In hindsight, I would say these were microlending programs, but no one at the time had given them that name, and there certainly weren't agencies regulating it. For us, it was just operations. We were helping someone start a local business in order to create more business for us. And our passengers reported high rates of satisfaction with these close-to-the-community experiences; they would rave about having the opportunity to take part in their trip, as though it was a privilege, rather than something they paid for.

The first two trips we ran changed the way even I had envisioned what travel adventure could be. Once we started seeing the benefits to the local communities that came out of this sort of thing, I was inspired, and so in 1995, we decided to take a bigger risk.

That was the year I was asked to speak to the World Bank in Washington, DC, which invited a bunch of local NGOs (nongovernmental organizations, a fancy way of saying nonprofit groups unaffiliated with governments) to come and listen. One of the staff who came was a young, fresh-faced representative from Conservation International (CI), a powerful organization dedicated to preserving ecosystems around the world. Jamie Sweeting was a kid from England living in DC, working in CI's new fledgling ecotourism division and trying to make a career in sustainability. We hit it off, and as we chatted, we discovered that we were so like-minded in our beliefs, it seemed natural for us to work together. As the first project that came out of our partnership, we developed a document that was a declaration of what we stood for.

In our brochure for 1996, before the descriptions of the trips, I wanted to break out from what every other company was doing. We included a one-page statement in our brochure that we called our Tour Operator Standards. At the time, every NGO was pumping out certification programs that would tell donors, service recipients, and consumers that their company had met certain standards set by that organization. Jamie and I wanted to take a different approach—by publishing our standards as a brand promise that these were the things we would deliver. It was a bold declaration of what we believed was important in creating tours that didn't just exploit the communities and the resources of the countries where we ran our trips. It was very forward thinking and most people thought it was ridiculous that we would consider putting this in our brochure. We were promising all kinds of things about using local transportation, using certain sized hotels, making sure they were locally owned, that all of the services that we were using were paid fair trade prices. (To read the full Tour Operator Standards, see the Appendix.)

These seem like obvious things for a company like ours to be interested in, but in 1996 the idea of sustainable or responsible travel wasn't really something people talked about. Ecotourism had arrived in the mid-1990s, and other companies were incorporating the buzzword into their marketing, but I never really identified with all that hype. I gave strict orders to our people to not use the word *ecotourism* in any of our brochures or literature. I thought we were doing much more than that, and I didn't want to be seen as riding a wave.

At first, ecotourism seemed to be focused on the preservation of nature; a popular motto was "take only photographs, and leave only footprints." With our small groups and general commitment to the environment, we were already doing that. But I felt that our model would be better described as *community tourism*. We built our programs around not just having great tours but also creating local benefits for local people. At the time, the evidence was starting to show that as we became more successful, local communities were sharing in that success. We were getting noticed as an ecotourism company. We were happy to be recognized for having a model that was working, but I wanted us to push beyond that and go to the next level. In those early days, we didn't get much encouragement, but we forged ahead anyway.

Over the years we had led a number of initiatives, but our partnership with Conservation International was a different animal entirely—the for-profit world and the NGO world viewed each other with suspicion if not outright distrust. It was a labor of love for myself and the company, but, of course, I also thought at the time that people would be more interested in us, that it would be a competitive advantage, and that people would want to know that we stood for something. Everyone I would speak to for business advice would tell me that, as a business, you should always try to maximize your market. To me, that seemed to translate into being as generic as possible. I was coming to the realization that I was living in a niche market world. Our fans weren't interested in a generic travel experience. Why not put the difference between our business and our competition front and center, right where our customers could see it?

All this being said, publishing the Tour Operator Standards was not well received: A lot of people criticized it and the rest ignored it. We were going way beyond even what people consider ecotourism at the time, and when I went to suppliers around the world presenting this, I remember getting incredulous reactions. "People don't give a shit about this stuff. Get that out of your brochure," one of our partners exclaimed to me. "You're just scaring people away from booking your trips. People don't know what these Tour Operator Standards mean!"

Around the same time, we started putting people's faces on our brochures—and not necessarily pretty ones, if you catch my drift. I wanted people to feel the real essence of the countries we ran trips to and to represent that in our marketing materials. That also met with quite a lot of resistance. I remember a partner once asking me, "Do you have another wino on the cover of your brochure this year?" If we did, he and some of the others wanted to produce their own covers.

They had all the leverage, and unless I wanted to lose access to the international market in order to communicate our brand promise the way I envisioned it, I had no choice but to give them their own covers. I guess I couldn't complain: We were still growing by leaps and bounds.

I wasn't about to sit around waiting for other forms of validation. I knew we needed to go further; we had to put together a compelling brand promise because I knew our success was going to be in exporting our tours internationally. And when the internet became publicly widespread, suddenly the idea of exporting tourism didn't seem so far-fetched. Over the course of the next eight years, we would set about integrating these projects into our selling proposition and building what we call a sustainable or responsible tourism model, though even that would change and continue to be redefined as we went along. People had to believe that this collective group of travelers was capable of changing the world.

Through our partnerships with Conservation International, we committed to a promise to our customers that all of our trips would visit world heritage sites and find ways to give back. After we developed the Tour Operator Standards, we evolved a triangular theory that illustrated how a nonprofit could work with a for-profit company to create sustainable projects within the communities where we ran trips. The nonprofit would regulate the projects; the for-profit would make it successful and bring in the revenue; and the local community would work with both entities. We were going to institutions like the World Bank for funding, and we had to show them how the relationship would function, because these three groups had never worked together in this way.

For our first project, CI approached a community in the Petén region of Guatemala, through which many of our customers traveled to see elements of Mayan history such as Tikal National Park and other Mayan ruins. The communities around the ruins, however, derived most of their income from logging. Due to unsustainable practices, the quality of the wood was going downhill, and clearly their future in logging was threatened. At the same time, however, the women in these communities were homeschooling their children, and they had become very good teachers. So the idea was floated that it would be best to start a project that could utilize their natural skills—teaching their kids to read and write. From that, the Eco-Escuela Spanish School was born. There's no better way to enhance our customers' cultural immersion experience than to teach them a few words in Spanish.

At the time, a lot of nonprofits were running ecotourism programs with local communities, but often neither group knew how to make them work as businesses. In Petén, the school would be run by the community and the nonprofit; CI would train the community members; and then we would be the ones promoting and marketing the school and its programs.

Our groups would stay with a local family and take Spanish lessons for a few days. They would spend time there and learn a bit of the local language to enhance their experience with us for the rest of their trip. When we started the Spanish school, we did these homestays with the women only. The men ignored us at first, but once they saw that the school was making money, they were eager to start teaching as well.

Next, we aimed for bigger prey. In the jungles of Bolivia, we had been running trips into a region where there were numerous lodges for travelers to stay in, and all of them were foreign owned.

Very little of the money spent there remained in the country. Many of the locals in the surrounding areas were involved in either logging or the drug trade. Some of these communities had been at war with one another for generations. We decided to try to bring them together and see whether, by helping them build a jungle lodge of their own, we could make a difference.

Conservation International found the funds to build the lodge, while G Adventures planned a route to bring customers through the area. Remarkably, the training process even helped unite our own people on the ground; many tour leaders were willing to devote some of their time off to helping train the local communities on how to welcome our customers. Through our collective efforts, the Chalalán Ecolodge was born. It was a lot of work but a huge success, drawing thousands of travelers and winning accolades within the industry.

Working with an NGO as big as Conservation International was a new and much more difficult experience than I had antici-pated. In some ways it brought me back to those initial days in my business classes, in which the solutions they proposed somehow seemed to create even more work than I thought was necessary to get stuff done. In terms of our respective philosophies, there was constantly a conflict between the for-profit company and the nonprofit, though not in the ways you might expect. At any rate, by 2000, I felt that working with external NGOs was slowing us down.

Working with nonprofits involves a lot of bureaucracy. All of the reporting, all of the justification they have to deal with in order to get things done, was something we hadn't experienced before. We were used to doing things as quickly and efficiently as a small company can, not being weighed down with paperwork and reports and justifying spending money. I, for one, just didn't work like that. I was fighting to keep our company nimble and made decisions quickly.

I started openly musing about building our own organization to accomplish the same things we had been doing with NGOs since 1996, something people criticized me for even thinking about. They argued that a business couldn't have a nonprofit arm that served a private company, saying the arrangement lacked integrity and distance. But, by 2000, I didn't want to put up with NGO red tape any longer. For the first time, I hired people to work in the office who were going to start building projects for us and looking at ways that we could work with nonprofits locally as opposed to through a partnership.

I craved a return to the way we built our first projects with Delfin, Diego, Jimmy, and many others with whom we effectively sealed the deal with a handshake. These were successful examples of the kinds of community projects that NGOs were trying to create, but they couldn't seem to see how their way of pursuing them was getting them bogged down. I admit, it was very enticing to be asked to speak at the World Bank or to jet off to meet with officials from the People's Republic of China as a delegate of the UN. But in the end, it was mostly talk. When you're spending someone else's money, you devote endless amounts of time to justifying your decisions and reporting on your findings. To me, that takes away any sense of creativity, freedom, or flexibility. My business was built on innovation and swift execution of our ideas, while still respecting the local communities we worked with.

After my experiences with institutions and NGOs, I was starting to realize how unique we really were. I knew there was a place for us to work together, but I couldn't put my finger on what had to change. I would have to pick up that path again at some point in the future.

On September 1, 2001, I went with three of the travelers who were with me in Tibet on a trip to Guyana on a quest to meet a legendary woman, Diane McTurk, who had befriended giant river otters in Southern Guyana. Giant river otters are extremely rare in the environment; they are among the species that are particularly vulnerable to habitat destruction, so there are very few of them left. And they're massive otters, they're four feet tall. They're truly amazing creatures.

I went with a group to meet Diane and stay with her at her farm, Karanambu Ranch, where she rehabilitates and studies these giant creatures and returns them to the wild. Being around her was a unique experience; she's cut from the same cloth as Jane Goodall, plus she's a real character. Diane's ranch had no electricity, no power, no radio. It was one of a very limited number of times when I was completely out of contact with the company—I couldn't call even if I had wanted to.

We spent the days roaming around with Diane in canoes as she sang songs she had made up to go with the names she had given these wild animals. "Bluto, Bluto, Bluto," she cried, and, to our amazement, we would see the massive heads of the giant river otters emerge from the water, surrounding our canoe and coming to say hello to their friend. It was an incredible display of the potential of humankind's relationship with nature. I have a picture of me taken on the eleventh day of our trip: I'm feeding a giant river otter, and I look as happy as can be.

Two days later, having left the ranch, we learned about September 11, 2001—the same day that my river otter picture was taken. We hadn't had a clue that anything had happened.

Even when I saw that infamous video of the Twin Towers on TV, I always felt that I had missed the force of the event on some level—because I didn't experience it until days later, I never felt the true, harrowing emotion of it. People were still in a panic, of course, wondering what happened and who was involved and whether there was going to be more violence. Ultimately, it didn't matter so much how I felt, but I did come back to a changed world.

When I got back to Base Camp in Toronto, there was a feeling of complete panic in the air. The travel industry was being ripped apart. People were terrified to fly, and as a result, tour companies were going bankrupt. Flight bookings dropped by upwards of 30 percent, and the airlines collectively laid off seventy thousand people in the week following the attacks. In some ways, the travel industry would never fully recover.

Not long after I returned, I called my management team together and asked for a report. We didn't have access to the kind of customer information that we do now; I knew that we had a lot of repeat customers, but I didn't have numbers on how committed people were to our brand.

The management team came to me with their hands up in the air in baffled delight! Even with the downturn in the industry, our business remained up 34 percent from the previous year. I asked them for passenger numbers; we did some studies on where the business was coming from, and the results showed that it was the same mix of people we had always had. At that point, people were still traveling with us but going to different places; regardless, they kept booking in full force and remained committed. In retrospect, 2001 was merely a slower year. We had never had anything under 40 percent growth in any year up until that point, so achieving 30 percent growth was considered underwhelming.

That's when I started to understand a bit more about the resilience of the market and how dedicated people were to G Adventures. All the things we were doing, things that I didn't necessarily hear people talk about—all the projects and the Tour Operator Standards—were now rewarding us in our time of need. It was the first time that I saw real evidence that paying it forward worked. We were hearing that other companies in our market space were not experiencing the same growth. People were committed to our brand in a time of uncertainty.

These days, we have access to extensive research about who our customers are, and much of it has confirmed what we've believed for years—that travel is a big priority in their lives and that seeing other cultures and meeting other people is an important pillar of their journeys. I've always known that for our travelers, experiencing the way other people live is more than just a lifestyle choice. They see it as a way to not be isolated in their thinking.

Our customers don't see a trip as a luxury item, but instead, as a necessary part of their lives. And so, despite the fact that people had started pulling back on luxury spending, we kept growing.

Now, we've changed over the years to open ourselves up to different types of travelers with eight different styles. They range from our young YOLO (You Only Live Once) brand and our Active brand to our G Plus comfort collection, as well as a number of packages oriented toward families, and a lot of other different styles of trips for different markets. On the higher end of the scale, we have $10,000 Antarctic small ship cruises and even a $20,000 Africa expedition cruise or on the other end, a seven-day local-living homestay with my friend Delfin in the Amazon for less than $500.

We constantly convert people to our way of thinking about travel; in fact, we pride ourselves on being the future of tourism. And if we don't win fans of conventional tours, we often find that we appeal to their kids. A lot of people who've been raised to think an all-inclusive is the ultimate holiday are starting to realize there is more on our beautiful planet to experience. G Adventures now offers more than fifteen thousand departures to more than one hundred countries every year, and we have a great adventure for everybody, but they're all framed within a brand promise. It's all still within the same philosophy of what our company stands for.

After making it through 9/11 with the business relatively unscathed, 2002 became another turning point for us. The United Nations declared 2002 the year of sustainable tourism, and they asked me to come to their headquarters in New York to open the year and to address the entire UN.

My association with the UN had started with a trip I made to China. UNESCO asked me to speak there in 2000 about cultural heritage preservation. They had government officials from every province in China attend, so it was a major initiative to try and convince the Chinese government that it was important to pro-tect their national treasures. UNESCO had asked me to speak specifically about cultural heritage preservation through tourism, something our company is a living example of.

In 2002, when the United Nations asked me to open their year of sustainable tourism with a speech before all the member countries, I was the only tour company presenting; indeed, that's when my profile started to rise. For years we didn't promote all of the things we were doing because we were afraid that people would think we were doing them just so we could market and exploit our relationships. I would be horrified if people thought we did what we did purely to make money. Our mission is bigger than that and always has been. We didn't want to seem insincere or exploitative, so if the subject came up in interviews, I became quite skilled at guiding the questions back to selling our trips.

My 2002 speech having been received well, for the UN's 2003 conference in Quebec on sustainable tourism, they asked me to deliver the keynote, in which I advocated more recognition of companies in the sustainable tourism market. At the time, it wasn't a category recognized by governments and tourist boards; the boards in particular tended to fund big companies running things like cruise ships and to malign the image of the backpacker. Officials couldn't track spending by backpackers as easily as they could with coach tours, and backpackers were viewed as cheap, as well as disruptive due to their supposed hard-partying habits. (In my view, backpackers were the original ecotourists, because they were most often paying fair trade prices with cash in hand.) In my keynote, I argued that supporting sustainable tourism was a long-term investment that might take more than a politician's four-year term in office to show results, but that it would eventually pay real dividends to local communities. They needed to pay it forward. I believed that indigenous tourism was the future of wealth distribution and that coach tours were just commodifying culture at the expense of local people. Audiences would get excited during my talks, but they didn't have the impact I wanted.

* * *

With the company's visibility increasing by the day, and our nonprofit projects also beginning to take on a life of their own, I believed the time had come to really support our initiatives by spinning off that side of the company into our own nonprofit. Some of my own people argued that we should work with existing nonprofits on the projects we wanted to do—because we're a for-profit business, they said, and we shouldn't control a nonprofit. After having had this discussion internally over and over, by 2003, I just said, Why not? Ford has the Ford Foundation, I insisted, so why can't we do the same thing? Obviously Ford's model is very different from ours, but I refused to accept that there was anything to be ashamed of in starting a nonprofit that would build community projects centered around the company's business model. Companies spend so much time telling people *how* they do what they do, but I wanted our travelers to know *why* we do it. Everyone thought it was impossible or that we shouldn't do it, but I did it anyway. My daughter Terra was born that same year, and as I announced that we would name this nonprofit after her—Planeterra—I declared to the people in my office that Planeterra could one day be bigger than G Adventures.

From the start, Planeterra was a distinct entity from the travel company, employing a separate staff. I wanted the relationship between the two to be at arm's length, with Planeterra operating as a stand-alone entity that could work with other companies. It wasn't that different from the projects that we had already been doing, like giving microloans to the people in Placencia so they could buy boats and equipment to run kayaking trips for our customers. The whole town was involved in that program, from repairing boats to preparing food. For us, creating that initiative was just the cost of operations.

Planeterra's original goal was to harness all those relationships that we already had. It was very aggressive, but it was also very innovative, I believed, and it gave us the freedom to work faster and to be quick to market with the ideas that we had. Unlike when we were partnering with other NGOs, Planeterra allowed us to be decisive; because we funded everything ourselves, we didn't need to constantly justify spending other people's money.

Then, of course, our competitors started to mimic the way we were associating ourselves with sustainable, ethical practices. Although they tried to do the same things, you could tell their efforts were somewhat insincere. A lot of them started creating programs with some of the world's most heavily marketed charities like Amnesty International or World Wildlife Fund, but in effect, our competitors were just giving the charities money as opposed to developing a truly sustainable business model. They were using these charities and NGOs to evoke an emotional response from their customers. These organizations had spent millions on ad campaigns to create a brand that the public would identify with; the companies were thinking that by aligning themselves alongside them and putting the logo of one of these megacharities on their product, they could buy a bit of the positive feeling people have toward the charity's activity.

I never understood how the customer wouldn't see through this. If they wanted to donate to any of those charities, couldn't they just do it themselves? Why would they need a travel company, or any company, to do it on their behalf? I felt that we needed to do a lot more than that.

Besides, while any company can give money to an organization like Plan or Amnesty International—or any of the most marketed NGOs in the world—and try to buy a bit of that emotional reaction, it won't make up for the fact that the brand of the company making the donation doesn't produce that warm feeling. Sure, the panda in World Wildlife Fund's ads evokes a fuzzy emotion, and then travel companies donate upwards of $5,000 a year to use the WWF's brand on their brochures, but they do it because these companies' own products aren't inspiring in themselves. The companies don't make people feel the way WWF does, so they use their donation as a means to kind of "greenwash" their business. (Greenwashing, for those who aren't familiar with the term, means to give the impression that your business is sustainable or eco-friendly while, in fact, another arm of the business is damaging the environment or not behaving sustainably.) We were doing something completely different—we were building projects and spearheading them ourselves.

I went to Peru in 2003. I hadn't been there since 1998, after I had gambled everything and gone all-in and committed myself to rebuilding the company. The last time I was there, I was closing offices and firing people who were doing things other than travel. It was a tough time.

Cuzco is the main traveler's town in Peru, and the center of the once-mighty Inca empire. It was where all of our groups hung out and is one of my favorite places in the world to just chill. When I came back to Peru for the first time in five years, I went around one night to see four or five of our tour groups that were in town and out socializing in Cuzco. Because I don't get to interact directly with our customers very often, it was a good opportunity for me to get a feel for the mood of our travelers and to make sure they were having a good time. It turned out that everyone ended up in the same bar, so it was easy for me to go to the place everyone went for a drink after dinner.

When I walked out of the bar at the end of the night, I was blown away by the number of kids on the street. There were dozens of children lined up outside the bar, some of them as young as four or five years old. It was particularly heart-wrenching for me because my life had just changed, having children of my own at the time. There had always been kids on the street, but never this many.

I started asking the kids what they were doing out, and then I realized why they were there: They were all waiting for our travelers to leave the bar so they could sell them junk food or cigarettes. In fact, throughout the plaza there were children selling everything from candy to kitschy souvenirs.

I remember one kid who must have been about seven or eight coming up to me and following me for an awkwardly long amount of time, knowing that I wasn't going to buy anything but still following me. Someone had told him that I was *el jefe*—the boss—of the company that everyone was coming to know in Cuzco. Finally I stopped walking and just started chatting with him in my broken Spanish, asking where he came from, where he lived. He told me that he had no place to live, and when I asked where he went to school, he replied that he couldn't go to school. "My parents are both drinkers," he explained, and because they drank, they couldn't take care of him. They also abused him, and so he left home and lived on the streets—at seven! He sold three or four chocolate bars and a couple of bags of chips a day, and that was his only way of making money to feed himself. He had learned it from other kids.

Hearing this story, I remember feeling overwhelmed. We're not necessarily perpetuating the problem, I thought to myself, but there's got to be something more that we can do.

After asking around, I found out that a woman named Luis Maria was trying to get kids off the street and make them go to school. She was trying to be the mother of all of these children. I asked a group of kids to take me to her. As they led me out of the gringo hangout area of Cuzco, the cobblestones soon gave way to unpaved streets. We were now in what I would call a traditional slum. It wasn't safe for me, let alone for those who called the area home.

I was led to the tiny apartment where Luis Maria had been housing all of these kids and was greeted with a friendly smile. It was almost as though she was expecting me; I think she imagined I was coming to volunteer my services. After hearing about the struggles she was having looking after these kids, I told her that through our foundation, Planeterra, we would support her work and efforts to get these kids away from the streets and back in school. The kids' heartbreaking stories really got to me. While Luis Maria and I spoke, some of the little ones would grab my hand just to hold it for a moment, to feel a connection. I told Luis Maria we would support the school, and then I asked her, What more can I do? What did she need?

I need a house, she replied; a place to call our own. Luis Maria explained that more and more kids wanted to come and stay with her, to go to school and to learn. She and the kids had been evicted from their last three apartments and the kids didn't feel like they had a home. The tiny place that she could afford, with the help of a few local benefactors, was too small for the kids to play in—they couldn't run around. I told her I was going to help. In that moment I didn't know exactly how, but I would do what I could.

To take this on, I knew, would be a real commitment. At the time I suspected it would be the biggest project we'd ever done, but once something is pointed out to you, you can either choose to not engage or get involved. How could I continue doing what we were saying we were doing without *doing* something? I couldn't. To buy a house big enough for all of them would cost in the range of $450,000. But again, I was determined. I was going to appeal to all of our customers and try to transcend just being a travel company.

It was a daunting task given that Planeterra was only six months old, but we managed to put a plan together that would engage our customers to a higher purpose. As I began to send word to our growing legions of supporters that we needed their help, I remembered the importance of storytelling to entrepreneurship. This was not about being a travel company; it was a human story.

It was amazing to see our customers start to rally, and continue to rally, once we launched the campaign. People were doing incredible things, like getting their own kids involved. We had people doing skydiving, climbing Kilimanjaro, and getting sponsors, as well as kids doing "Pennies for Peru" programs in their schools. There were no major donors, just a lot of passion and purpose. Bit by bit the donations came in, and at times I really didn't think it was going to happen, but it did.

At last, in October 2009, we bought a house for Luis Maria and the children, moved them in, and gave them a one-hundred-year free lease. All the former street kids moved over to the new house. They were absolutely elated.

The kids in the house have to go to school, and they have hot meals served every day. There are music teachers at the house, so the kids get to play instruments and dance. They are also learning new skills like leather-making, sewing, and embroidery, which they use to make the products that they sell to local vendors. Since we got involved, the People of the Sun project (that's what it's called) has also received donations to cover food and other supplies for the house.

We continue to donate to fund the house through Planeterra, and we also order some goods from them; the kids make different paper items and laundry bags for our customers to use in their hotels. It's a truly phenomenal project, and it cost G Adventures nothing. I donated, though I didn't donate an exceptional amount—many people donated more than I did. But we did it; we raised the money. And we did it by creating a movement and transcended being just a travel company.

*Scan this QR code or visit Looptail.com
/streetkidsperu to visit the House of the People of
the Sun in Cuzco, Peru, and see the impact made
by donations from around the world to Planeterra.*

This was when I first started to put everything together about the Looptail. I saw people's heartfelt efforts to do what they could for these street kids, whom they had never even met. I also observed that the donors made their contributions through our company, and some may not even have traveled with us. I learned that it was possible that people could identify with your brand without having a commercial relationship. By providing them with the vehicle to give back, they were more emotionally engaged with us than they were previously.

Around the same time, I had started reading about happiness and how the secret was the ability to find your own personal happiness through the happiness of others. I had become so jaded in many respects, until I started getting letter after letter from people who felt honored to be part of something much greater than themselves. They would actually thank me for doing such great work; I really wasn't doing anything except creating the playing field. Again, it cost me nothing, and it engaged everyone who touched our brand to a higher purpose. One day we received a letter from the estate of an older woman who had passed away. In her will, she had left money to our foundation. We were becoming more than just a travel company, and I was consumed with what we should do and what we could become. There certainly wasn't a well-trodden path to follow, so we would have to blaze the trail. I learned that we had to stand for something, because believing in everything amounts to believing in nothing. As we started to reinvent our business I began to realize that, if we wanted to change the world, we would have to change how we looked at our business in general and push past our industry.

We love changing people's lives. It's one of our core values, and the way our company has embraced the meaning behind it extends beyond our tours. I thought I knew just how much our people were committed to our values, but when a massive earthquake struck Peru on August 15, 2007, I learned the true strength of the G Adventures community. Let me introduce you to when I knew we were becoming a movement.

By that time we had two hundred employees in Peru, and seeing the devastation through their eyes really hit home for many of us. After the earthquake struck on a Wednesday, in the immediate aftermath there didn't seem to be a lot of international aid coming in. There wasn't a huge death toll, mercifully, but there were quite a lot of displaced or stranded people. Certain areas had no food or water. We knew there was a crisis on the ground. As the news rolled in, we learned that all along the coast of Peru, people's lives had been destroyed and that many had lost everything. On that Friday, we decided we had to do something, so I instructed the Planeterra team to send an e-mail to all of our customers, telling them that this earthquake had happened and that we were seeking donations in order to buy tents and fresh water.

This was an emergency disaster relief mission, which wasn't something we really considered part of G Adventures' core purpose, or even Planeterra's. But the people of Peru were devastated, and when you engage people in a business model that's based around happiness and freedom, sometimes these things have a life of their own. Overall, we were hoping we'd raise maybe $25,000 to show our support for our friends in Peru.

On Monday morning, we came into the office to find that all of our servers were so jammed, they had completely shut down from people donating through the weekend. All told, we had raised $100,000 dollars, which just amazed us. I remember being absolutely staggered by the outpouring. I looked at the list of donors and there wasn't a single major donor; they were all small- and medium-size amounts. We realized we had this huge responsibility to give away the money, but, although it sounds strange, we didn't necessarily have the structure in place to do it. In many ways, responding to the Peru earthquake was Planeterra's first big test. We had to make sure that that money was used properly, which was challenging because we didn't have the infrastructure to handle that many donations.

Ultimately, we got a whole bunch of our staff in Peru to set aside their jobs, because we had promised our customers that we would deliver that money in services, not just donate it all to a large NGO as everybody else did. Pretty soon we had people buying skids of water and going around the region handing out bottles. I don't think people even realize the enormity of it when they give $5. In the end, we were even able to fund some Red Cross efforts, but we were also able to do a lot on our own. I think we all realized the truth in a saying I once heard from Warren

Buffett—sometimes it's much easier to make money than it is to give it away responsibly.

The thing that really made an impact on me, though, was how we as a company were engaging people and also how we rallied the whole company together around a single cause—everyone had to take part in making that happen. The power to get things like this done is something that we've tried to harness. While many of our projects are about finding a sustainable solution to a business problem, the Peru earthquake was a completely different situation. People trusted our brand enough to donate to help out their fellow man. Again, we transcended our core business and engaged people beyond travel.

By the time G Adventures' twentieth anniversary rolled around in 2010, Planeterra had started getting donations from our customers rather than being funded solely by the company. We started offering that option as a service to our customers, to direct their donations to specific projects and match donations to a yearly maximum. And, because the tour company paid all of Planeterra's administrative costs, we promised that 100 percent (doubled by our matching) of the donations that people gave would go to the specific projects they chose instead of going into a larger organization-wide pool.

We started to softly push our customers to consider giving more by starting a dollar-per-day program that, at the time, was revolutionary—the idea that a travel company would solicit a donation from their customers at the time of booking. People thought we were crazy and that we might scare away the clients or make them feel uncomfortable by somehow pressuring them into giving. It was just a simple question that we asked after they confirmed their trip: Would they like to give one dollar to Planeterra each day for the duration of their trip to help make the world a little more perfect?

PART III
COMMUNITY

CHAPTER 6

Success Doesn't Happen by Accident

A lot of people think I must be some kind of hippie, founding an adventure travel company and talking about creating happiness and community all the time. They imagine when I talk about our company culture that everyone drifts into work whenever they like or that we're always playing foosball in the middle of the workday or something. In some ways, we did have a hippie-mentality kind of culture in the early years. We believed in having flat, nonhierarchical management structure and giving equal treatment to performers of all stripes. At one point there was a company-wide bonus for salespeople that was equal for all salespeople if the company performed at a certain level. Ultimately, though, that approach didn't serve the organization well because there are always people at the top end of the spectrum who do amazing work and carry the load for people who are less effective. Because everyone benefits, you're supporting poor performance and inefficiency.

There is a hard side to business, making sure people are

effective and want to be there for the right reasons. I mean, you still have to be good at what you do. And while a lot of the people working for us in 2005 were good at their jobs, once I started taking a hard look at the company and at what was working or what wasn't, I began to realize that if we were going to survive and thrive through the next set of big shifts I had in mind, we had to make some more tough decisions.

Seven years had passed since I went all-in and took on all of our debt in 1998. In those seven years, annual revenue went from $7 million to more than $50 million. The business was still growing, we were still running great trips, and we were being garlanded with awards. Between 2002 and 2005, I don't think anyone won more industry awards than we did. We must have won a hundred. And the people who had come into the business were more committed.

My employees were very happy with the growth over the past five years, and they thought I should be happy, too. People would tell me that I should be the happiest man on earth. They would come up to me, shaking my hand, sometimes even crying, and say, "You should be so proud of yourself; your parents must be so proud."

But when I took a closer look at the business, I saw things I wanted to change. That meant starting with a hard look at myself and some of the decisions I had made. In order to keep control of the business and not be beholden to creditors, I made a lot of choices, particularly in staffing.

After a lot of thought and reflection, I came to realize that after years of bootstrapping and making decisions based on what I could afford as opposed to what was best for the company, the company was becoming something that didn't reflect me anymore.

I believe building a company is a very emotional process. Entrepreneurs are the artists in the business community—they're often quiet or socially awkward, and they march to the beat of their own drum. To me, someone creating a company isn't any different than an artist who writes a song or creates a painting or a magnificent sculpture. Art is about putting your ideas, thoughts, heart, and soul into your work. And regardless of what you do, it will be a reflection of who you are and what you stand for.

At that time, my fundamental philosophy about business was changing. I started to believe that how you view the world is inextricably linked to all of your influences and that the world is just a reflection of your own consciousness. I know that sounds a bit lofty, but I really believe it: Whatever you see, that is what you are or will become. And I maintain that the process of creating a truly innovative company comes from an inspired place, and the cathartic process isn't dissimilar to that of an artist. Building a company is personal, emotional, and ultimately, in its truest sense, reflects the founder as well as the people who bring the idea to life.

Because I had built the business myself and had control over it, it mirrored my personality and what I believe in—it's inevitable when you build a company from credit card debt. But by this point, even though we had great people and a great business, and we were winning award after award after award, I felt like we didn't deserve the accolades, because I didn't completely know what we stood for. We were trying to be everything to everyone, and as a result, I felt that we effectively stood for nothing. We had a lot of values, but most weren't documented and our business model wasn't centered around them.

For the first time, I felt like I was being challenged in terms of my own personal leadership. I was seeing weaknesses in my ability to bring us to the next stage as we had become a multi-national company. I started taking leadership courses, reading up on the topic, and traveling to attend leadership conferences around the world. I saw Jack Welch, the legendary former CEO of GE, speak to small groups of people in New York, and he struck me as a fearlessly creative leader who was able to direct hundreds of thousands of people, all housed in separate companies, in one unified direction. I also took a two-day leadership course at MIT's Sloan School of Management went to some classes that His Holiness the Dalai Lama did on the art of happiness; and, during a trip to England to speak at the London School of Economics, I did a short leadership seminar there.

I started to understand who I was doing all this for. It wasn't for myself or for anyone on my management team. It was for the people on the ground who worked for us and who relied on us every day for their livelihoods. We were getting reports back from the field as we grew, saying that we were lifting an increasing number of people out of poverty. It was my responsibility to lead the company and to do what was best for the health and growth of the business. That was the hardest lesson I had to learn.

By the time a business matures to the point where you have to make those difficult changes in order to keep scaling up— sometimes reorganizing or reimagining the company at the deepest levels—most entrepreneurs cash in their chips and sell the company. That way, someone else has to make the tough decisions to amplify and further develop the business.

(Some years later, in 2009, *Forbes* magazine contacted me to do a story called "The Founder's Dilemma" on this very topic. More about this is available at www.looptail.com; be sure to type in "runningwiththebulls.")

In 2005 the signs of complacency were plain to see. For the first time, we had hired people who were just clock-punchers, for whom it was just a job. Our human resources (HR) practices were formulaic, and we spent most of our time managing underachievers. One indicator was in the "Think Tank Pizza Parties" or "TTPP" I used to hold at the time; they would last as long as it took for people to order and eat pizza, during which we'd brainstorm on a topic or just generate ideas. I'd randomly invite people in the company to sign up. In addition to the TTPPs, we also had other, more regular volunteer committees consisting of people doing various Planeterra projects, company functions, and that sort of thing. As I observed these committees and think tanks, I started to notice that some people never showed up to *any* of them.

In any workplace, you can tell which of the employees genuinely enjoy the environment and which of them are just there for the paycheck and what the company affords them. And, to my surprise, I also noticed that the people who were very keen to participate in the company culture weren't necessarily the people who excelled at their jobs.

Worse yet, some people were silo-ing their departments and hiring their friends within the company, effectively building subcultures inside the business. They thought they were somehow bigger than the company and that it couldn't function without them. By building teams or tribes that were loyal to them or their friends, they created a support group that stood behind that person and not the company as a whole.

I knew that we were on the verge of finding our true purpose and that there were tough decisions I would have to make to get us there. I wanted to change our course and to commit to a set of priorities that was important to the business; but the people around me thought these were crazy ideas. Members of my executive team even came to me saying that there were groups within the company who were asking them to vote against things I was proposing in our meetings.

I had gotten used to people rolling their eyes at one another when I spoke, thinking that I didn't notice. I felt alienated within my own company.

I once heard Madonna say in an interview that if you want to be a trailblazer, there are periods where you have to accept that you're going to be unpopular. I know it's weird to quote Madonna, but sometimes you hear things that resonate with you, and it doesn't matter who said them. I'm not a fan of her music but, really, no truer words were ever spoken.

Being popular or unpopular as a leader comes with the territory, and it ebbs and flows with time. I have always believed that if your intention to drive change is pure, then you will always ride back a hero, even if sometimes you have to be the villain within your own company. Winston Churchill once said, "You have enemies? Good. That means you stood up for something, sometime in your life." You have to do what is in the best interest of your business; it isn't always pleasant, but when things aren't firing on all cylinders, it's your job to fix it.

For me 2005 was the toughest year (at least, up until that point). I felt that the management team I had had in place since 1998 had reached its limit. There are many reasons I came to this conclusion, but out of respect for the people I worked with, I won't list any specific ones here. Let's just say that things had to change. I had assembled this group over the company's most challenging period, and they had come through in our darkest hour. But, because of that success, a feeling of entitlement and a distinct lack of urgency had set in. You learn a lot about people when you're in business. Mediocrity breeds mediocrity, and mediocre people hire people who won't threaten their own position by turning out to be better than them. It's a cancer that can take hold of any company. I always tell my best people that they should constantly be looking to hire and develop their replacements, because that will allow them to move up. You need to create leaders in order to be successful in a change-oriented environment like ours. If you have people who don't produce and recruit other leaders, you can't grow.

I started to initiate conversations with everyone about their future at the company, but I made a point of doing it in the most compassionate way possible. In some cases people were asked to leave, and we paid double the legally required amount of compensation. Another person relocated to a different region to find a better place within the company. For the most part, though, the people I met with came to the conclusion that it was best for them to move on. I offered to redefine their positions to give me the space I needed to make the necessary changes, but when you're on the management team of a spectacular company like the one we'd become, some people start to feel a bit entitled, believing that the company can't exist without them. So when I tried to move certain people around, they either left or we peacefully agreed it was time for them to find another job. Of the six directors I had at the time, four were gone before the year was out.

The changes in my management team sent tremors through the whole business. Some people who were dedicated to those managers no longer felt they had a place in the company, and they also decided to move on. The people who left were popular and, in a lot of ways, were really leading my business. They were charismatic people who were loved by everyone. Change is hard, and I was feeling a vibe from people who thought I was selling out, that success had gone to my head. Nothing was further from the truth. I was more committed, focused, and determined than ever before.

With the departure of so many senior people I thought there would be a big hole in our institutional memory and knowledge and that I didn't know enough about how everything worked. I had to get back in touch with where we were from an operational standpoint; it was just as I had felt in 1998.

A few years beforehand, I had written out a blank check for $5,000, placed it on my desk, and told everyone that the money was theirs if they could hurt my feelings. It was a way to encourage people to speak openly and honestly and to tell me the hard truth. As I started to investigate the business, I would remind people of the check on my desk because I wanted to get a better idea of what people were thinking, and I needed to hear what everyone had to say. As I brought people into my office to have a chat, I would mention the fact that they could leave our meeting $5,000 richer if they could hurt my feelings. It was a great icebreaker, and it certainly made people more comfortable speaking their minds because they knew I really cared about what they had to say. I don't think anyone ever went gunning to hurt my feelings in order to get the cash, but it has always encouraged people to be open with me and not be afraid to tell me the good, the bad, and the ugly.

Today, that $5,000 check has become something of a mythical creature. But recently, when I moved offices at Base Camp, I made sure it was still there in my drawer. It has our old logo printed on it, but it's still there, and I remind everyone now and then before meetings that it's still up for grabs. Maybe I should rethink the amount and up the ante to $10,000? You know, what with inflation and all.

Success doesn't happen by accident. Despite all the talk of freedom and happiness in a business model, success rests on getting responsible people in every seat. Ironically, one of the most critical aspects of creating freedom and happiness is this: *You have to hire slowly and fire quickly.* It seems harsh, but firing someone does not always have to be a negative thing.

Parting ways with someone who's not happy in their environment or who's not contributing, because the job they are doing doesn't suit them or their skills, should be seen more positively. I know that I'm nothing but grateful when someone comes to the conclusion that they are not into what we're doing and decides to move on. Far too many people know they don't like where they are and just hang around like a bad odor until someone has to remove them by force with a hammer and a stick of dynamite— and that never ends well. That's what I learned during this period in the life of the business: You must make it easy for people to leave and even encourage it. If someone isn't finding happiness in your workplace and they think they can find it somewhere else, you should be happy for them and let them go.

A person who leaves of their own accord is doing you a massive favor by not dragging it out and becoming a negative drain on your culture. And sometimes—in fact, a lot of times—people just don't work out, or they just run their course with the company. The sooner they come to the realization that something has to change, the better for everyone involved and everyone who works with or around that person. It's a thing of beauty to celebrate when someone has enough self-awareness to come to the conclusion that they need to move on.

Some people have described our culture as a bit fanatical; the word *cult* has also been bandied about. But the truth is that our business model is actually based on freedom, and unlike in a cult, it's easy for people to leave. That's what you have to do: Make it easy. Encourage people to leave, either by having good compensation packages or just by mentioning frequently that change is welcomed. When you do this, the people who stay, or those who choose not to leave, end up being more committed. They buy in because they are silently committing to stay, by working harder and letting their efforts speak for them.

CHAPTER 7

My ESPN Turning Point: 2007

I know many people who say they can pinpoint a single moment in time that changed the way they view everything. For me, it was a year: 2007 was my ESPN Turning Point.

That year, we were starting to become a real business: We passed the $80 million annual sales mark; we were gaining market share and continuing to outpace our industry; and all of it was happening while our industry was consolidating quickly. Massive publicly traded holding companies were buying up companies in our space. To me, it was the greatest thing ever—all of our competitors were getting bought out, and as soon as their once-passionate founders left with their briefcases full of money, those companies would more or less disappear from our radar.

The conglomerates that were chewing up small companies were seeing the fast growth of adventure travel, and they wanted a piece of it. The threat to everyone in our market space was real; many owners of adventure companies were cashing out in fear that they would not be able to compete against these emerging juggernauts. And with some of the insanely huge offers being thrown around, you couldn't blame any of them for taking their golden parachute and heading out of Dodge. More than twenty companies, all of which on some level were competitors of ours, were sold. Various groups created conglomerates to streamline operations, consolidate buying, and squeeze profit out of what had become the fastest growing sector of the tourism industry.

We started getting offers at G Adventures as early as 2006, but the conversations were always short. I'd simply say, "We're not for sale—move along, nothing to see here." The offers got bigger, and as we continued to skyrocket, we suddenly became a real target. The meeting requests from venture capital firms and serious investors started coming regularly, at times, more than one a month. I never really paid attention and in many ways was in my own world. I started ignoring most of the inquiries. That actually produced some angry, even venomous follow-up letters saying that I was being irresponsible to my employees by not even replying. Who did I think I was? Recession talk was in the air, and I was being scolded by rabid bankers who thought I had lost my mind by not agreeing to meet with potential buyers. I found it kind of funny.

When I did agree to sit down with these suitors, every meeting had a similar pattern. The company reps would start off very pleasantly, then slowly move to making passive-aggressive threats. One firm suggested that, as a Canadian company, we were at a disadvantage because people don't see Canadians as adventurous and that this would limit our growth on a global scale. Then came the inevitable spiel about how "we've got billions to dominate this space, and we will, and our consolidated buying will slowly destroy you." They would say that they were focused on us and that if they wanted to, they could lose money for the next five years until we went bankrupt. I don't know how many times I stared down the barrel of that particular gun. "Do you even know what you're buying?" I would reply. "Why would you want to pay this ridiculous multiple for my company when it would just start to shrink shortly after you paid me for it?" Our brand was built around a relationship with our customers that is tough to put a price on; it was hard to explain to them.

I have always believed that, as a brand, we're only as good as what people think of us. The whole 1980s-view of brand and brand equity died with Kodak and Atari. Our culture is our brand, and the only thing we own is our ability to work hard every day to earn a place in the hearts of our followers and supporters. I would tell these investors that I represent a group of people, real people who touch our brand every day and who depend on me to make the best decisions for their happiness. Really, there is nothing here to sell—I don't own anything here that is for sale. We don't own our brand, and I have been telling my people this for years. Our brand is what people think of us. *Our culture is our brand.* That is priceless.

This type of talk would often drive the suits on the other side of the table into a rage. They would bristle and huff that they were different and that if I sold, they would leave me alone to do my own thing, and I could just continue to grow the business. In fact, they would usually offer to put ridiculous incentives in place for me to continue doing what I was doing.

Everyone I had grown to know in our industry was getting big offers, and, almost without exception, they were taking their payday. The peer group that had formed over the years was heading into early retirement. I would actually hear people say to one another, "Did you get your offer yet?" as though it was perfectly okay and expected that these big shops were bent on buying up the whole industry.

Then in May 2007, in a meeting with a more suitable strategic partner, someone put a number on the table. A big one: $70 million. That was quite a jump from the $1 million offer from back in 1999. And they wanted to act fast and could close everything in a month.

For the first time, I flinched. "Maybe," I said. And we began to talk. At this point more than fifteen companies in my market space had already been consumed, and this suitor made it clear to me that they were creating a juggernaut and wanted me onboard to be part of it. I was confident that I didn't want to sell, but $70 million is a lot of clams!

They had caught me at a weak moment, and it sent me into a tailspin. Not long after the offer came in, I was reading an article about Edvard Munch's famous painting *The Scream*. When I turned the page, I saw another Munch painting, a lesser-known work called *Despair*. Where the figure in *The Scream* is obviously panicking, the person in the foreground of *Despair* is hunched over, eyes cast downward. I stared at it. I swear the guy in the painting looked like me. That was the pose I saw when I looked in the mirror.

My malaise had been brewing for a while, and now it was coming to a head. The more I thought about it, the more I felt that the company had grown in a way that didn't represent what I believed in and, worse, that I might not be the best person to lead it. Despite all our success, for a while I had felt adrift. I couldn't shake the sense that we could be doing more, that we were becoming complacent. To me, instead of transcending our industry, we had gone slightly off course. We continued to grow and had gone from $6 million in annual revenue in 1997, even as I lay there that frozen night in Tibet, to $80 million. Instead of focusing on our business model and the things that mattered, we were focusing on handling our growth. Meanwhile, some members of my team were wondering whether I had lost it—again! They'd say, "What's wrong with Bruce? He's never happy. Why does he always have to push?"

I don't know if I knew the answer to that question at the time; I wasn't being clear about the direction I thought we should go in because I didn't think people could take any more change. We had a bunch of new staff and everyone was happy with the numbers. We had been through so much upheaval, I feared people thought I was pushing just for the sake of it and that if I articulated where I thought we were going, perhaps they would lose confidence.

When I was scraping together the cash for that $15,000 government matching loan in 1990, I didn't know I was signing up for the complex leadership challenges it would take to build a multinational organization. Being a leader was easy when we first started, because the lead-by-example leadership role is a comfortable fit for me. I work hard, you see me work hard, so you work hard. This is the form of leadership that comes most naturally to entrepreneurs, as most of us are defined by our resourcefulness and work ethic. To this day, I make it my first order of business to show that nothing is beneath me when it comes to every aspect of my company. I'm down in the trenches with my team every day.

When we continued to grow and I experienced the challenges of our becoming a multinational brand, we began to need people within the company to lead in their own right. I call that "coaching leadership" because at that point the main challenge is to get the best out of people, to encourage them to achieve their full potential. Just like a coach, your role as a leader is to share your own experiences and give people the confidence to stand up and lead. That way, they can learn from their mistakes and grow as people. Coaching leadership was always my strongest area.

For me, the toughest form is what I call "inspire leadership." This is much more difficult in general, but I find it particularly hard. Here is my problem: We're approaching two thousand employees in more than one hundred countries around the world, and about half of them are people whom, in their entire careers with this company, I will never have a chance to meet. In fact, even of the remaining half, I will meet most of them only in passing. We might say hello or maybe have a quick conversation about what they do to make us great. As open as I try to be, these encounters slip so easily into the world of casual contact— they aren't meaningful connections. To lead these people and to inspire them to deliver on our brand promise, to work hard every day, to wake up every morning and love the company, and, most importantly, to reach *their* potential in *their* lives—this is where "inspire leadership" becomes critical. Happiness becomes a weapon in your arsenal to create community by uniting people regardless of their background or what they do for the company.

We had come a long way from the maverick model I had employed in my early days, which was flat and focused on being quick to market and promote something we called an "open innovation" concept. I have always been aware that the company could only grow as fast as I could. If I didn't personally evolve, we would stall. I know that sounds rather heady, but that is how I felt. It's a sobering place to be when you're a self-centered entrepreneur and you have to constantly reevaluate your weaknesses to get better, stronger, and faster. It is without a doubt one of the most important lessons I tell new entrepreneurs. It is a painful process of continuous self-evaluation; you need to get over yourself if you want to apply the theories of the Looptail to your life or the business world.

I had entered what I called the summer of despair, and I was feeling pressured. My development as a leader was stalling. And now, suddenly, my golden parachute was right in front of me, and I knew I had to seriously consider for the first time whether my staying on was in the best interest of the business or of the people whose shoulders I stood on to achieve what we had up until this point. I always thought a time would come when the company would swell to a size where we might need a traditional CEO, a professional who could manage us at the highest level, even if that meant slipping into incremental growth.

When you do the math, it's very simple; as the numbers get up there, eventually you cannot continue recording double-digit growth. At some point, the company would have to be oriented around systems and a structure that celebrated single-digit growth. Deep down, I knew I wasn't that person. I spoke to a senior person who worked at KFC who told me that when they hit 3 percent growth, they threw a champagne party for everyone to celebrate. When he told me that, I threw up a little bit in my mouth. I admire the CEOs who have that skill, but that wasn't the world I lived in; the thought of it made me gasp. I'm a builder by nature, but all that said, with a recession looming, I started to really wonder whether this might be my time to step aside. I didn't know what I was looking for, but I wanted a sign—any sign.

Then, in the middle of the night on November 23, 2007, my phone rang. I lurched up like I had that night in Tibet ten years before, but this time there was no water on my face—just a whole lot of water in my future.

It was Jeff Russill on the phone, my director of operations. He told me that he had just received a call from the US Army in North Carolina. The Coast Guard had picked up an emergency distress signal coming from the M/S *Explorer*, a ship that we owned and operated and used for tours off the coast of Antarctica. Jeff said that the call was probably nothing, but that he just wanted to let me know, and that he would contact the ship and see whether he could get hold of anyone this late. We both agreed that the alarm must have accidentally tripped or that there was a malfunction of some sort. I hung up and quickly fell back to sleep.

Twenty minutes later, the phone rang again. If Jeff was phoning to tell me not to worry, I was going to be annoyed. I heard him take a deep breath. Jeff explained that the ship had either been struck by or had struck ice. The information we had was limited, but one thing we knew was that the ship was taking on water and that even though they didn't think it had taken on much, Jeff had been in touch with our VP of Operations, Frank Schuran; our Chief Operating Officer, Saul Mandel; and our Operations Coordinator, Rich Heller. They would meet in the office in thirty minutes; I said I would be there, got dressed, and hurried down to the office. It was the beginning of what would be our company's greatest test.

I have never spoken at length about the sinking of the *Explorer*. I've refused interviews with everyone from Larry King to Regis and Kelly, and turned down speaking offers at conferences on topics ranging from risk management to leadership. Over the years, I've read a lot of speculation about what happened. For a number of reasons, I'm reluctant to go into detail about the incident, but I do want to mention it here because it underscores a key lesson I learned about the importance of transparency.

In our office, I was trying to get my head around the details. Our executives had set up a war room in one of our boardrooms, and we were hearing from ship operations people in Sweden as well as from the ship itself. The hole was fist-size, they told me. Our certified A-1 ice-class hull should have been impregnable—ships in the Antarctic hit ice all the time—but one thing turned the puncture into a freak accident. For some reason, the power on the ship had gone out. Normally, the bilge pumps would have been able to pump out the water from a leak, but without power, they couldn't spring into action.

I had a big decision to make at that point. Specifically, based on the information we had in that moment, whether to wake up the passengers (it was the middle of the night there) and offload them or have the crew try to fix the electricity. They could have repaired the power in ten minutes, half an hour, or it could have taken twenty-four hours. We'll never know. The question I faced was whether to try to save the ship or to move to protect the safety of the passengers first. Many have said that I made the wrong decision that night and that we should have tried to fix the power. But you can never know how you'd react in a moment like this.

As a company, we had studied every situation imaginable to prepare for a critical incident. For seventeen years we had been preparing ourselves for this kind of moment, but when it came, it was nothing like what we rehearsed for. We had Critical Incident Management (CIM) manuals and instructions to follow in case of emergency, but all of those things went right out the window. Rightly or wrongly, the decision was made to offload the passengers. Since they were sleeping, they weren't dressed or prepared, so it took some time to gather them together and get them ready to disembark.

Less than an hour after arriving in the office, my personal cell phone rang. I had resisted the cell phone movement for many years and had gotten my first one only a few months earlier. At most, three people had that number. I answered the phone; on the other end, a male voice introduced himself in a British accent as a reporter for the *Sun* newspaper in London. I was shocked for a moment. I told him I was in the middle of a rescue mission right now and that we'd be in contact soon with an update. Within twenty minutes, *News of the World*, also from England, called me, also on my cell. To this day, I have no idea how either of them got my number.

By 3 a.m. the various members of our global executive team were in touch with one another. We were waiting in the war room, ready to deal with anything that might come our way. My managing director for the UK and Europe was on his way to our office in London, when he also received calls from the *Sun* and later, the BBC, asking him for on-air interviews. We started seeing images of the ship pop up on websites around the world. By then, our marketing department members were arriving, and our director of marketing started to take calls. One at a time, every media agency jammed our phone lines.

The next morning, the *Explorer* was on the cover of every newspaper on the planet and was the lead headline on every media website in the world, reporting that the ship was sinking and that the 154 passengers, crew, and staff had been evacuated into lifeboats. Given the international nature of our company, it seemed like we had a passenger and crew member from every country in the world—the UK, US, China, Australia, Canada, Switzerland, Denmark, Sweden, Finland, South Africa, Germany, Japan, Philippines, Turkey, Hungary, Ukraine, Poland—you name it. Needless to say, that only exacerbated the extent of the media frenzy. It was an international sensation, and as we looked on from the war room, we saw shows in the UK being interrupted for emergency updates. What made it so much more dramatic is that the *Explorer* didn't just sink immediately. The actual hole was small, which meant that it could take days for the ship to fill with water and actually disappear. By then, every news outlet in the world was showing live footage, taken from the air as the *Explorer* twisted, danced, and flipped around the frigid Antarctic waters before finally vanishing from sight.

Just outside of our war room, people were arriving at our office to start the workday and, as they learned what was happening, the anguish spread through the building. The phones lit up. As I went back and forth from the war room, I could see the looks on the faces of our people. For a big part of the first day, we weren't sure whether the *Explorer* was going to sink.

I remember one of the young guys in the office looking at me, his eyes wide with fear, saying, "The *Explorer* isn't going to sink, is it, Bruce?"

"Not if I can help it," I replied. "We're doing everything we can." And with that, I saw tears well up in his eyes. I realized right then how my dream of showing people Antarctica had become everyone's shared dream. I can't express how proud I felt, in that split second, to have this group of people behind me.

While the media scrambled for fresh angles and the story took on a life of its own, we had much more pressing issues. We were now in the midst of executing a three-day rescue mission; ninety-one passengers and sixty-three staff and crew were in trouble, and we had to get them home safely. Nothing else mattered.

The first big decision I had to make was if I should head down to Punta Arenas to work with the Chilean navy in person and to handle the world's media, which was migrating south to report the biggest story of the moment. Collectively we decided I was needed at Base Camp, so we immediately contacted everyone in the region to head down to Punta Arenas. Within twenty-four hours, we had four people on the ground under our direct instruction. Our sales teams mobilized to set up global phone queues to handle all the calls from the passengers' families, and they made contact lists to give updates and support to people who anxiously awaited news of their loved ones.

We located the nearest ship in the area, the M/S *Nordnorge*, a cruise ship owned by the Norwegian company Hurtigruten. They were in the area and had extra space, and soon I had the CEO on the phone. He was a kind man and, after a brief conversation, he confirmed that they had space and agreed to reroute their trip and pick up our passengers. (In the frenzy, I never had a chance to thank him for helping us that day, so let me say it now: Thank you.) Still, they were on the water for four hours; it seemed like an eternity for us, so we couldn't imagine how long it seemed for the passengers themselves. The *Nordnorge* arrived as promised and picked them up successfully. By then we had arranged to have them dropped off on King George Island, one of the few areas in Antarctica that had both a community of scientists who lived there year-round and a landing strip.

All Antarctic trips run through Argentina. It's the place where the ships leave from, and where the passengers leave their luggage, when joining any Antarctic cruise. I won't comment on the lack of responsiveness of Argentina's government, other than to point out that the Chilean navy were doing everything in their power to help us. With Chile's assistance, we set a rescue plan.

First, we would get the passengers to King George Island, then we would arrange to have them flown by Hercules plane to Punta Arenas in Chile. There was a skirmish going on with insurance companies over who was covering costs, but none of that mattered. We would resolve it later.

The crises that this company has been through have taught me a lot about humanity, about the good and the bad in people. In 2007 I got to see both extremes up close, and while there were certainly moments that inspired me, I also struggled to comprehend the ugly side of human nature that surfaced around us. Maybe I'm naïve to think it could be otherwise, but I was shocked at how our job turned out to be avoiding a witch hunt.

Punta Arenas swarmed with media. Crowds of news crews with cameras lined the streets, looking to speak to anyone who knew anything, and everyone seemed to know something. Every major news company in the world had sent people to the small, sleepy town within twenty-four hours, and they all wanted a story.

Now that the passengers and crew were safely stationed on King George Island, the first reports starting coming in. There were satellite phones and even cell phone service, so people started giving interviews. To our surprise, the interviews were positive. The passengers said that they were being well taken care of; in fact, I remember hearing an interview with one British lady who said, "We're having the time of our lives." There were even passengers who took the opportunity to get engaged. While I was relieved to hear that everyone was all right, we still would not sleep until everyone was off the island.

The plane was finally ready, but now we had to be patient and wait for a safe weather window. The climate in Antarctica is unpredictable and unforgiving. We'd have to be able to fly there and get out; a window might open up in an hour or in a month. They couldn't give me a better estimate than that.

As we waited for our weather window, we knew that when it came, we had just one shot to get in and out to transfer everyone safely to Punta Arenas. The plane held 155 people, so we knew that when we arrived, we would have just enough room to bring everyone back in one trip. It was going to cost us hundreds of thousands of dollars to hire the Hercules plane to come and pick them up, so we knew there was no room for error. At last, we got the call that there was a break in the skies and the plane could take off. On to step two of our rescue plan. We all waited anxiously for any feedback about how it was going. At this point, we knew that everyone was safe, comfortable, and, in fact, no one had caught so much as a cold.

The first report came in from one of our staff members on the ground. The Hercules plane had arrived as scheduled! We breathed a sigh of relief. Then the bad news: When the doors opened, a scrum of reporters piled out of the plane to get the first breaking stories of the rescue. Ten of them had bribed their way onto the plane somehow, which meant ten fewer seats for our passengers. There would have to be two trips.

I was screaming mad and wanted the reporters left behind. At that point, though, it was officially a Chilean navy rescue mission, and we were just paying the bills (or the insurance company was, anyway). Since there was so much media attention and everyone was watching, the Chileans wanted to show the world they were doing a great job. My protests went unheard. After enduring such a long wait, now we had to decide who would stay longer and have their ordeal continue.

We arranged for a second flight, and after a couple of white-knuckle days, the plane touched down in Punta Arenas. When the news hit our war room that everyone was back safely, many of the people on our team dropped to their knees in tears. We were tired and disheveled. It had all been such a serious situation that for days we spoke only about the issue at hand. Though we tried at times to lighten the mood a little, the level of stress on everyone was tangible, right up until we got the phone call that the second flight had arrived.

Once we knew for sure that we'd got everyone back on land safely, there were a lot of high fives and cheers throughout the office. But we weren't finished. Though the passengers were safe in Punta Arenas, they weren't back in their homes yet; our job wasn't done until everyone was home safe. The insurance companies and legal teams were astounded at the resilience and the positive energy shown by our passengers, who all received settlement checks before they got home. More reports and interviews started coming in and, to my utter amazement, people went out of their way to talk positively about the experience. I was astounded.

There was one scene in particular that brought a tear to my eye as I spent a quiet moment by myself watching the news. Because the rescue was so hurried, our passengers had arrived in Punta Arenas with nothing but the clothes on their backs. We arranged for the biggest department store in town to open up for them and gave each of them $200 to buy what they needed until we could get them home. At this point it was about customer service and making sure everyone was as comfortable as possible. Someone locally tipped off the media, so they set up their cameras inside the store to film when the doors opened and our passengers flooded in cheering. I was watching the report on CNN, and I smiled and welled up a little. The camera focused on one passenger who was in a joyful frenzy. She had a smile on her face and said to the news crew, "We all booked to have an adventure, and that's just what we got. I don't want this to end; I don't want to go home yet." I dropped my head and quietly choked back my emotions. I don't know who that woman was but in that moment she gave me strength.

I don't think I really knew before the *Explorer* sank just how much people rely on a leader in a time of crisis. Everyone in our office was on edge until the moment the second plane landed in Punta Arenas, and one show of weakness from me would have caused everything to tumble down like a house of cards. Being put in such a pressure cooker, some people might go off and do all kinds of strange things that they otherwise wouldn't. One of the many things I learned was that if you can keep a calm head and focus on solutions, not problems, you can get through anything life throws your way.

Staying cool really is your most crucial task. One of the biggest things I learned during this crisis was how to stay out of the way and let everyone do their jobs. I've mentioned before that leaders in general, and entrepreneurs in particular, are notorious control freaks. Some business books say that this is your time to shine, that you should take control. The old school command-and-control leadership style you see in movies all the time is popular but ineffective. Plus, I'm no Alec Baldwin, and this isn't *The Hunt for Red October*. The kind of control you need to exert isn't the kind you might think. You need to regulate the mood, keep the energy positive, and have everything moving forward, but everything else is up to the people around you.

Inevitably, you'll have to be the one who makes the big decisions, but only after gathering information and advice from everyone around you, in an inclusive way. Greatness shows up in so many forms during a high-stress situation, but the most important thing I have learned is that, in general, people will rise to any challenge if they're guided in the process, and if they feel safe to do so. The minute any form of panic hits, it's game over—the decisions from there on out will be based on fear or else purely based on clinical information. You have to remember that the contributions of everyone on your team are what you hired them for. It was amazing for me to see, in a relatively short period of time, how my people rose to the challenge. Once they felt that they were being heard, everyone stepped up and met the challenge. And as I accepted my role of being the information center and the voice that had to make the important calls, I think everyone really stood beside me and focused on just getting the job done.

People want to know how a relatively small company like ours was able to handle such a massive crisis, particularly without hiring an outside PR firm to deal with the attention of the world's media. My advice to anyone in that situation is simple: Be transparent. We had nothing to hide; we had just spent more than a million dollars on the ship while it was in dry dock only three weeks before. We didn't cut any corners. We had all of our certifications and safety certificates, and we were completely compliant with every law and every restriction—that's how we do business. In the end, the story the media told was a positive one because this little company that could showed the world what we were capable of—getting everyone back safely and making the right decisions under fire.

Not that the media made it easy. My wife was being followed and harassed by reporters as she dropped off our kids at school. Our nanny was called and offered money to give an interview about what life was like in our house. I started getting e-mails from people I went to high school with—I didn't even remember them—who were being contacted to find out what their relationship with me was and if they wanted to comment on what I was like growing up. (Call it the Facebook factor.) At one stage of the crisis, wanting to clear my mind, I decided to go to my local gym to have a quick run on a treadmill. The row of machines at the gym ran parallel with the row of televisions, and every screen had images of the *Explorer* still swirling and spinning in the ocean. Within a few minutes of starting my run, I saw someone approach me from the side. I ignored them, hoping they would notice that I had headphones on and was listening to music and would go away. Then another person appeared, then a third. I took my headphones off, thinking they were gym patrons interrupting my run for some reason. Nope—they were newspaper reporters who had followed me in. I darted straight out the side door to my car and headed back to the office.

As I said, the ugly side of human nature came out during that time. When we had our first taste of success as a company, I was shocked and disappointed by the negative attention we received from some people. What I'm referring to shouldn't be confused with genuinely constructive criticism, which in my view is one of the most valuable things someone (particularly customers) can give us—because it's an opportunity to improve. I'm talking instead about the haters, people who just like to hate, no matter what you do or how pure your intentions are. There was this relentless search to find something, anything that could be construed as dirt.

At one point we were in the war room looking at all the media reports when the BBC interrupted their programming for an emergency update. They said that they had just discovered the safety report from the last inspection of the *Explorer* and that there were two safety infractions, the details of which they were working to find out. I immediately asked everyone to find out which report they had and which port had issued it. When your ship docks in various ports around the world, it's pretty common for representatives from that port to come onboard and do an inspection before allowing you to dock. We located the report and found the two infractions: There was a loose rug in one of the hallways and a broken lamp shade in our onboard pub that the inspector thought could be a safety risk. I instructed our staff to release the report to every media outlet we had contact with. The story fizzled; though they said they were "waiting to hear more information," there were no follow-up reports.

A similar thing happened a couple of days later. The BBC reported that someone had received medical treatment on the ground in Punta Arenas. We immediately got on the phone to our team there; apparently one of our passengers had twisted an ankle. It was the first we heard of it. Naturally we had doctors present, just in case, to meet the passengers when they landed, and, because they were there, the doctor had taken a look at the passenger's ankle. I asked our people on the ground to find the person and to find out what was wrong. The report came back that they were fine and needed no attention. We sent out the message to our press contacts, and once again, the report disappeared. I told our marketing and PR department to release all of our service records and every detail of our routine service that we had just completed. The media outlets seemed shocked at our transparency, but we were just determined to fight one fire at a time until we could get our people home.

In a short conference call with our insurance company, they said that if we settled 60 percent of these claims and 40 percent went to legal action, we would be doing well. I was staggered by that and braced myself for the worst. I have heard over and over from people in the insurance industry that what ensued over the next few days was something they had never seen before. Of the 154 passengers, staff, and crew onboard, 153 settled and with very little back and forth. There was only one hold-out. Overall, it showed the incredible resilience of our customers and their unique relationship with our brand.

One night not long after, I was home alone and still feeling shell-shocked. I logged onto our company message board, The Watering Hole, and saw the pain people were feeling over the loss of the *Explorer*. They had grown attached to her and were making tribute videos and paying homage to her like she was a friend. In a weak moment, I went against everything my PR people had told me and posted:

"Today the *Explorer* is leaving us in very dramatic fashion. She could not just go quietly in the night but instead is hanging on and dancing her way out of commission.

"She made everyone in the world watch for just a minute to remember her history, hanging on long enough to allow all of our passengers to disembark to safety. I would expect nothing less from her. The *Explorer* was a big part of our history as a company and is a reflection of what we are . . . original, innovative, and a world leader."

I signed it with my real name and logged off. Just a couple of hours later, I was watching the evening news when the anchor announced the top story. The CEO of G Adventures had given a statement about the sinking ship off the coast of Antarctica, they said. There was my message on the screen, with a horrible picture of me from when I was about twenty-five. I smiled for a minute and just marveled at the speed that we work today.

In the wake of 2007, the doubters were out in full force. Everyone thought that this might be the end of G Adventures. The buzzards were circling, and I took a few calls from people asking whether I was now more open to talking about selling the company—though the price, of course, would be discounted compared to previous offers. People I had never met would send me messages asking how I was doing and saying that, if we needed a new partner, they would be open to helping out. Instead of rolling over, we would instead make our biggest acquisition and spend $20 million on a new ship, the M/S *Expedition*. I was not willing to give up on our Antarctica dream, and within a year we would sell out the tours and show the world again what we were capable of. It would surprise everyone, and the talk of discounting the value of the company would vanish and make way for more people being even more impressed.

Scan this QR code or visit Looptail.com/Explorer to view a dedication to the late M/S Explorer.

The third major test that arrived in 2007 came when I received a letter from The Gap Inc., the clothing company, saying that they wanted to take legal action against us over our name. When the lawsuit was first filed, I was incredulous. As with the sinking of the *Explorer*, there has been a lot written over the years about this situation. And in truth, it's something that I really don't like talking about because it's so filled with negativity.

Here's what happened: We had been called G.A.P Adventures for more than seventeen years.

They were suing us on two counts, one of trademark infringement and another of trademark dilution. (I'm not a lawyer, but the difference as I understand it is that where infringement is alleged, the test is whether someone might be confused by one company's use of a trademark into thinking the product or service was connected to the other company; where dilution is claimed, the use of the trademark doesn't have to cause confusion, but it does tarnish the reputation of the other brand—for example, in 1996 Toys"R"Us successfully sued a porn website called AdultsRUs.com for dilution.)

The judge ruled against us on the confusion charge and in favor of us on the dilution charge. In my view, he was effectively throwing up his hands and saying, "Either settle or fight it out in appeals court." We launched an appeal and said that the battle would continue, but as I learned at the time, the way appeals courts work in the US meant that the legal wrangling could have gone on for years. The verdict was only for the United States, a market that, at the time, made up less than 10 percent of our business. It would have been easy for us to change our name in the United States only and use IP address technology to show American customers a different website.

Those four years included some of the worst days in my working life—specifically, any day that I had to spend in offices with lawyers. No offense to the legal profession, but there is nothing on this earth that irritates me more. I would take a lifetime of listening to nails scraping on a chalkboard to get out of a single afternoon in a lawyer's office.

When the US judge handed down the initial ruling, it came as a rude awakening. I thought to myself, Wow, I'm in for more years of fighting with lawyers, and I just couldn't take it. I was losing my core purpose, spending company money that we could have used to change people's lives and have a positive impact on the world. It wasn't the right decision.

If our culture really is our brand and that, as I've been telling people for years, it doesn't matter what we're called, I should have listened to people in our company who said we should think about a name change anyway. In the UK in particular, the "gap year," which refers to taking a year off before starting university in order to travel, was becoming a fixture of the travel industry landscape. We were being stormed at trade shows by teenagers looking for gap-year holidays, and that wasn't really our target demographic. This was a glaring problem we had for years. It had reached a point that at some trade shows, we registered as Great Adventure People in order to avoid the teen stampedes.

So, in 2011, I decided one night that we would change our name, of our own accord. I have learned in business that you cannot control the motivations of your enemy, and I didn't identify with their thinking or how they were using the legal system.

So on September 27, 2011, which was the UN's official World Tourism Day, we held an event at the Winter Garden Theatre in Toronto that we called the Future of Tourism. Live, in front of one thousand people (and simulcast to forty-six universities around the world) who wanted to hear our presentation about our plans for the upcoming season, we announced for the first time that we were changing our name, on our own terms and without any settlement.

The other people who work at G Adventures are extremely entrepreneurial in their thinking. They're innovative, they are passionate about their jobs, and they run this company as though it was their own business. I love working with them. That said, everyone has their limit.

I wish I could share with you the looks on the faces of my executive team when I brought them together to tell them that I wanted to change the name. I saw a whole lot of deer-in-the-headlights stares. Here I was, face-to-face with all the brilliant people whom I rely on, and they were behind me 100 percent. But I could see that they were stunned by the decision.

When it came to deciding on the new name, we paid a big branding company hundreds of thousands of dollars to come up with different possibilities. G Adventures wasn't even on the list. Numerous members of our staff said G Adventures meant nothing to them, and that we should just change the name completely. Since the letters in our old name stood for Great Adventure People, the natural thing for us would have been to call ourselves Great Adventures. I bought the URL from Mattel for greatadventures.com (they had a line of Fisher-Price toys in the 1990s called Great Adventures), and it looked for a while as though we were headed down that road. But I was concerned; I felt that it would limit our freedom as a business to do other things, because Great Adventures is only a travel company. And, when you get right down to it, I thought it was a bit boring.

The marketing company came back with their data and recommended we become GO Adventures, and again, I bought the domain name goadventures.com. (I still own it. I paid a fortune for it.) And when the testing came back from our customers, everyone liked the name; they thought it was an awesome idea to be called GO. I was particularly attached to the idea because in an earlier attempt we designed the logo we still use today. Most people just see the G, but in fact, it's what's called a "looptail g," one of two kinds of lowercase g characters. Unlike an "opentail g," which just has a simple curving tail, the tail of the looptail g forms a closed circle below the "bowl" (the top half of the character).

If you notice, the looptail g in our logo comes all the way around and forms an O. That's because the logo was inspired by that Dalai Lama biography called *Great Ocean* that I had picked up on my 1997 trip to Tibet. So, to me, calling ourselves GO seemed like a fitting tribute. Great Ocean is actually what "Dalai Lama" means translated into English—the full translation is "Great Ocean of Wisdom."

We were all about being GO at the time, and though I didn't realize it, we had inadvertently come up with a name for the theories of business that I had been developing—and, later, this book. As I was thinking about *Great Ocean* and where we had come from as a business, as well as my trip to Tatopani all those years before when I had discovered the book, I decided that I wanted to read *Great Ocean* again. The book was long out of print and was very rare by then, so my assistant and I scoured the internet looking for any copy we could find. The copies for sale that we unearthed ranged in price from $10 to $500, and I ordered them all. Within a few weeks, I had stacks of them on my desk and more coming in every day.

One night when I was reading over the various reports from the branding company, I noticed that many respondents commented that it wasn't as original as they thought our brand represented. The overall feeling was that GO Adventures was, unfortunately, a boring name. Then later when I looked up the registered trademarks associated with it, I found hundreds of companies. This bothered me to no end and I couldn't let it go. I started to do my own research.

And so, at the very last minute, without consulting with any focus groups or anything like that, we just decided to go with G Adventures. It wasn't the most popular decision, but I was determined. I just always believed that if I was going to live the motto that our culture is our brand, I was going to breathe life into whatever our name was. I looked at the examples of W Hotels and M Resort. I studied how overstock.com had recently rebranded to O.co, and I liked the daring approach of being known by a single letter. Besides, even the Beatles is a bit of a corny name for a band, but when we hear the name, we breathe life into the words because of everything we think of when we're reminded of what they meant.

And when I thought about it, we had paved the way toward becoming G Adventures over the years. We had our G Hotel and G Lodge in the jungle; our ships in the Galápagos were numbered G1 to G6; and I'd grown to love our G logo, its connection to the looptail concept, and how it signified Great Ocean or GO. That meant something to me and it stood for something. We just needed a bit of courage because we had paid the branding company a lot of money to tell us what to call ourselves—and now we were going off-script. No matter what it is we're called, my goal is to create freedom and flexibility for the future, and with that in mind, G was the answer. In the end, I had fought a huge lawsuit for two letters, an A and a P that, for so many reasons, didn't mean anything to us anymore. Once the decision was made, it was a mad dash to acquire the website URL, Facebook, Twitter, and do global name searches to make sure there weren't any conflicts. With a bit of a push, it all just came together, and it just felt right. It was original, gave us freedom, and would stand for whatever life we gave it.

The gasp heard in the packed house at the Winter Garden Theatre at our Future of Tourism event in 2011 when we announced that we were now called G Adventures proved that what the branding company came back with, after questioning thousands of our travelers, partners, and employees, was exactly right. In effect, our brand meant something to a lot of people, but it didn't matter what we were called. It was all about how we made people feel. Our culture truly was our brand and it didn't matter what we were called. I keep saying that freedom lies in being bold. This was without a doubt one of the boldest moves we've ever made, and finally we were truly...free.

PART IV
CULTURE

CHAPTER 8

Leaving Las Vegas

I had made it through 2007 and the *Explorer* incident, but the strain was taking its toll on me. It was clear in my mind what I wanted to do if I stayed, but I really didn't have anyone else around me who understood. That's not because anyone was resistant. It stemmed more from the fact that I was awful at communicating where I wanted to take things and what I wanted to do.

My choice was stark; I could sell the company and move on, or I could make one last attempt to steer it to where I wanted it to be. On the one hand, I still had something to prove at G Adventures. I had to be clear in my mind that I was the right person to lead the company and that I really wanted to do it. On the other hand, I thought that if I sold the company and went off to start something else, I could do something to show the world that all of my philosophies on business, customer service, and culture could be translated to other industries.

Sales continued to rise, and by the end of 2008 our sales had passed $100 million. The bounce had returned to the steps I heard in the hallways. The recession was in full swing, yet we were still kicking ass and taking names. All of the vultures who were circling for a feeding frenzy after the *Explorer* incident went quiet for a while, but before long the phone began to ring again. From deafening silence, the recession of 2008 turned the urgency to acquire us into a raging bull. Maybe it was our resilience or the fact that we were defying all odds as we continued to show explosive growth while our competitors downsized or sold out to conglomerates in a last-ditch effort to save their failing businesses. The offers intensified, and then, one day, we reached new levels of insanity. This offer was a $100 million package that sent me reeling into deep thought. My summer of despair that began in 2007 would linger into 2008, and I struggled with what I wanted to do. Investors started to chuckle at me—with wry smirks on their faces—when I stared them down and refused $100 million. We were in a full global recession by this point, and there was talk of it becoming a depression. Inside, I felt a burning desire to reinvent our business model again, yet I still wasn't sure I had any more gas in the tank.

By the summer of 2008, I knew that, if I was going to stay, it was going to take a revolution. *A cultural revolution.*

I had to be sure. I had to be sure that I was the right person to lead the company, and the only way I could do that was to clearly understand what I wanted to do and meticulously communicate that to everyone around me who were just getting used to me being the grumpy guy. As I thought about it, though, I got a sinking feeling when I began to realize the dramatic change that would have to take place for me to find my and the company's intention and purpose.

At the time, I felt that I had very little firsthand knowledge of my business. Sure, I knew what we did as a company, and I worked closely with our management team, but what I really needed to know about was what was happening on the ground. I needed to bring our people together, to unite us around our common purpose, and to define our company culture so that it transcended the differences between our national and regional cultures. And for me to do this, I needed to know what our employees thought of themselves and how they fit together as a community.

This was, and still is, my greatest management challenge. We had reached the size at which I needed to move from coaching people to inspiring them, as I explained in Chapter 7. What I was also coming to grips with, however, were the massive cultural differences between Africans, South Americans, Central Americans, Asians, Europeans, Australians, you name it. Every cultural group has a different view of work and of the relationship with the company they work for, yet even though their perspectives were so widely varied, our front-line employees in all these different cultures were the most important people in my business. They delivered service to our customers and embodied our aggressive brand promise. And the simple truth was—I didn't really know them.

With the growing influence of things like blogs and crowd-sourced review sites—what we would soon be calling social media—I saw that there were new tools that liberated people from the limits of geography. If we could harness them, we would bring people in the company together.

I also wanted to explore using social media to rally our customers around our brand. While we were going through the process that led to changing our name, my views on branding itself were changing. Social media was creating a level of transparency that allowed companies to develop the most intimate relationship with customers and brands that had ever been.

The way branding traditionally was understood was that, when you went to the store and saw a Nike jacket, it would trigger an emotional response from you. You would see the Michael Jordan commercials in the back of your mind, and you would relate the idea of being the best that you could be to the feeling of seeing that brand, and that would increase your desire to purchase the item. What I had observed recently was that branding was changing at a rapid pace. People had so much information at their fingertips (and with today's smartphones, access to everything via the devices in their pockets). They could communicate with brands by blogging about them, leaving comments on other sites about them, discussing them on Facebook and, eventually, on Twitter. It gave brands a human dimension; the consumer could have a more intense relationship with a company or brand based on their business model and what they stood for, not just their product and their one-way advertising. I started to believe that, with all of the social tools that are being intertwined in our daily lives, consumers were changing. People don't buy from companies anymore. People buy from other people. Brands now have a face because of the intimate relationship the consumer is afforded through being social. I knew this was a significant change in thinking that was in contrast to the way most people thought about modern marketing and branding.

Though some companies weren't necessarily doing the right thing, they chose to concentrate on having the best product as the basis for their relationship with their customers. Now, there was growing concern among these companies that, because your customer could look you up on Facebook, or read and contribute to blogs and message boards talking about your product, you couldn't necessarily control the discussion of what your company was doing and what you stood for. That was now largely in the hands of the customer. (This is what I had begun to see when our customers responded to our plea regarding the Peru earthquake and to our appeal for funding for the street kids home in Cuzco.)

Before today's social media, a brand could be created by just making a product and spending $100 million on an ad campaign. A good example of that was Accenture. Where did they come from? Andersen Consulting, the product of a vicious legal battle with its former parent company, Arthur Andersen (of Enron accounting scandal fame), distanced themselves from their former incarnation in 2001 by adopting the new name, Accenture. They launched an aggressive $100 million ad campaign, hired Tiger Woods as their spokesman, and, overnight, became a brand.

Then there's Dove. As an immigrant kid, I grew up using Dove. It was a cheap discount brand; one of the cheapest, in fact. Along with Irish Spring, you could get a long row of ten bars of Dove for $3.99. In 2006 Dove launched a movement around their brand using social media to get people to vote on how they defined beauty. Instead of the usual skinny models, they hired women who were middle-age or older and photographed them in the nude. They started a movement by using these striking black-and-white ads, the women appeared crouched down and showing the natural curves of normal humans, as the ad asked the question, "Wrinkled or beautiful?" It created a viral sensation that turned Dove into a premium brand. I started to wonder what brands really meant. With the transparency of social media and my thoughts on social innovation, I saw an opportunity like the space in the market I saw back in 1990 between the backpacker and the mainstream traveler. I knew we could combine our social entrepreneurship, social innovation, and social media and reinvent the company around my theories of social enterprise.

At the time, I was still developing my notion about how a brand is only as valuable as what people think of you. In fact, you don't really own your brand. Your brand is defined by how people discuss you among their friends and how they post about you on the internet. It's what they say about you when you're not in the room.

I had started offering to speak at technology conferences to share my views on branding and social media, but my talks received only a lukewarm reaction. It seemed that, in the early stages of the social media revolution, companies were still more concerned with shaping the message around their brands and figuring out how to deal with the power of people's comments on the internet. The popularity of TripAdvisor was a hot topic; execs observed that people were less likely to post something on the site if they had a great experience with their products, yet people were *very* motivated to write in if they had a bad experience. So even if their business had five hundred satisfied customers, the execs would generally focus only on the one unsatisfied customer who had posted about a negative experience.

Personally, I was more interested in the idea that, if you could figure out a way to transcend your product and even your industry, people really would be motivated to talk about their positive experience. In fact, you would be able to build an army of support-ers and rabid fans who were powerful enough to define the value of your brand through what they said about you. Those people are what we would later call Ravers: people who relate to you positively through their experience dealing with you and who, using today's technology, create a more intimate relationship with your company.

The ultimate goal of all this, though I didn't realize it yet, was to turn my travel business into a social enterprise. Social innova-tion is a term that describes using new ideas to tackle problems in society, though it was generally reserved for nonprofits. To me, that was what we had been moving toward all along. The time was right to transform ourselves. We would use the power of our community, which we would build and strengthen using tools like social media, to rally our company and our customers around social innovation. Alleviating poverty, empowering local communities, and all the things we had already been passionate about would become a core part of our business. It was about creating a business model based around happiness and freedom, and truly believing that we could really change the world.

If this was going to turn out properly, I thought to myself, I had to strip down the company in order to harness our energy, and all of the great things we were already doing that transcended what people thought of as the basic function of a travel company—things like the earthquake appeal for Peru—and clearly define what we had become. I was fascinated by the idea that G Adven-tures could grow into something different and truly become the definition of a social enterprise, but if that was to be our vision, it would take a lot of change to implement. We would take all of that and use these new tools to make our culture and our people the main driver of our brand. We would finally create the Looptail.

The summer of despair had consumed me. I wasn't sure I had the energy to make the changes I needed to become what I wanted us to be—a better version of ourselves. I put together a plan to see if I could get us back to good. If I was going to continue, we would have to start down the road of redefining social enterprise, and I knew in my heart of hearts that I couldn't get there with the team I had.

The transition I had to make was going to start from the top. So in 2008, I gathered my global core executive team in Las Vegas to hear what was next for us as a business.

Inside the conference room where we assembled, everyone was sitting around a table. Some of my execs were commenting on the serious tone and jokingly likened the environment to the famous Robert De Niro baseball bat scene in *The Untouchables*. I started to detail my concerns.

I started with a blunt observation: I had realized that our competitors ran really good trips. For the first eighteen years of the company's existence, I used to get up on stages all over the world and say that we were the best, that we ran the best trips in the world. And one day, it occurred to me that, actually, this wasn't quite true. I can honestly say that nobody does it better, but there's a glass ceiling to how great a tour can be, and there were a lot of companies now that ran great trips.

There's also a fine line between what a customer experiences as a great trip and a truly incredible experience. If you hold onto your customer satisfaction scores as the benchmark of your success and use them to guide your direction as a company, people are always going to tell you what they already know—in their experience, this was a great tour. They can't draw from what they don't know; so if you let that lead you, it's an innovation killer. It was driving me a little crazy. Henry Ford once said about feedback from his customers, "If I had asked them what they wanted, they would have said a faster horse." I really believe that the most meaningful dialogue you can have with customers is on issues of customer service. Everything else has to be gained through disruptive innovation, and your customers can't help you there.

I wanted to actually challenge the consumer, I said, and to put something in front of them that they've never experienced. I wanted us to be saying, "Here's something new; here's something you've never seen before, and you're going to like it."

So when these holding companies started coming in and consolidating the industry, I knew we couldn't beat them just by saying that we had the best tours, not with their capacity to out-spend us. Who cares if you're the biggest—is that really something anyone wants to hang their hat on? We now had to beat them with a brand that stood for something. We had to outsmart them.

I told the executives around the table that I knew where I wanted the company to go but that I didn't think I could get there with this team. So, I explained, I wanted to offer them the opportunity to move on.

"We have to work harder," I said, "to transcend our industry and to engage our customers to a higher purpose." I needed to build relationships with our customers that centered around our company's core values, and we would spend the time to see if we could come up with a draft of what our core values were. I also told them I would be bringing randomly selected groups of employees from across the company to Las Vegas for a series of meetings in order to document our core values and to gather all of the energy of our company.

"I know where I want to go," I said to my team, "but I think I almost have to restart the entire business. I have to go back to the very beginning and figure out where we stand. I want to harness this all together," I told them, "and I don't think I can do it with this group, because I need new energy." In fact, I didn't even know whether I myself had the energy to do it. I told them about my summer of despair and the need I felt to distill our core values and rally the business around a common purpose.

"I'm going to be relentless in my pursuit of this," I continued, "and I don't think it's going to be fun; I can understand if people don't want to be part of it. Because everyone thinks we're doing great, and they want to know, 'Why isn't Bruce happy?'" I told them this wasn't about anyone not working hard; nor was it about people not doing their job amazingly well. But as Wayne Gretzky said, "I don't skate where the puck is, I skate where it's going." And people get tired of doing that, which I totally understood.

It was like the air had been sucked out of the room. Many of the people there had been with me for a decade, and I don't think they had seen this coming. The sense of shock was palpable.

"Let's enjoy this weekend in Vegas," I continued, "and we can talk afterward about what the solution is."

It certainly wasn't about people getting fired, and I made that very clear. That said, I needed everyone to recommit to the business, and if they weren't willing or able to, I wanted to give them the chance to go find something else and to pay them double the legally required severance. Getting another job wasn't going to be a problem for anyone: Because of how we were positioned in the travel industry, our staff was constantly getting offers to work for other companies.

It sounded harsh, and I'm sure to certain members of the team it was. But there were some people who believed in me and believed in the company, and there were some who, upon hearing my ultimatum, decided this was their parachute. In the end, I think people know their limitations, what they're capable of and what they're willing to give, or not. I was leaving it up to them to make the decision, and I took the risk that some people who I thought would stay would decide to move on, and vice versa. But I needed the team to buy in again, to find new energy or leave.

Everyone shuffled out of the room. Within the year, six directors would leave the company.

After my announcement in the boardroom that day in Vegas, the executive team and I regrouped in the afternoon and started to have a conversation about core values. I cited a few examples of companies with a clear, well-defined sense of what they stood for and tried to get my team to identify the spirit of what everyone thought our purpose was. Great ideas were flowing, and I was surprised to find that everyone there really knew what G Adventures was about. The fact that the execs had a better idea of our purpose than I had anticipated says more about my being out of touch and disconnected from the reality of the business than it says about them.

Next, I gave everyone a lesson in risk. I told them that, as the leaders of the company, I needed them to take risks and that they needed to take those risks with the company's money. I gave each person $200 in an envelope, and we went down to the hotel's casino. Whoever turned their cash into the most money, I told them, would get an extra week off work. Entrepreneurship involves a high tolerance for risk; I get excited by the opportunity of high-risk and high-reward projects. I wanted the exercise to surprise them and to give them and me an opportunity to see how they viewed and handled risk.

As everyone fanned out around the casino, some people took to making $5 bets, while others took the entire amount and divided it into a few bigger bets. I was taking part, too. Near the end of the night, I jumped on a blackjack table and went all-in, putting down my entire pile of chips on a single bet in silent recognition of my all-in bet on the company, which had happened in 1998, almost exactly ten years earlier. Everyone gathered around, I hit twenty-one, and, in celebration, I danced around the table churning the pot! This put me in the lead, ahead of everyone. Some people had already lost everything and were out. I thought at the time that it was probably a bad idea for me to play and that, if I had beaten everyone, it would demoralize them and defeat the purpose of the entire exercise. In the end, though, we're a competitive bunch and it just seemed to fuel everyone. People kept playing long into the night, well after I went to bed. In the end, we came up with a winner.

Scan this QR code or visit Looptail.com/Vegas
to see how Bruce and the G Adventures crew
roll in Vegas.

Another lesson I wanted to get across in these meetings were my feelings on value innovation, a concept from the book *Blue Ocean Strategy* by W. Chan Kim and Renée Mauborgne, which I had asked everyone on my executive team to read. Briefly, value innovation is when you transcend your industry by creating value for your customers in areas that competitors don't even realize they need to compete in.

One of the greatest examples of this, and one reason why I chose Las Vegas for our meetings, is the dominance of Cirque du Soleil. The creative group behind that company had redefined the circus, moving into an area unique to them. Studying their company is like a master class in value innovation. Every night we were there, we went to see a different Cirque performance and afterward we would discuss what they did to transcend their industry. It was magic. We had a great time celebrating what we had done together. I wanted to mark a moment in time, a milestone, knowing change was on the horizon and that we wouldn't be the same team in the near future.

A few months after our meeting, my team got together and had a custom-designed snowboard made for me to show their thanks and appreciation. The design along the front tail featured our new G logo—complete with a looptail—as well as scenes from Vegas in our brand's color, purple. It was so well thought out that, in fact, it was one of the best gifts I have ever received. When they all walked into the office one day to give it to me, I was touched to know that I had been heard. Everyone understood. And even though some of the team members would leave a short time later, there was still a mutual respect. It was powerful.

On to phase two of our transformation. I held a series of meetings with different groups, again in Las Vegas, only this time they were drawn randomly from throughout the company and the world. The goal was for us to develop the framework of our new core values. I wanted us to be absolutely clear about what our core values were. Many companies have documented their core values, but the employees don't pay any attention. The document sits in a drawer somewhere, or the list is too long to remember. Enron famously had their core values etched in Italian marble in their office lobby: Respect, Integrity, and Excellence—they obviously meant nothing. At the meetings in Vegas, I brought in examples of companies whose statement of core values were up to fourteen pages long. We ran similar exercises to those done with the executive team and set out to redefine our values.

In this new group, I now had people from all over the world and from various different cultures telling me what our brand meant to them. It was mutually decided that we would have only five core values and that, unlike other companies' some-times lengthy documents, our five core values would consist of just a few words each. We agreed that it was important that our core values transcend cultures and that we had to make it easy enough for people to understand, no matter whether you were a cook on a truck for us in Africa or a horse stableman in Mongolia.

During the process, we came up with a lot of different ideas. There were some that I liked and others that I felt were redun-dant. But after a long deliberation, we finally settled on five core values that we would hold dear:

Every year we run a company-wide core values video chal-lenge through which we engage departments in a global compe-tition to make short movies of what our values mean to them. They are hilarious, outrageous, and very clever. You can see some of the best ones here:

Scan this QR code or visit Looptail.com
/ValuesVideos to see the best in G Adventures
employee-produced core values videos.

These core values guide all of our decisions. We print them on our t-shirts, plaster them all over our promotional literature, and generally make sure that everyone knows that these are the things we stand for as a company. Sometimes people half-jokingly throw the core values back in my face, like when they want a raise ("That's creating happiness for me, man!"). But for the most part, our core values provide a way for us to stay focused on what we stand for. Our lifetime deposits are a perfect example.

Once we had a group of people in our office who started talking about customer deposits on trips and how, when something happens in their lives that prevents them from going, we keep the deposit. They asked, "Isn't that taking advantage of people's misfortune?" It's standard practice in the industry; travel companies make millions of dollars on these deposits because people get excited about their trip and put down a sizable deposit months in advance. But then, if they get sick or have a bad breakup or get a new job or get fired, they end up canceling their trip and losing their deposit. As the internal discussion went on, someone in our office started flying the values in our faces, saying, "That's not Doing the Right Thing." And they were right.

That's how we came up with the idea of the lifetime deposit. Now, if you put down a deposit for a trip but end up not being able to go, you can apply it toward a new trip, or give it to someone else, or even donate it to Planeterra. But it won't expire. That deposit is yours—for life.

The concept was revolutionary, and it still is. (It was also the first time we got a registered trademark on something that we had come up with.) We did a great service to our customers, and it all came out of our core values and trying to stick to them.

I wanted to change our business model even further and sat down one night to think about disruptive innovation—how we could totally reimagine the way we defined business success to better suit our business and to recognize our unique culture and people. Until this point, we followed what's known as the triple bottom line philosophy. This had become a widely adopted way of looking at business that many companies who sought a sustainable solution were using. I had started to think we would have to expand the spectrum of triple bottom line thinking.

We're all taught from a very young age that you measure a company's success by how profitable it is. In business school, you learn that as a company becomes more profitable, it's considered more successful. In the 1990s, a pioneer in sustainable business models named John Elkington came up with the triple bottom line; instead of focusing only on Profit, a triple bottom line company expands the spectrum of how they gauge their success to include two other Ps: People and Planet. These sustainable companies view the effect that they have on people (that is, those affected by the operations of the business in the local community as well as the people inside the company) and on the planet (the environment) as a measure of their performance. Some companies might even create balance sheets to measure how by the existence of their product affects each of their three bottom lines.

That model had been working well for us, but I felt that we needed a better way to gauge the success of our people and to understand the human side of the business. So I began talking about expanding the spectrum to include not just People, Planet, and Profit, but also to incorporate two other elements: Purpose and Passion. It sounds kind of crazy, but I wanted to have a quintuple bottom line. Our success would be measured by how we could drive our people, planet, profit, and passion around our core values, and their purpose around why we do what we do. It was very important to rethink how we did everything, and it started with our business model and an expanded spectrum of how we gauged success.

By the end of the summer of 2008, I was all-in once again. I knew I was the only person who could drive the company in the direction we needed to go. I turned down the offers to sell the company that I had been half-heartedly entertaining; there was nothing for sale here. Instead, I jumped back in with both feet and needed a forum to let everyone know about it. So I redefined a company global conference we used to call Product Training Weekend to become the global cultural extravaganza that we call G Stock.

Many years ago, we ran an annual or biannual event called Product Weekend. Back in the early days, we sold other people's tours in addition to our own core products in order to round out our global range. Product Weekend was our opportunity for the people behind the other products that we sold to come in and train us about new products and new things they were doing. We did that for several years.

Product Weekend began to evolve in various directions and to include a strong social element. For the most part, though, these gatherings were attended by people based in our head office. But with G Stock, I wanted to bring people in from around the world, in order to start to bridge what was then a massive gap between the people in the field and the people in our sales offices.

In November 2008, I decided that I would share with everyone my new plans and deliver a harder message about the need for change and upheaval, how we needed to outsmart our competition, and how to transcend being just a travel company. Leading up to G Stock that year, I also made videos of some of the amazing things we were doing around the world in order to bring to everyone's attention what we were and what we had to become.

At the event, I launched our new core values and gave out awards to people from around the world for their commitment to our brand and our culture.

Over time, G Stock's success became so great and such a beacon for the rest of the company that I decided to take G Stock on the road and bring it to people around the world. With that, Latin Stock, Asia Stock, Safari Stock (in Africa), Euro Stock, Central Stock (Central America), and Oz Stock (Australia) were born. I would travel more than seventy-five thousand miles in about three months, and it would cost almost a million dollars to put on these events globally. But I thought they were important. I wanted to meet as many people in the field as possible and present my ideas and aspirations around redefining social enterprise. And I wanted it to come from me directly, not handed down from on high.

By now, G Stocks were becoming really big events. People would be flown in from within each region to attend. I used the opportunity to tell people what I thought we needed to do in order to really achieve something special—something that had never been done before.

I also delivered a similar message to the one I had given the executive team—that the next period was going to be a painful era of change and that if people didn't want to be part of it, I needed them to leave the company. I said to everyone, "If you don't have that fifth gear that we need, I totally understand, but you should find another job and move on. I need to have every seat on the bus filled by people who understand our core values and who are motivated to do extraordinary things." To be successful, I needed people who really believed they could change the world. If they didn't think they had it in them, or they didn't care enough to want to make their mark on the universe, I wanted them to leave.

The truth of the matter is—and this is something that came to light in our sessions in Las Vegas—people around the world have their own reasons for their level of engagement, whether

Bruce and the bus that drove him through the tumultuous roads in the Himalayas (1997)

Bruce, removed from the harsh reality of September 11, 2001, meeting new friends in southern Guyana on September 11, 2001

At the United Nations headquarters in New York, officially opening the Year of Sustainable Tourism (2002)

Following in the footsteps of Roald Amundsen (2011)

While it took longer than he expected, Bruce made it to the South Pole in what was his latest and greatest adventure to date (2011)

One year after the initial meeting with His Holiness the Dalai Lama that inspired Bruce to write *Looptail*, Bruce presented him with the book when they met again in Portland, OR (2013)

Happy Tibetan monks after receiving stickers as a gift from Bruce, confirming that His Holiness the Dalai Lama is alive and well (1997)

Delfin is a proud warrior and dear friend of Bruce (2010)

Delfin and his family, who have been responsible for providing G Adventures' travelers with unique homestay experiences in the Ecuadorian Amazon since 1990 (2010)

Delfin covering Bruce with mud as part of a sacred soul-cleansing ceremony (2010)

Proof that the "crazy" monk was telling Bruce the truth about his photo not being able to be taken (1997)

The CEO in Vietnam, who at the recommendation of a very happy G Adventures traveler was the recipient of a custom purple suit as a random act of G-Appiness (2012)

The emotional meeting of Bruce and a stableman who prepared the horses for His Holiness the Dalai Lama's escape from Tibet in 1959. The stableman has just been reassured of the well-being of His Holiness the Dalai Lama (1997)

Speaking at Ignite the Night, the fund-raising event that raised $160,000 for Planeterra (2010)

high or low. The reality is that the travel industry is not the best paying one, and some of our people have to work hard just to take care of their families. But for us to really become what I knew we were capable of, I needed every person to believe in what we were doing and to buy in; there was no room for clock-punchers anymore.

Getting out around the world to see everyone and to address the crowds at our G Stocks was exhilarating and gave me another view of what our brand meant to people. It also had the intended effect. The year before G Stock 2008, we had less than 5 percent employee turnover in our head offices. After it, we saw a mass exodus of people. The level of turnover rose above 15 percent—and I couldn't have been happier. I started getting calls from people I respected in the industry who were asking me what was going on? The word on the street, they told me, is that you're losing all your people and that everyone is saying you've lost your mind. Now people were underestimating us. It was fantastic.

One of the most significant changes that I made around that time was to give up my CEO title. To be honest, I was never especially fond of it, and I no longer identified with it. I was doing a lot of interviews back then, and whenever someone from the media called me the CEO, I would flinch. Through all my research into how the company really worked and what went on in the field, one thing I was convinced of was that I was the least important person in my business. In the traditional business world, the CEO title was reserved for the most important person in the company. Well, I certainly didn't believe I was the most important person in my business. How could I be the most important person in the company when I didn't have any face-to-face contact with our customers?

I was being interviewed by the *New York Times*. At the end of our chat, the writer politely asked me what my title was.

"Founder," I said.

"Are you not the CEO?" he asked.

"No," I said, "I am not the CEO," and when he asked why not, I replied that I didn't relate to that title because I wasn't the most important person in my company

At this point, the writer got a bit flustered. He thought I was playing around and being facetious. He told me that if he didn't refer to me as the CEO, the readers wouldn't understand my position with the company, and the story would be meaningless.

In fact, they didn't run the article because of my objections over my title. That's when I decided that, if I needed people to feel happy and free enough to deliver the best customer service on the planet, each one needed to be empowered as a CEO. So, while giving my talks on stages around the world, I declared to the company that I was giving away my title to everyone who comes in direct contact with our customers. I explained that I wanted the world to know that each customer-facing employee is the most important person in this company. From then on, anyone who answered our phones would be a CEO. Most importantly, in the field I wanted to redefine the traditional tour leader role and transform it to become what we would call a Chief Experience Officer.

There was a lot of resistance against this particular idea, again because there were many cultural issues around it. In many countries, it was considered a high honor to be a tour leader, and people worked hard to gain enough education to become a tour conductor or guide. Locally, the title "tour leader" supplied a level of status for them, while "CEO" meant nothing. I even read comments on our message boards of people saying, "I don't care what Bruce says, calling myself a CEO means nothing to me and means nothing to our travelers. I am not using it."

So, I sat down with my marketing and creative team in order to figure out how to create a brand and status in our sales materials, about what it means to be CEO at G Adventures.

I wanted everyone to understand that this was the birth of a new era and that it was a great time for such an unorthodox change. In the field, we were already the employer of choice for people who wanted to work in tourism, and we were attracting the best talent. People wanted to work for us because we were not part of the conglomerates that were consolidating operations for profit while driving families into poverty.

I needed people to understand that this wasn't a gimmick but a way for us to fundamentally change our thinking about who are the most important people in the company. We had to offer the best customer service in the world, and we could only do that if we created a culture of excellence. The first step was getting everyone to understand who we worked for—and that it wasn't me. It was everyone who delivered on our brand promise. Our CEOs are both the face and the voice of the company.

After putting that message out there in our brochures and in our sales materials, we eventually started to see that, around the world, people wanted to be a CEO. And, at the same time, it was a term we owned. No other travel company had multiple CEOs; it created differentiation from everyone else. Our CEOs came to be seen as an important part of our business, and, over time, we built whole marketing campaigns around our CEOs. We had created something that belonged to us and created the status I felt we needed in order to push our operating culture further and link it to what our brand stood for.

Not to mention the delicious irony that it started causing all kinds of confusion when it happened, especially in the business community. One of our greatest joys as a business is when people call and say, "May I speak to your CEO?" We usually say, "Which one?" Then the caller asks, "How many do you have?" And we respond, "Oh, we have hundreds."

CHAPTER 9

The Death of HR

The next thing I needed to change was how we managed our people. As far as I was concerned, we were doing a lot of things wrong. You can't just treat human beings as though they were administrative files. I needed to develop a better understanding of what we were doing in this area, and, by the end of 2008, I knew I had to blow it all up and start over if we were going to create a cultural revolution. I told everyone working in the human resources side of the business at the time that I would have to reevaluate everything, which likely meant I was going to hire new people.

When I started to really dig into how we managed people, I was stunned by what I found. Our practices weren't at all in line with our core values. We managed everyone to the lowest common denominator—making decisions that applied to the whole workforce based on the behavior of a few bad apples and, as a result, punishing everyone in the organization.

Our Facebook policy was a crystal-clear example of this. One day we learned that a few people were on Facebook for four and five hours every day. Our head of human resources

(HR) responded in a way that made perfect sense, from an HR perspective—she came to me and asked for approval to lock everyone out of Facebook. And I gave it. At the time, it seemed like the easiest thing to do; I had so many other things on my plate, it seemed like a good solution. Today, though, I realize that this was a classic example of managing to the lowest common denominator. We were limiting the freedom of the entire company—most of whom weren't abusing Facebook—in order to punish a few offenders.

We also didn't manage or get rid of people who weren't contributing beyond the bare minimum. A large percentage of the people who worked for the company at the time chose to be there because of the lifestyle it afforded them. We had a young, vibrant, fun culture that attracted great people, with varying degrees of how they contributed to the success of our business and company culture. At the extreme end of the spectrum were what I call Culture Vultures—people who were huge culture promoters, but that didn't mean they were necessarily that good at their jobs.

I'm a firm believer in the importance of company culture, but I also know that you can't run a company by focusing only on having happy people and a fun work environment. Performance matters.

So, if you think about it in terms of the Looptail, along with creating passion and purpose and paying it forward, you also have to nurture an environment that demands excellence and celebrates achievement. It's not glamorous; even with a great culture, we still sometimes have to fire people or restructure departments. Ultimately, though, it's part of being a fast-growing company. There's no way around it.

To start the process of transforming how we managed people, I decided to implement the teachings of Jack Welch, the former CEO of General Electric. I consider Jack Welch one of the greatest leaders of our time. Many people find it strange that I can relate to a company like GE. To be honest, I can't. What I can relate to, however, is the innovative leadership of someone who managed to achieve incredible results while getting hundreds of thousands of employees to believe in his ideas. To me, leadership is about getting a group of people together from different backgrounds, with different ideas and different beliefs, and getting them engaged and moving in the same direction. Few people have ever done this as well as Jack Welch did. I spent time studying Jack's beliefs on management, and while I had to refine his teachings in order to mesh with the needs of our business, eventually we tailored it enough so that I believe it is truly unique to G Adventures.

One of Welch's best known management approaches (which were outlined in detail in his best-selling business memoir, *Jack: Straight from the Gut*) was called the 20/70/10 rule. It says that every company needs 20 percent of its workers to be high-potential people; 70 percent who are the most important people in terms of getting the daily work done. The last 10 percent, Jack believed, are the people you need to identify and figure out how you're going to manage them out.

I call this the Lord of the Flies law of nature—in any group of people, there will naturally be 10 percent at the bottom of the food chain, and they have certain characteristics. Even if you take the most high-performing collection of people, there will always be a group that forms at the bottom, for the simple reason that everyone can't be on top. It's easy to understand: No matter how elite the members of any group are, once you bring them together, individuals tend to view themselves in relation to the others, rather than to the world outside the group. Fifty percent of the group members are, by definition, below average. And that has a real, tangible psychological impact. I have found that people fall into their roles, start to accept their destiny within their group or surroundings, and then manifest that destiny. It's a shocking reality, which brings me to one of the most important lessons I learned in managing people: the value of differentiation.

The mistake most organizations make is that they don't properly identify their bottom 10 percent, yet end up spending most of their time and resources managing this group of people because they are generally harder to maintain. The startling revelation I had as I began to apply this concept to my business was that often, the group of people in the bottom 10 percent were also Culture Vultures. They were popular among their fellow employees and took part in all company extracurricular activities; they were often first to volunteer for any committee. They protected themselves from being called to account for their deficiencies at their actual job by making themselves irreplaceable as culture leaders.

What companies should really be focusing on is managing their highest performing people. The biggest mistake we make is not paying attention to the top 20 percent because by nature they are generally self-managing and self-motivating. They work hard because they are more conscientious and committed to achieving anything they put their minds to. So, we tend to leave those people alone or to manage them with performance bonus plans that will allow them to make more money than everyone else based on their hard work. I call this the Mary Kay style of management, after the American cosmetics company that employs women to sell their products to their friends and acquaintances in their local communities. The company puts on these massive conventions, at which the top sales people are given pink Cadillacs and fur coats that they parade in front of the people who didn't do as well. That's what I call an aspirational culture, one that creates an environment consisting of people aspiring to achieve the pink Cadillac and fur coat. People go mad at these conferences, which are really a blatant celebration of differentiation—it can all be yours, the message goes, if you just work harder.

There are many studies, however, that show it's generally a bad idea to motivate people with money alone. While people need to feel valued and to have a compensation package that respects their value to the business, it's not a very good tool for motivation. A study by a group of US researchers published in 1997 showed that there are three kinds of work orientation: jobs, careers, and callings. People who consider work to be a job are just out to earn a paycheck. They are the type of people who work because they have to and spend most of their time looking forward to spending time away from their jobs. They are the least productive people, and they are motivated only by their own personal gain. People who view their work as a career don't work as a necessity, but instead to advance and succeed. They want to do a good job because they want to advance their careers. Then there are people who view their work as a calling. This group wants to achieve happiness, and it is important to them that their life is fulfilling—not because of external rewards or self-interest, but because they want their lives and work to contribute to the greater good.

Those who see work as a calling are more committed to it and work both harder and longer, because their life is rewarding and they are happy. They are the people who generally get ahead in the world, and these are the people you want to make sure you create the right environment to attract and retain. That's relevant to everyone, no matter what their position; studies have shown that there are doctors who view their work as a job and house cleaners who view their work as a calling.

Back to our 20/70/10 rule. As I say, linking pay to motivation doesn't really work. It's really just a way to leave the high-performing group alone in order to focus on the most needy group. In terms of building a business model based around purpose and performance, that's a big mistake. You're effectively paying extra for the top 20 you're ignoring, while at the same time, focusing on your bottom 10 is costing you more and sucking up even more resources.

This might sound surprising, but the middle 70 percent is your most important group. They're the worker bees, the ones who generally do a lot of the heavy lifting and get work done.

Within the 70 percent group, there are always two fringe groups, one on the top end and one on the bottom; the one on the top consists of people wanting to push up to the top 20 percent category, and by contrast there's always a group in danger of falling into the bottom 10. It's a ladder that people move around on every day, depending on so many variables that might change or shake your business.

In my experience, you will never find anyone who can jump from zero to hero—who can go from the bottom 10 to the top 20—but you will find people who will fall from the top 20 all the way to the bottom 10. It doesn't happen very often, but I have seen it. Usually it's because of a bad decision in terms of promoting someone who is really good at their job into a different area, and it turns out to be one where they struggle. This is often the case in sales. When someone is an outstanding seller, you'd think the next natural progression would be to put them in sales management; but really, that takes such a different set of skills. Someone who was a great salesperson isn't necessarily a great manager of sales people. If they're not a good fit, they start to struggle, and it's hard for them to go back. It's an old phenomenon; *The Peter Principle*, the legendary business book that describes how people are promoted into jobs that are beyond their ability, came out in 1969.

You see this often in the investment world, in which they take hotshot traders off the floor and put them in a management positions. If they really don't have those skills, they will fail—or, even worse, they may be terrible at their new jobs but nobody does anything about it. They may have been great traders, but as terrible managers, they end up destroying a company's culture along the way. It takes a long time for a manager to admit that, after promoting a rising star, that person fell from the top 20 to the bottom 10, and now you have to do something about it. Sometimes this problem can take years to address. By the time you do something about it, there may be a long trail of carnage.

You may have lost many great people who left because they were tired of being managed by someone who wasn't good at it.

I used to pride myself on nurturing a very flat organizational structure. I called it the Maverick structure, after the title of a book that influenced me in my early days. The author, Ricardo Semler, is the chairman of a Brazilian industrial conglomerate called Semco, and his book details how he developed a massive company around a very flat organizational structure in which there are few layers of management between the people on the ground and the people making decisions at the top.

Semco was one of the first companies I read about that promotes freedom in the workplace and demonstrates how freedom connects to getting more responsible people in every seat—by allowing employees to set their own hours, design their work environment, and share information. I think what surprised me the most is that employees also set their own salaries. In doing so, they had to consider similar positions with equal responsibilities in other companies, and all salaries were posted and made public. I was taken by the freedom it created and how it rewarded responsible behavior. But I was starting to question whether that flattened structure would serve us the way we wanted it to.

The other thing that is critical to leading people is building a brand around your leadership. As I was rebuilding my team, I needed to look at them as assets to the business and build a brand around our leaders, to take the pressure off just a single founder. Ditching my CEO title was one move; the next was to make sure that everyone around the world who works for the company, as well as our customers, knew that we had some of the best and brightest people behind our purpose-driven culture. So I decided to bring together our leadership in a group called C.O.R.E., which stands for Chief Operating and Reporting Executive. This would be my top global leadership body. They would meet twice a year and be responsible for maintaining our global culture, which was a big part of our company strategy.

They would also be involved in think tanks and would be part of most of our big decision making and execution for the company strategy on a global basis. I also formed an extension of this group, called G Force, that included a wider group of executive team members. G Force would meet annually to share thoughts and contribute to some of the company's thinking and direction. Most importantly, I wanted this team to help me and C.O.R.E. better understand the needs of the regions and give us a better sense of the pulse of G Adventures as a multinational organization. The clarity that internally identified our C.O.R.E. group was an important internal decision, one that created clear lines of reporting and gave everyone immediate access to me through their C.O.R.E. representative.

Your structure becomes critical to creating clear chains of command. How you communicate and the access people have to the top decision-makers of any organization is one of the most important things you can do to create the confidence needed to generate all of the great stuff like connectedness, innovation, happiness, and freedom. The traditional ivory tower, military command-and-control style of leadership I was contemplating during the *Explorer* crisis is dead, and while you might get some results employing such tactics, you will forever remain vulnerable to being beaten by an organization that is more social and engages employees and customers differently.

Our chain of command is unique because we had what I call an owner-centric system that was more circular, one that kept me and C.O.R.E. in the center of decisions but created enough freedom to drive innovation. Unlike traditional organizational charts, which run horizontally and create silos that in turn promote division, we developed our own organizational structure that we called a "halo system." It was designed to be simple, removing as many layers of management as possible in order to give everyone access to leadership and me, the owner. The first halo is of people at the VP level, then the senior management level, and so on. Our halo system looked something like this:

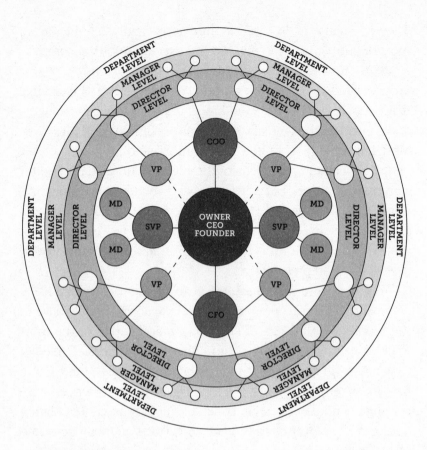

I started to research companies with winning cultures that led their industries and found the three main attributes they had in common were directly related to our basic pillars of happiness. These organizations focus on:

A collaborative environment (connectedness)
Ethics and values (passion)
Purpose and mission

Another component these companies have changed is what they look for in the people they hire. In our own hiring process, we needed to redefine both what a superstar looks like and what transcendent leadership looked like. If we were going to rise above conventional workplace thinking, we had to be clear about what traits defined a socially ready workforce that combines the cultures among family, team, and tribal groups. That definition is what I call the "Seven Cs" (catch the travel reference?).

All of the people we hire embody these three characteristics:

1. Creative
2. Collaborative
3. Communicative

In addition to those three, transcendent leaders must also have the following:

4. Curiosity
5. Courage
6. Confidence
7. Consistency in their beliefs (integrity)

Why do all this high-concept stuff? Because high-performing organizations often have a more open structure, and like them, we aim to create more freedom as we get bigger. Replacing those traditional office-based structures is how we put a stronger emphasis on our company culture—and how we avoid putting our employees in an organizational straitjacket.

Now that the lines of communication are fully open in our company, it was time to start using them to sing the praises of differentiation. So we started developing theories around my views on what we would call Star Mapping. I had to truly get to a point where I understood that while people may be born equal, by the time they became employees, managers, and teammates, they were not.

At the time, bonuses in our sales department were equal for everyone; if the company hit its target, everyone received the same amount. When I started to investigate how that was working, however, I found that almost exactly 20 percent of the sales personnel were propping up everyone else. In effect, our culture was also protecting the bottom 10. When I went to speak to managers about this, they were quick to defend the practice of rewarding everyone equally. It was a world of happiness and unicorns where everyone pitched in; there was no competition to answer phones, to close sales faster, or to have multiple people helping one another out on a single file. Some people told me our equal bonus structure was the only reason they worked here. I knew I needed to find a balance, but the status quo would have to change.

I started by having meetings with my C.O.R.E. team and speaking to everyone in the company about differentiation. In any talk I gave, I brought up the concept and said that we would start developing programs to reward people based on performance. I asked all department heads to start by giving me a list of the people in their departments divided into categories of 20, 70, and 10. I wanted to know where everyone was, and I wanted us to be mapping out our talent.

The resistance was immediate. I sat down with my managers to hear their thoughts on where their people belonged, and I was staggered by what I heard. I didn't personally know everyone who worked for the company, but I had a good idea about the people who stood out. One at a time, each manager walked into my office saying they really didn't have anyone in their bottom 10. I sat and debated each employee with them. There were a few exceptions, but generally this was my red letter day. Everything about how we dealt with people would have to change, and it would have to start with redefining what we thought about people management. That's how my one-man battle against Human Resources began.

A couple of years earlier, I was featured in the cover story of a business magazine. When I got my hands on a copy, I saw myself on the cover, with a quote to the left of my face: "HIRE PEOPLE

YOU HATE." I was quite shocked; I did say it, but it was taken out of context. To make matters worse, a few of my managers had seen the magazine on the store shelves before I did; one by one, they came to my office holding a copy and saying, "I guess this means you hate me?"

What I really said is this. For years, I had mentored young entrepreneurs, and one of the big mistakes I found was that when people first started to grow their business and they need to recruit their first employees, they would always hire people whom they liked, regardless of skill. At this early stage in the life of any business, money is usually tight and you need to make sure you bring on someone who will have the greatest impact on your company. Hiring people you would like to be friends with makes sense because, as human beings, we're generally attracted to people who are like us. They are people with similar traits and, usually, similar skills. It sounds great to hire someone that you would like to have a beer with at the end of the day.

But hiring someone who's more of a friend is often a bad idea. In fact, that is the last thing you should do at such a critical stage. You should hire people who are *not like you*, and, at times, even people whose style is so different from yours that they irritate you. These are generally individuals who have the skills you don't. For example, I have very few friends who are fastidious and obsessed with details in their life or their work. Such people sacrifice getting a greater volume of work done because they are motivated by detail and accuracy, and they're the ones I often need to seek out for my company. Some of my best people can take my blood pressure from zero to one hundred in a flash because I find them so incredibly tightly wound and conservative. It drives me nuts! But you have to have people like this in your organization because you need all types of people to build the perfect team.

So, I used to joke with young entrepreneurs that they should hire people they hated. I was exaggerating for comic effect. And yet, when I started my search for a new vice president of human resources, I didn't know that my theory was about to be put to the ultimate test.

At the beginning, when we put out the call for candidates, we got an incredible response. I was handling the search myself; I wanted to see every single résumé and do all the calls and meet every candidate personally. When I heard Jack Welch speak, he said that HR had to be represented at the highest level of any great organization. He said that one of his closest confidants was his human resources person. I believed if you truly wanted to create a company defined solely by its culture and its people, that would have to be the case. I decided at the start that there was no way I was going to settle for a candidate who was just okay. I needed to find someone who shared my views on people management and talent mapping. I was starting to develop a philosophy that seemed counter to everything I was reading about in the world of human resources, and I wanted someone who felt the same way.

I began the search, and after the first round, we received more than five hundred résumés. I met with about forty of the applicants; there was not a single person I would even consider hiring. Not even close. I didn't share any common views with any of the people I met. I started getting worried and doubted my ability to recruit someone. It wasn't just that I had a few differences of opinion with the people I met—I didn't share *any* views. It was scary. Within a minute of my asking them for their views on human capital and managing people, I would be gasping for air and aching for the meeting to end. Sometimes I was even rude and would end the meeting abruptly, because I was getting more and more agitated.

My feeling was that traditional HR departments are set up to keep people from making errors. It's the science of locking down people's freedom and taking away their ability to think for themselves by setting detailed rules to handle any situation, all in order to avoid making a mistake. And as companies got bigger,

HR would create more rules and more oppression, taking away more and more freedom. It went against everything I believed in.

I actually found that I didn't like the people attached to such views, and it angered me. I started to question whether the HR person I was in search of really existed and thought maybe I really did need to hire someone I hated! I wondered if I should forget about finding someone who intrinsically shared my views on creating freedom and happiness in the workplace.

The hunt for this unusual HR person had gone on for more than five months. Thinking that I might be recruiting individuals who were too set in their ways and who really came to these interviews to try and teach me the best tactics for good people-oppression, I decided to re-advertise the job at the director level, to see whether I could find someone with experience yet with a bit more of an open mind. Another six hundred résumés flooded in. All told, 1,100 people had applied for this job, and in all candor, I couldn't find a single decent candidate that I would even consider for the job. But then again, I wasn't looking for the typical or traditional HR professional.

This was now getting serious. It was going on ten months that the search had been dragging on. By then, some of the people I had wanted to leave were gone, and our HR department was being held together by a few loyal people in the department who were pulling ridiculous hours just to maintain the administrative side of HR. They were swamped, frustrated with me, and just wanted some leadership.

There was a point when I thought the problem was me. I hadn't been so closely involved in recruiting for a long time, so I thought that maybe my expectations were unrealistic. So, I brought in the top four candidates that I had seen and gathered my C.O.R.E. team to meet them and to see what they thought. Maybe we had changed so much by this point, or maybe my team and I were starting to share the same views; either way, there was a stampede to my office door after each interview, with my C.O.R.E. team members saying, "There is no way we can hire that person." We shared so many funny stories on the views some of these candidates had in common about the management of people, and yet, we all knew the stakes were high because this position would be the next step in our transformation.

After ten months, I thought I had finally found a couple of good candidates. They were not perfect by any means but I liked them enough. I was simply exhausted and started to remember my "HIRE PEOPLE YOU HATE" cover story. The C.O.R.E. team had much the same view. The people we had seen were all good candidates, but the team's comments on them were only mild praise. They could do the job, and they seemed nice enough. Finally, I offered one of them the job, and then she asked whether she could take a week to think it over.

This is the worst possible thing you can do to me. You see, I want people who work closest with me to be driven by a burning desire. I want people to want not just *a* job, but to want *this* job. So, it bothers me when people can't decide. It casts doubt and shows indecisiveness, which I don't want at my highest level. I called a few of my friends who ran companies and asked their advice; they all said that I was overreacting, that people process things differently, and that some of us needed to think things over. Well, on the last day of the additional week our first candidate had requested to make her decision, I received a résumé out of the blue, and—quite frankly—it looked good. We were due to receive the final word from our prospective hire that afternoon. But for some reason, I still decided to call the number on the new résumé myself. It turns out that this person lived just a few blocks from the office, and when I asked her to come by, she agreed. Hours later she showed up at Base Camp. She introduced herself as Amanda and within five minutes of meeting her, I knew this was the person I had been searching for. I quickly rounded up the C.O.R.E. group, all in the same afternoon, and right after they met her, they came straight to my office and said that she was the one and that we needed her on our team. I had to make it happen. So when I received the call from the other candidate after her week of pondering the idea, I said I was sorry, but that the position had been filled.

This was one of those moments when I believe that karma appears in business and, like Tibet in the days of the oracles, you have to sometimes follow your heart. Nothing happens by accident, and again, everything happens for a reason.

CHAPTER 10

Your Culture Is Your Brand

As we began to work together, Amanda and I found that we shared many of the same views on human capital and the importance of culture in any purpose-driven organization. There were only two concepts that I regarded as important in HR: talent and culture. When I thought it over, I realized that HR had two basic functions, neither of which it was particularly well geared to: hiring the best people and fostering a healthy work environment. How can you have a healthy office culture when you manage to the lowest common denominator and when everyone else's freedom is taken away because of the actions of a few? I wanted to do away with traditional HR. Through the painful recruiting process for Amanda's job, I learned that traditional HR departments were adverse to what I wanted to accomplish. It had to go. So, we created two departments that we would call the Talent Agency and the Culture Club.

*Scan this QR code or visit Looptail.com
/TalentAgency to see how G Adventures announced
the death of traditional HR to its employees.*

We also moved some of the administrative functions of HR into our finance department. Significantly, we decided that we would have the Talent Agency and the Culture Club as the departments in charge of the important elements that I wanted to foster and develop in the company. These are the areas that, I felt, had a meaningful impact on the people side of my business and that would clearly deliver on my goals of creating a socially innovative business model—one that would define what our brand meant to anyone who came in contact with us.

For some reason, people can't understand how a business can function without a traditional HR department. I have no problem with people who still believe in a traditional HR setup, but to me, it just isn't necessary. And, it doesn't really fit in with the culture I wanted to create, one that transcended our industry and created differentiation.

We knew we had to change how we brought people into the organization. It was not only important to attract talented people but also to make sure we had the right people who would contribute to the company's culture. We put systems in place to build on our existing practice of interviewing candidates to see whether they'd fit in culturally and turned it into what we called the "G Factor Interview."

The purpose of G Factor was to ward off what we called "brilliant jerks." When you're a fast-growing company, or when you get as much attention as we have, you generally attract a parade of people who want to be part of it. And in truth, many of them have preexisting relationships or channels of business that, if you hire them, they can bring along to benefit your company. Brilliant jerks are high-performing, influential, and usually admired by everyone around them. Unfortunately, the problem with them is that they center everything around themselves and are terrible at creating winning teams or contributing to any culture—let alone a culture driven by purpose or the relentless pursuit of excellence through differentiated customer service.

Brilliant jerks are actually culture killers, using their influence to create divisions within the company. They're disablers; a growth company needs enablers. If we were going to place our brand value in our culture, it's just too expensive, in terms of time and effort, to try to manage brilliant jerks—people who, no matter how much business they can drive, just can't fit into your culture. I have learned this over and over in my time—it's just not worth it.

G Factor would change the way we conceived of the ideal candidate; they had to contribute not only to their job but to the building of our brand and our culture. After a candidate had gone through the regular process of interviews by their managers and it was decided they were the best person for the job, they then had to go through a G Factor interview, no matter how senior or junior the role. If they didn't pass, they didn't get the job—no exceptions.

In a G Factor interview, we randomly select three people from across the company to conduct the interview. These people come from various departments and levels, from the executive level to the mailroom. We installed a Crown and Anchor wheel in our G Factor room, and the candidate spins the wheel to choose from a series of questions that attempt to take people out of their comfort zone. The questions are sometimes silly, sometimes more thought-provoking. Some examples:

> If you could only eat one thing for the rest of your life, what would it be?
> If you could have one superpower, what would it be?

What was your favorite toy as a kid?

Who is the last person you would want to be on a deserted
island with?

The interviews also include some casual banter, aimed at getting to know who you are. At the end of the interview, the interviewers score the candidate by giving them a green, yellow, or red light based on criteria centered around their ability to be fun, friendly, and contribute to our culture. Green obviously means this person needs to work here right away. We usually get excited when someone gets green lights all around because it means "Yes! We found them!"

Yellow is an indication that there are some warning flags and we need to take a closer look. We haven't hired anyone after a yellow light result yet, but that decision usually comes back to the manager, who then speaks to the Talent Agency and/or their C.O.R.E. member.

The idea of the G Factor interview is to put people on the spot, albeit in a friendly and comfortable environment. In truth, we were surprised how some people just couldn't do it. In the first quarter alone after we began holding these interviews, four people were rejected by G Factor. I had VPs pleading with me to bend the rules because the candidate they wanted failed the G Factor interview, but I've stood my ground, because I believe we have to live by the values we've set for ourselves as a company.

We began to further our development of our earlier work with the 20/70/10 concepts. Our new talent team came together, and we released our new method for conceiving of our talent breakdown, the Star Mapping System (SMS) to match our Talent Agency theme. It was the same idea, but we made it more understandable by calling the three groups Stars (middle 70), Shooting Stars (top 20), and Black Holes (bottom 10). We were never happy with the Black Holes name—it was kind of an internal joke for a while—but it seemed to stick as we began to implement the program because the bottom 10 consumed so much more time relative to their contribution. Eventually, we renamed Black Holes to be Rising or Falling Stars. The goal was to manage them up or out, and they could go either way.

Pretty soon, it became clear to everyone which people belonged in which group, and an amazing thing began to happen. Once we packaged it a bit better, our once-resistant hippie culture started to truly accept differentiation—even demand it. You see, Shooting Stars prefer to work with other high achievers, and when you give them a taste of what it's like to have superstars in every seat on the bus, it fuels people's appetite for working smarter and being more committed. They become insatiable. The change was hard to push through at first, but suddenly, it became so widely adopted that the culture became self-regulating. People didn't need to be told they were Falling Stars—it would be apparent even to them, and often they would leave on their own. They didn't need to be managed out. Meanwhile, the people who really cared and wanted to stay came to the Talent Agency and wanted to work toward moving up; they wanted a road map on what they needed to do.

Also, our Stars and Shooting Stars were tired of carrying the load for the Falling Stars, and once the system began to take off, they became more invested in who we brought into the company. It was the most amazing thing to see the tone and opinion change. There was a group of people within the company that I called our "oldies but goodies," for whom these changes would breathe new life into their relationship with their work. We woke up the giant in some of them; they were ready to recommit and stand behind our revolution, to seize their opportunity to grow, and to finally have a department that saw them as talent. They knew it was their time to shine, and we wanted them to have the chance to do it.

One lesson I have learned that I try to impart to anyone wanting to build a winning culture is that great companies celebrate. In the case of someone who needs to move on, we're talking about the celebration of growing and coming to terms with moving on to better things in life. But in general, there are all types of celebrations that contribute to building a winning culture. Great companies go out of their way to make a big deal of every time they do something better than everyone else. We have many different ways of celebrating these things, and it's especially important that we put some thought and creativity into them. There's no better way for a boss to send the message that her people mean nothing to the company than ordering a few pizzas as a way of saying, "This is for a job well done." It's like putting cash in a birthday card; it says you didn't give an ounce of thought to how to commemorate someone else's special occasion. I have said over and over that people will always remember how you made them feel. Everyone wants to be part of a winning team, and celebrating successes is not only good for building connectedness with your people, it also helps to attract great people and to engage your customers.

One example is Haircuts and Hot Dogs, a day we hold a few times a year as one of our many different ways of celebrating. We bring hair stylists into the lobby of our building and have hot dogs and ice cream vendors outside for lunch, all of it free of course. We often plan one when we win something, and not to sound cocky, but we win so many awards that we can schedule these regularly. Along with our core values, we have what we call below-the-line values, and here's one of them: Be smarter, faster, and celebrate winning.

Scan this QR code or visit Looptail.com
/HaircutsandHotDogs to get the inside scoop on
this deliciously stylish celebration.

*Scan this QR code or visit Looptail.com
/CelebrateWinning to see how the G Adventures
staff celebrates winning.*

Once we really got our culture driving the business, it was a night-and-day kind of change. It polarized some people, but those who remained were stronger, and the new people who came in were charged. We were heading into the height of the recession, yet while our competitors were reporting record losses and rolling back their staff levels, we grew more than 40 percent and continued down our aggressive path to changing the way we looked at the business.

In the course of my studying how to reinvent business, I learned a lot about what drives and motivates people; one of the greatest drivers is happiness. I began to think back to the second part of my trip in 1997, when we left Tibet to go to the kingdom of Bhutan for the Paro Festival. If anyone knows about what happiness really is, it's the people of Bhutan.

Like Tibet, Bhutan was another place that shook me to my core, because everything they believed in 1997 were things that we in the West considered backward. Bhutan is located in the middle of the Himalayas, which lent it a degree of isolation. Unlike its neighbors, Bhutan had never been invaded—most conquering armies weren't strong enough to make it through the harsh Himalayan mountains. Even in 1997, the Bhutanese had no televisions and their newspaper came out only weekly. And yet, though Bhutan is governed by a monarchy, the king himself was very modern. Rather than tracking the country's development in terms of Gross National Product, the king of Bhutan measured Gross National Happiness.

When I got off the plane in Paro, I walked up to the customs officer, who sat in a little booth made of glass that looked like a phone booth, and checked in. My name was written on his clipboard. He said, "Oh, we're expecting you." It felt like visiting an amusement park. When you visit Bhutan, you pay a per-day rate, and kids stay and eat free. Back then it cost $250 US per day, which you paid the government by wire transfer to a New York bank account. Once you did that, they took care of everything. Whatever you wanted to do, they'd set up; you would get a guide, a vehicle, and stays in government-run hotels. So after checking in, I met the guide assigned to me, whose name was Karma, and set off to see Bhutan. To be honest, I just didn't know what to expect. And that was thrilling.

I had heard all kinds of crazy things about this country: that they had no concept of mental illness, no sexually transmitted diseases, no problems like peanut allergies, juvenile diabetes, and asthma that are so prevalent nowadays. What I saw fascinated me. You would see prisoners doing the manual labor of the country, painting the monasteries every day, so that the palaces and such were absolutely pristine. When we went on walks, you could drink out of the rivers and the lakes because the water was so pure. Their main means of exchange was barter and trading. It's also the only country that I've been to where men could marry as many women as they want, but also, where women can also marry as many men as they want. Women could have multiple husbands. I met some of them who did.

In other ways, it was so advanced. For example, they do a recycling day every week, which the whole country takes part in. The one that amazed me, though, was Family Planning Day: Once a week, every street corner had a kiosk where they gave out birth control to everyone. They also gave out little booklets about family planning in Bhutan. It was so forward-thinking. There was one day at the Paro Festival that I'll never forget. These little kids were goofing around near us, and we were taking pictures with them. One of the kids gave me a piece of candy, and they all said,

"Candy! Candy!" and told me to eat it. They were all giggling; I didn't eat it because they were laughing. Turns out they had tried to get me to eat a birth control pill.

Again, by Western standards of progress and development, these people had so little, yet they were so happy. It just seemed like heaven to me, and I don't think I can understate the importance of that trip when it came time for us to focus on happiness at G Adventures.

In the office, we started to discuss building our business model around happiness. I had spent a lot of time since my trip to Bhutan learning about their country and their king's Gross National Happiness model.

Around the same time, *National Geographic Adventure* had announced that they were going to search the globe for their list of the Best Adventure Travel Companies on Earth. *National Geographic* doesn't do anything halfway, so it was a rather extensive process; they were speaking to customers, suppliers, and employees of all the companies around the world. I lost track of what was happening with it. One day I was in Wisconsin speaking at The International Ecotourism Society Conference, when an individual from *National Geographic* approached me after my talk and told me that, after all of their research, we were ranked number one as the best all-around adventure operator and given the grand title of Best Adventure Travel Company on Earth. They had many specialist categories but we came out on top overall, he said, and the results would be in the next issue of the magazine.

I was obviously excited to hear the news. Right at the moment when we were finishing our conversation, however, I felt a tap on my shoulder. I turned around and I had to adjust my eyes, because right in front of me was Karma, my local guide in Bhutan from more than ten years ago. Standing there in his native robes, he looked at me with his kind eyes and asked if I remembered him. "Of course!" I said, as I gave him a big hug.

Karma and I caught up quickly, as though we had never been

apart. He was at The International Ecotourism Society Conference to promote the company he worked for now and was representing Bhutan. It was great to see him, and it warmed my heart to reminisce about our time together in his magical country. He was telling me about all the changes in Bhutan, and I began to ask him more questions about their Gross National Happiness. He knew much more than I would have thought. He told me about the views of his king and about how happiness was still the basis for their government. I told him how that had influenced me and that I thought it was relevant to my business and what we do; that I had been researching it myself, and that I wanted to build my business around the same ideas. He was very generous and kind with his time, and he encouraged me to come back to Bhutan soon. I was only at The International Ecotourism Society Conference for the day in order to do my keynote and had a plane to catch, so he walked me out to my taxi and we said good-bye once again.

I studied many different views of happiness and also met a brilliant fellow named Tony Hsieh, who was taking over a new company called Zappos that was getting a lot of attention. I heard about Tony a few years before meeting him, when we both appeared in *Entrepreneur Magazine*. We actually spoke on the phone during that time when the writer of the story, who had interviewed both of us, suggested we should link up because we shared similar views. We lost contact after our initial conversation, but later Tony and I would reconnect and share ideas. And later still, he took a trip with us. Tony and I share many of the same beliefs about people and happiness. We apply things differently to our respective businesses because we are in different industries, but our views are still very much aligned.

When you ask people about what makes them happy, most will say things like spending time with their family, getting a new car, or hanging out with their best friends. These are all things that create happiness, but in truth, these feelings of happiness are fleeting. That's why in today's society, people consume so much—they're endlessly trying to chase happiness by stringing along moments of temporary happiness and doing things that offer only temporary relief.

When I started to research happiness, I realized that most people believe that we are the center of our universe and that our happiness revolves around us. The truth is, the basis for happiness in our life is the base of our existence, so happiness is actually at our core, and our lives and successes revolve around it. This isn't revolutionary stuff. There have been endless scientific studies on happiness, and this wasn't anything that I made up. My model of four pillars of happiness, however, is directly related to business.

What it boils down to is four conditions that create the environment in which you can achieve happiness:

1. The ability to grow
2. Being connected
3. Being part of something bigger than yourself
4. Freedom

If you're put in an environment that has all of these elements, they don't make you happy on their own, but they do allow you to achieve happiness if you truly want it. Something I often say to our people is that happiness is free and available for anyone who wants it. You just have to decide that you deserve it and that you want to achieve it. I have learned from my experience that you can only create the playing field—people have to want to get in the game.

I was amazed that when I started exploring elements of happiness, I saw immediately that they could be directly related to any business. The first pillar, having the ability to grow, is obvious. Everyone wants to feel that they can grow and develop. In the workplace, this is especially true, because I think everyone wants to feel that if they work hard, they can progress. It's a very basic component of happiness and is directly relatable to how every company should run its business.

Companies need to have programs in place to help people grow and develop. As a human being, you need to feel that you can grow to achieve happiness. We launched three extra days off annually for everyone in the company. We called them Me, We, and G days. One day to better yourself (Me), one day to better your community (We), and one day that represented our core values (G). People can apply for them at any time and use them to grow within themselves, their community, and the company.

Being connected is the second pillar of happiness and one of the most important in order to create community. People can never achieve happiness without being connected to the people or company they work for. It might be your colleagues, or the product or service you produce, but being connected is important. Today, with the rise of social media, there are more tools than ever to keep people connected. In many ways, I think the popularity of social media is directly related to people's search for happiness through social connectedness. But it is important for people to feel connected at work—to their employers, their colleagues, and/or what they do.

At G Adventures, we use Twitter to connect our global family. Twitter is perfect for business use because it is quick, concise, and simple. We have more than one thousand employees now on Twitter, and everyone is trained how to use it when they join the company. Everyone gets breaks during the day to tweet, and we encourage people to communicate through Twitter, which also creates freedom. And, we use it to promote transparency by having all of our company tweets posted live on our website, because we're proud of our people and what they have to say about the company. I'm not sure there are many companies that could do the same thing. One of my favorite sayings is:

> Twitter taught me how to love people I have never met.
> Facebook taught me to hate friends and family I've known
> my entire life.

The third pillar, being part of something greater than yourself, is one of the most important aspects of a business model based on happiness. No matter what you do, whether you're a receptionist or an executive, you should share a common purpose and have a united understanding of your company's greater mission. Whether you drive this message through your core values or through programs you implement in order to bring people together, you have to enable people to find purpose and happiness through their work, regardless of their function on your team.

Happiness is about creating a movement, one that revolves around finding your happiness through the happiness of other people. This is a very powerful thing, to bring a group of people together and to motivate them to truly believe that their individual well-being revolves around what they can do for others. This should be the way of the world, but it isn't. The true key to happiness is being in the center of your existence, and you revolve around what drives sustained happiness. Being part of something greater than yourself is about building a community whose members are committed to doing what they can for others and being aware of how our work impacts everyone around us.

Freedom, the fourth pillar, is the basis of happiness. If you are not free, you can never achieve happiness. From the manager's point of view, if you take the long road and manage your people such that everyone knows where they fit, particularly the bottom 10, you will eventually have more and more responsible people in every seat, which gives you the ability to create more freedom. If you manage your people carefully and create programs and an environment where people can grow, and if, over time, you work tirelessly to put a star in every seat on your company's bus, you will have fewer people who work for what the job affords them and who constantly look at how they can advance by taking advantage of any system. Instead, you will see freedom grow along with the company, and everything will open up to create more freedom as you get bigger.

I have to warn you though, it's a rough road. It's unpopular at first; the hard and sometimes unemotional side of business rears its head when you decide on a culture of hiring slowly and firing quickly. You need programs in place like our G Factor interview to get the people already vested in the company to buy into the recruiting process. Half the battle is getting everyone to truly want to contribute to the success of new team members. To be successful in a purpose-driven business model you have to hire people who want to change the world. It is tough at first—this is the part of the Looptail that involves paying it forward—but it will all come back around.

It doesn't happen by accident, either. Building a great team involves careful planning and flawless execution. But people eventually see the benefits, and, as your culture stays true to this vision, it is amazing to watch it become self-regulating over time—when your culture is so strong, people who don't fit or are underperforming will seek help or leave of their own accord. And while that may sound harsh, it's the greatest gift when someone realizes that they want to be somewhere else. In that situation, you should make it easy for them to exit and see it as a celebration of freedom. That freedom allows both parties to move forward: The person will find happiness somewhere else, and the company will find the right person who will contribute to creating freedom by being responsible and doing what is in the best interest of your company every day.

Culture Club is a group whose job is to promote our culture all day, every day. They set up all company functions, run all internal communications, and organize all the very cool things we do.

When we came up with the idea for Culture Club, naturally we called the people who work there Karma Chameleons. We then decided that Culture Club needed a head representative; someone elected by everyone, who would speak for all employees. In short, a mayor. We put out a call for nominations and ran a two-month campaign among the candidates. It was fantastic. Our city was having an election at the same time, so we brought in one of the actual mayoral candidates to moderate a debate among our Culture Club mayoral candidates and filmed it all for a video we shared throughout the company in order to bring everyone into the process.

Scan this QR code or visit Looptail.com/Election to watch how the first mayor of G Adventures was elected.

There were posters all over the office, websites set up, and various election scandals along the way, but after two months, we elected a mayor of the company who would be part of Culture Club. We obviously found the right person, because he's been reelected in every election we've held since. And after three terms, our mayor became so popular that he was given a permanent role in Culture Club.

It might sound goofy, but Culture Club's role is absolutely critical. Put another way, Culture Club is an organization internally that looks for ways to support and enhance our company culture. But that description is boring, and the last thing culture should be is boring. So instead, the members of Culture Club try to make our company's culture fun. For example, G Adventures is a big promoter of gamification—using techniques from games and game design to drive certain desired behaviors. One example of gamification would be Foursquare's badge system, where people compete to see who can check in the most in a single location. So many of the things we do at G Adventures are gamified, from our annual Guac-off Golden Avocado Championship to our global work-exchange programs to our create-your-own-adventures.

Scan this QR code or visit Looptail.com/Guacoff to get a taste of a fierce but friendly G Adventures culinary competition.

These days, Culture Club seems to get involved in everything and often leads company communication. They now manage a global network of twenty Culture Club ambassadors, who are stationed in every office we have around the world. The Karma Chameleons create videos and organize various global office functions, like the Family Lunches we hold, which take place every Wednesday in many offices. They also manage touch points in our office when we have visitors to Base Camp, and they have taken on the mammoth task of organizing G Stock. They promote and run everything from bring-your-kids-to-work days (which we call Little G Day) to the Haircuts and Hot Dogs days I mentioned.

One of our most recent Culture Club initiatives came during the 2012 Summer Olympic Games. We ran our own G-lympic games over Twitter, challenging our people in the various regions to represent our core values on the ground, in order to be awarded gold, silver, and bronze medals that we gave out daily. We had a running medal count and the winning team would get a region-wide celebration. Our regions went wild. They sent in entries ranging from pictures to crazy videos and generated almost three thousand tweets during the games alone. Not only did it create even more engagement, it united us both regionally and globally.

*Scan this QR code or visit Looptail.com/Glympics
to experience the G-lympic celebration.*

I'm also a firm believer in the idea that sports are the best way to bond people, and not only to build a supportive team environment, but also to emphasize the importance of building a winning team. Within our head office we have six sports teams which are coed, with members recruited from every department. We also run occasional dodgeball nights just for fun, in which we divide up the teams based around company core values. Besides promoting a healthy, active lifestyle, they contribute to our need to build connectedness, which contributes to our happiness business model.

*Scan this QR code or visit Looptail.com/dodgeball
to see athleticism and camaraderie come together
in the form of an epic dodgeball tournament.*

Communication and video are another big part of what Culture Club does. G Adventures has our own biweekly news broadcast, which we call GNN. GNN is a lighthearted and funny look at what's up in the G World every couple of weeks. This was an internal form of communication for many years, but after we started getting requests from our travelers to see it, we eventually made it public for anyone who is interested to check out.

*Scan this QR code or visit Looptail.com/GNN
to get a glimpse at what G Adventures newscast
is all about.*

I started to see the confluence between social innovation, social entrepreneurship, and social media. I realized that we could transcend our product and our industry by blazing a new trail, one that combined all of these influences in order to become a social enterprise—a company that is driven by purpose while still benefiting from traditional business philosophies.

The Looptail is about stringing everything we were thinking together into a new business model, one that would stand for something and that would drive us to be passionate about our calling, to be a group of people creating a movement, and through that movement, to change the world. It sounds crazy, but it's possible. This is where the philosophy of karma comes into business, and into the Looptail. The idea of the Looptail is that, if we get everything in our business right, with our people and our culture, you have to believe that everything else will fall into place. To believe in the Looptail, there are elements of karma involved: the idea that your every action will have an effect. If you get everything else right, all the other good things that are traditionally viewed as gauges of success in business will come.

Walt Disney is seen as the visionary who, among other things, created the "happiest place on earth." But he was also a shrewd entrepreneur. Disney's ideas would have been merely ordinary if he hadn't had a philosophy that transcended just an animation studio built around a talking mouse. He started by getting the people around him to achieve happiness if they wanted to create happiness. In fact, Disney's beliefs are kind of karma-like, in that if you deliver excellence and believe in what you do everything else will take care of itself. He once said, "Do a good job. You don't have to worry about the money. It will take care of itself. Just do your best work." This ties together with my philosophy that people do their best work when they are in an environment where they can achieve happiness and have the freedom to express themselves.

Walt Disney also said, "Whatever you do, do it well. Do it so well that when people see you do it, they will want to come back and see you do it again, and they will want to bring others and show them how well you do what you do."

When you create an environment in which excellence is expected, and when you believe that, if you get your business model right, everything else will fall into place, people will engage with you beyond your product.

Let's be honest. Companies have to make money. If you decide you want your company to be a social enterprise, however, the more money you make, the greater positive impact you can have in the world—and that's a powerful motivator. Things like customer satisfaction, staff retention, attracting the best of the best to work with you, profits, repeat customers, and brand loyalty will all follow, if you get your culture right. I am not a Buddhist—and I get asked all the time whether I am—but I do believe in the Looptail. We get back what we put in. If we pay it forward, it will pay dividends. You just have to believe that what you're doing is important, that it's worth the effort, and that you're doing it for reasons more than just to make money.

When I talk about these things in my public talks, sometimes I see a bit of eye rolling going on. People groan at the mention of happiness and freedom in the workplace at first, though by the end, after I build a story and put my ideas in context for people, I get rousing applause. Still, not everyone understands it at first; especially among the cynical, it's a tough sell. You can't do it half-heartedly. But the Looptail will create a business that gives you an intangible advantage that can't be measured on a balance sheet or in a weekly report. It is that fifth gear, the one that creates engagement between you and your customers, the one that breathes life into your brand and into your core values, and the one that tells everyone what you stand for.

Life is about putting together a string of meaningful connections. Many indigenous tribes believe we have a certain predestined amount of heartbeats in our life, and when we reach the last beat, we die. I believe life revolves around our meaningful connections and how we make people feel. That's what your brand should be focused on. The Looptail is about how your brand makes people feel.

When you're at a corporate party or some kind of networking event in a room full of hundreds of striving up-and-comers, you can really see how people operate. It's the best people-watching opportunity. Some of them work the room and shake as many hands as possible; others take their time and make an impression on a few select people. Your life, and your company, is like that party. When you leave, the people you interacted with might not remember what you do, what you said, or what you tried to sell them, but they will always remember how you made them feel. At the end of that party, you probably have a pocketful of business cards and contacts to follow up on, but if the connection wasn't meaningful, the people you spoke to probably won't remember who you are or what you talked about.

If you find your purpose in the world, either personally or as a company, and believe in the Looptail and how your brand makes people feel, you won't be that forgotten networker. Gauge your personal success not on how many people you meet but on the truly meaningful connections you create and your company's success on how its existence impacts the world. Create a place where people don't just come to work, but where they feel that they are contributing to something greater. Do that and their work, no matter what it is they do, becomes a calling.

With all this change afoot, I knew the next step was getting my top people to understand the importance of company culture and how it was responsible for driving excellence—for change to work, it has to be intrinsically believed from the top down. After careful planning on my part, I developed a program centered around two of the world's greatest brands, which are known for delivering excellence: Apple and Google. Both companies are dominant in their respective fields, but they embody polar opposite company cultures. Google has an open culture that has taken on the heady task of organizing and sharing the world's information, while Apple drives innovation and has a closed culture that famously keeps their own employees in the dark about the things they are developing.

Having spoken at both campuses, I had become friends with a few key people in both organizations and asked them if I could bring my team to their offices for a tour to meet with their executive teams and to talk about the importance of company culture. After a bit of pleading, I got the green light and announced to C.O.R.E. that our next meeting would be in Silicon Valley. Over the course of those four days, we toured their facilities and had lunch and met with some of the most interesting and brightest people who were very open about what drives their culture and how it lends to their individual success. It was a perfect platform to open the discussion about my vision of how we would transform our business by putting our company culture first and how we could transcend our product and our industry. In the evening we were lucky to also get a luxury box at a concert for the band Green Day, which happened to be playing on their home turf at the end of their world tour. It was a magical experience that drove home the importance of company culture and why it is important to attract the best people, engage customers, and create brands that transcend your industry.

What I learned is something that I mention throughout this book and reaffirmed my belief that success doesn't happen by accident. While you have to remember your core purpose and where you come from, you need to know what you stand for and that even your company culture has to be carefully managed. They are critical parts of the social revolution that allows people to identify with brands on an unprecedented level. They create loyalty to brands that make their customers feel a certain way. The values and company culture are anchored in what the business represents and not just the outstanding products or services it offers.

Scan this QR code or visit Looptail.com
/SiliconValley to see the C.O.R.E team visit Silicon
Valley on the trip that redefined corporate culture
at G Adventures.

It's all about people. Defining the type of people that will best represent your brand becomes critically important. And it goes beyond skill set. So at G Adventures we would have to meticulously evaluate what characteristics we would need to bring to life our designs to redefine social enterprise.

CHAPTER 11

If You Don't Love Your Customers, Someone Else Will

It is important to people inside and outside of any company to define why you do what you do. For years, one of the most asked questions from within the organization was, Why do we want to keep growing? Is it just about making more money?

It is, if you're a public company. That's not to say public companies can't be sustainable or do great things. Cemex, Ritz-Carlton, and some of the other companies I talk positively about are all publicly held. But the core purpose of a public company is to make money and to create value for shareholders, and everything else is secondary. For a social enterprise, however, the primary motivation that drives the organization is finding ways to have a positive impact on the world.

Once you clearly define your purpose as a company, and you build the right team of people who see their work as more of a calling than a job, that question of whether to keep growing just disappears. The more you grow, the more you can accomplish. This is the Looptail in action; as you find your purpose, pursue it, and pay it forward, you want to keep growing so that you can have a greater impact on a social level.

At G Adventures, I've explained how everyone who works here is motivated by our core values, our shared purpose, and all the things that make us a social enterprise. To keep growing, though, the customer has to buy in and believe in the company as much as our employees do. That's why customer service is one of the most important aspects of our company.

Customer service means something different to everyone in business, but nobody questions its importance. G Adventures is customer obsessed because the customer is the lifeblood of our success. I stress to my people all the time that "Lead with Service" is the most important of our core values; without our customers we would not have a company, never mind the other four core values. Being our customer has to be a remarkable experience, and I made it very clear that we would be relentless in our pursuit of this.

Between 2008 and 2010—the height of the financial crisis— our sales amazingly continued to grow and soon we soared past $150 million, and as people wanted a deeper relationship with our brand, our Facebook fans have exploded past eight hundred thousand. We were the market leader in our space and the distance between us and second place was growing as we continued to defy the odds.

As I was making changes to our business model and our culture, I needed to get everyone to believe that without our customers, we are nothing. We always had great customer service and our travelers had always told us as much, but I wanted us to do more. Our market competitors continued to consolidate, and I knew our customer service had to be a key differentiator—to be as great and as innovative as the rest of the company is.

So, I gathered C.O.R.E. in Paris for a series of meetings to talk about our customer service. The focus of the trip was strictly on the customer experience. We started our meetings by heading to Euro Disney's Disneyland Paris.

There are few companies that have mastered the art of shaping the customer's experience the way Disney has. Disneyland, Disney World, and Euro Disney transcend their industry. Before they existed, the county fair was the model for amusement parks; today, the industry mostly consists of Six Flags–style theme parks with rides for families. But Disney engages customers to a higher purpose than playing a carnival game or being scared by a roller coaster; they created an immersive experience with a message—that we're all part of a small world, a world of laughter and a world of tears, a world of hope and world of fears.

What I wanted to get across to C.O.R.E. was how Disney is able to package and export the Disney experience, because that is exactly what G Adventures does—we export experiences.

From the moment we checked in at the gate, we could see that Euro Disney's execution of their brand promise and delivery is flawless. It didn't matter if they were the security guards or people sweeping the streets; every employee was part of the cast and part of the brand experience. They all delivered something special, and the effect was that it took you away from your world, so that, for a moment in time, you could be a kid again.

We needed to create a similar kind of magic. Taking people away from their world is exactly what we needed to do with our trips. We lead people out of their comfort zones and into a place that is so different from anything they've ever experienced. For that moment, they are free and open to anything—whether it's food, culture, music, or the outdoors. They become receptive to having a life-changing experience. I wanted C.O.R.E. to understand that, if everyone in G Adventures was part of our brand delivery, then we had to have everyone in our company put our customers' interests at the heart of all the things we did.

The first thing that is critical to achieving great customer service is communication within the organization. I know that sounds strange, but hear me out. Everything you implement in your company, if you want to do it fully and completely, starts from the top down. Nothing in your business will ever reach core value status without the people at the top buying in. Everyone has to believe, and it comes from great leadership.

Next, you have to make sure your people are equipped to focus on the customer. There's nothing worse than being stuck on the phone with a customer service agent who won't solve your problem, either because they don't have the freedom to make the decision or because they don't care about their job beyond doing the bare minimum in order to keep it. When it comes to the part of the Looptail that's about creating freedom and paying it forward, initiatives like the Tour Operator Standards and our community and Planeterra projects demonstrate that we believe in what we do and strive to be different. But even with those projects, we still have to focus on communicating our commitment to the customer directly, through their interactions with us on a day-to-day basis.

Furthermore, today's consumers are becoming more and more savvy. They can tell the difference between traditional good service—which could mean low hold-times, quick call resolutions, and efficient answers to questions—and innovative customer service that affects how you make them feel. Modern consumers respond to more real or sincere representatives of your company who are committed to the customer's happiness because that in turn will contribute to their own.

In order to deliver a phenomenal customer service experience every time, one thing gives you that edge: happy and free people. We give everyone in our offices a free trip every year on one of our tours, but that's only the beginning of treating your people right. You need to not only make your culture your brand but also drive a united team to deliver exceptional customer service that exceeds your customers' expectations because it is being delivered with a tangible difference: Your customer service is being delivered by more engaged, happier, and united people who are sincerely willing to go beyond expectations because it is the purpose and calling of your company.

For years, people complimented us on our amazing customer service. Travel agents who sell our trips to their clients tell us how they love just getting the opportunity to get on the phone and call our people. But I always want the quality of our service to go beyond that, and the only way you can do so is to inspire people with your business and your "why." Too many businesses try to engage people with "how" they do things better than the competition; by trying to offer what people have grown accustomed to or what they think of as good customer service, they forfeit the chance to surprise their customers.

When I started reading more about customer service, I read a lot of things about how expectations of customer service are different in various regions and markets. I believe you can transcend all that with employees who are just happy and passionate about what they do. Part of the reason we focus so much on happiness in our people within the company is that I believe that happiness is infectious. If someone loves the company and believes passionately that working here is helping them fulfill an important goal in their life, everyone they come in contact with will be able to tell that it's genuine.

Getting our people and our company to be customer-obsessed—to go that extra distance at every opportunity that we have—is just the beginning. You also have to seize on every opportunity to improve. For so many years we lived in a bubble—we were this fast-growing company, we were on the cover of magazines, and we had a very cool product that people loved. But you have to be careful not to become complacent. I tell people constantly that we're only as good as our next unsatisfied customer and that, if we don't love and take care of our customers, someone else will.

When we make mistakes, it's a gift, because it allows us to learn from them. Whenever we have that opportunity to make things better for the customer, it's not considered a mistake. If you learn from it, you never make mistakes. It's all just a means to get better as a business. And, in our culture, when we get an unhappy customer, we see it as an opportunity to do whatever we can to win that customer back. We have found that there is no more loyal and more vocal fan than someone who has had a bad experience, gives you a chance to make up for it, and ends up satisfied.

Giving your people the freedom to make decisions—and to do whatever's needed to make the customer happy—is a big part of great customer service and the Looptail. In order to give our people the resources they could deploy when they thought it was appropriate to do something special, we created an entire department called Incite, whose job is to be an in-house group of customer advocates. Incite started a program called Random Acts of G-appiness that works this way. We invite our people to suggest specific situations that arise, which we then dissect in order to see if we can create a better experience for our staff or our travelers.

For example, one of our passengers told someone that they had the best CEO ever on their trip and joked that, because he was such a good example of what we were about, we should make him a purple suit, which is our official brand color. It was just an offhand comment, but we took him up on it. We had a purple suit tailored for that CEO in Vietnam, where he's from, and sent it to him. Then we took a picture of him in it and sent it to the customer with a thank you for the suggestion.

More recently, Incite received an e-mail from one of our people telling us about a customer who was booking a trip over the phone. This person was a repeat traveler who had taken trips with us before, but this time he was taking his daughter, so she too could experience our brand promise. The CEO in our call center noticed that the customer had contracted a bad cold and was coughing throughout the call, so she sent a message to Incite asking whether they could put together a basket of things you would need to get over a cold. Within minutes, Incite mobilized, sending over lozenges and some tea for one of our great and valued customers.

I want people to be *eager* to come back, not just saying, "Oh, I'll consider traveling with them again." I can't tell you how many letters I get every week from our travelers who feel it is their life mission to tell me that their particular CEO went way beyond the call of duty either before or after their trip. It's easily the most common type of e-mail I receive every day. It makes me so happy when I see that feeling coming back from the farthest reaches of the company. People are just astounded, and everyone needs me to know that their CEO is the best we have. I *must* know about it.

I always thank people who take the time to write me something negative. Nothing's worse than if someone has a bad experience—maybe one that doesn't necessarily ruin their tour, but something that lends a sour note to it at some point—and they don't take the time to tell us. We can't make it better for the next person. If one of our travelers has a bad experience, we hope that passenger will take the opportunity to let us know so we can fix it for the next person who comes along. We'd love it if they decided to pay it forward—we're big fans of that kind of thing. But if they only tell their friends about the part of their experience that was bad, it's not serving anybody.

There are unreasonable requests, of course. I get many letters from customers saying this or that happened to them, and they usually say something like, "I'm very surprised, you guys pride yourselves on customer service!" Then they go on to complain that it rained during their entire two-week trip and that because we didn't give them back their money, we're not giving good customer service. And even when they write in with a silly complaint like the one about the rain, we still reach out to them, as crazy as it sounds, and try to do what we can.

After revisiting our childhood at Euro Disney, C.O.R.E. reconvened in Paris to come up with some game-changing customer service ideas. We needed to generate strategies that would not only revolutionize our industry but would also send a strong message within the company that we were seriously committed to offering the best customer experience on the planet. Until then, we had been so focused on *how* we were going to show people the world; it was time to concentrate on *why*.

We needed to show everyone that we were serious about wanting to put the focus of the entire company on our customers. That's when what we refer to as the "Holy Trinity of Customer Service" was born.

1. Open 24/7: *When you're ready, we're ready.*

We wanted to put our travelers first, so we wanted to be there whenever they felt like reaching out and talking to someone about travel. That meant we needed to figure out a way to keep our global call centers open twenty-four hours a day, seven days a week. This might seem easier than it actually was; accomplishing it without breaking the bank to hire massive amounts of people to cover all hours in all regions was a huge operational challenge. But we wanted to be available 24/7 so that we could tell our customers, when they're ready to speak with us, we're just a phone call away.

2. Lifetime Deposits: *Travel now, travel later.*

I touched on this idea in Chapter 8, though it actually originated in our Paris meetings. Figuring out not just how to keep records of deposits over the long-term, but to allow people to re-gift them to others or even to donate them, was another enormous operational challenge, but it really paid off in terms of generating goodwill and giving us a competitive advantage. Customers are used to other companies not giving back their deposits when they can't travel; by making sure that they don't forfeit their deposit, our customers feel like we're giving them a gift—or, at least, not ripping them off. It reinforces in their mind how much we want them to have a great, life-changing experience, that we're willing to go above and beyond what the rest of the industry does.

After we announced the Lifetime Deposit, not a month had gone by before people started to try to sell their Lifetime Deposits on eBay. We were fine with that. A couple of months later, our competitors came out with lame versions of the same thing, only with all kinds of stipulations and conditions. Ours has no fine print. It's your deposit, and it's good for life.

3. *Guaranteed Departures: If you're booked, you're going.*

This was the biggest of the three promises, and it became a game changer for our industry. To me, it was a return to our disruptive innovation roots. We saw that the main building blocks of our industry were not working together to create the best customer experience; in fact, they created a nightmare. The two basic elements of booking a holiday are your land and your air. In our case, we sell small group adventures as land packages, and others supply the air service. It occurred to me that the way we were working ran in opposition to what our air transportation providers—the airlines—were doing.

As tour companies, we need to book a certain number of people per trip in order to break even. You can offer a myriad of trips in order to look impressive to a customer, but when they agree to book one, all group travel companies then leave the customer hanging—the trip isn't guaranteed until they reach their minimum numbers.

By contrast, you can't take any tour without getting there, which means booking your flight. The airlines, however, have a different business model than we do; it's accepted behavior for their airfares to rise and get more expensive as you get closer to your departure date. As our travelers waited to hear whether enough people had signed up for their tour, the price of their airfare was increasing.

As group tour operators, we were, in essence, expecting our customers to fund our business. But we were also making it harder on ourselves as we went. The longer it took us to get our minimum numbers for a trip, the more expensive the trip became to the potential customer (not to mention the customer who's already signed up), because the airline industry's model works in contrast to the tour company model. It was horrendous for the customer. How stressful was it for them to watch airfares skyrocket while they waited, forcing them to call in every week to see whether their trip had been confirmed and was guaranteed to run? And, because most of our customers are travel agents, these files would stay on their desks because they're just a pain to deal with. Even more strangely, tour operators wanted us to book as far in advance as possible, but we were encouraging the exact opposite behavior.

This is a specific travel industry problem, but it's the kind of problem that affects all industries. Every industry has things that aren't perfect, but they're accepted as par for the course because they're part of standard operations—it's just how it works. There, in itself, lies the opportunity.

When we launched this, it surprised a lot of people. No one else was doing anything similar. I went on a promotional tour through the US and Australia. In more than twenty interviews I talked about our 100 percent guarantee. I don't think anyone I spoke to truly believed we were actually doing it. One writer described it as attention-grabbing but said we could never really do it. Our competitors chimed in and tried to spin a story about why they couldn't do it themselves. We heard from two small companies who said they had been doing the same thing for years; one stated right on their website that they had conditions of needing minimum numbers, and the other carried roughly as many passengers in a year as we do in a day.

It was another example of brilliant execution by our team, doing the impossible and being driven by the sheer motivation of wowing the customer. I said to every journalist who asked me how much money we would lose doing this that I believed it should just be absorbed as the cost of doing business. I take our relationship with our customers very seriously. It should be our job to do whatever we can to improve the customer experience.

Before I launched "100 percent Guaranteed Departures" at

the Future of Tourism, I put this quote on a slide projected on
the screen behind me on stage:

> *"It's kind of fun to do the impossible."*
> —Walt Disney

The next thing we wanted to do was disrupt the common travel
brochure. It was time to change how we communicated with our
travelers.

The opening pages of every travel brochure are the same;
the section is referred to as "red ocean." The travel industry is
littered with companies whose message is all about how you
are going to have the best time if you travel with them, and in
those pages they detail how they're going do it and how they're
better than their competitors. They describe hotels as having all
the comforts of home and take away any ability to surprise their
customers. They have become so generic; to me, they all blend
into a mélange of mediocrity.

Our brand team put together a plan to feature our people and
our values in the opening pages of our brochures and to remove
all the monotonous text that promised you "real, authentic experiences from the best of the best blah blah blah." Instead of the
"how," we wanted to focus on our "why." It would take a crew
of three people a whole two months to travel the world, on a
back-breaking schedule, in order to gather material featuring our
CEOs in the field. They are the ones representing our values and
putting our culture on full display and showing why you should
travel with us.

Our new brochure won raves and awards from around the
world. I knew we did a good job when we debuted our brochures
at the annual World Travel Market in London, the same trade
show where I launched my initial ideas to export tourism all
those years ago. As our brochures sat proudly on display, one of
our competitors sauntered up to the table to brazenly take a copy.
Jokingly, he grabbed one and said in a condescending voice, "So

what does Bruce have you guys doing now?" Upon opening our latest piece of art, he let out an audible "Fuck!" Then he scurried away into the crowd, no doubt to go converse with his colleagues about our tenacity.

Scan this QR code or visit Looptail.com/why to see how G Adventures changed its brochures to incorporate its core values and culture.

Transcendent customer service goes right back to your company culture. One thing that is incredibly important for business leaders to understand is that, any time you want to make changes within your organization, the goal should somehow connect back to the success of the individual within the company, as well as to the company as a whole. And, as I said earlier, when you make big changes, communication is critical. You have to give people a detailed map outlining what it means to be successful in your organization after the proposed changes have taken place.

Big companies are notorious for moving the goalposts and not communicating the revised map about what success looks like in the new form for the company they've envisioned. This is a serious mistake, and one that leads to many programs failing. If your people cannot see their path to their own potential success, or to the success of the company in general, then ultimately they will be less interested in getting behind it.

With that in mind, I once again took to the stage at G Stock 2011 and delivered another very hard-to-digest message. This time I said that being good at your job is no longer good enough. "In order to be a star, you have to contribute in other ways. You can be good at your job to stick around, but if you want to grow and develop in the company, you would have to contribute to our culture, not just be part of it. You have to help develop it, and we want to hear your ideas."

But I couldn't just say that and not establish how it was going to work. We needed some ways to harness those ideas and to really create a dialogue between the head office and our culture stars in the field. After I saw the value of bringing those groups together in Vegas, I knew we needed to create communication vehicles to bring a global and more inclusive mix of voices to the company. As we were advancing toward defining social enterprise, it was critical that we should embrace a more social existence and give everyone the tools and ability to contribute. That's how we came up with the concept of CEO Leadership Camp.

We decided that we would invite our field Chief Experience Officers from all over the world to apply for a week-long camp. The idea was that the ones who were selected would work in a big group with our top executives and trainers so that we could make these CEOs better leaders with a comprehensive program. We also wanted to hear their thoughts about how we could get better, since these people were our culture stars, our most influential people. It became an exercise for us to learn as a company how we can get better at creating opportunities for our people in the field, as well as to train our CEOs to be not only better representatives of G Adventures, but also to enable them to achieve their own goals and to become better global citizens. Ultimately, we wanted them to be able to contribute to our business on a higher level—we wanted them to be part of the cast.

We held the first camp in Greece in 2011 and flew in people from all over the world for it. (I was only allowed to be there for one day, because apparently I'm disruptive and a distraction. I try not to take those things personally. Remember that $5,000 check if you could hurt my feelings?) The reports from everyone were that it was one of the most amazing things that we've ever done. There were so many tears and so much sharing that it became almost like a love-in. People talked about overcoming barriers, breaking boundaries, and going beyond their capacity. Within months after the camp, almost every single person within the company who attended leadership camp was doing some other job or had been moved to another division or something, because we saw that they had way more talent than we had realized.

The next one was held in Africa in 2012, and after what we had learned from Greece, the impact was even greater. The excitement had grown around the world and the number of CEOs applying increased by an incredible amount, but we could only take twelve people, so it was a tough decision. For many of them, it would have been the first time they or anyone in their family had ever left their country. We had people from Asia, Africa, Latin America, and Europe come together to be heard and contribute to our company voice.

Once again, I was only allowed to be there for one day, but the energy in Africa was electric, and the ideas coming out were incredible. Now that they knew we were giving them the freedom we had promised, the ideas came flowing like a river. The best part was getting feedback about our customers from the CEOs, the people who really lived our Lead with Service core value. All of the learning became valuable and stored in the halls of our intellectual property and just made us stronger as we brought our culture together to drive customer service to feverish levels. When we announced that the most recent camp will take place in the Galápagos Islands, more than eighty applications came flooding in. It truly changes people's lives and delivers on our brand promise.

*Scan this QR code or visit Looptail.com
/GreeceLeadership to experience Greece Leadership
Camp and what it means to Lead with Service.*

Scan this QR code or visit Looptail.com
/AfricaLeadership to take a look at the
impact Africa Leadership Camp had on
G Adventures' CEOs.

As I mentioned, the idea behind these leadership camps came when I started bringing groups to Las Vegas in 2007. Something I also realized during that time, however, was that only two of the people on my executive team were women. The company as a whole was about 50 percent female, and in our offices specifically, it was more than that. But our gender diversity wasn't reflected in the executive team or at the management level in general. And, to make matters worse, both of our female executives left within months of our cultural revolution.

When you think about it, women should be a huge part of our company, and not just for obvious reasons of fairness. The reality is that our clientele is 65 percent women. You might not expect that, given the stereotypes around adventure travel; but our research tells us that women who are adventurous are unique and that they're less likely than men to have a friend to go off traveling with. They're also less likely to travel on their own, for security reasons. That's one of the reasons why women choose group trips more than men.

The gender ratio of our customers is just one more piece of evidence showing why we should have been prioritizing listening to women in our organization. Instead, I realized, the company had gone in a very unhealthy direction. Not only were we failing to develop our female employees, our environment was not welcoming to them at the top level. In my experience—and I know there are exceptions to this, but let me generalize for a minute—men tend to communicate very differently than women, and when a bunch of men or mostly men get together, it can be very alienating. A lot of our winning-centered culture and bravado had created an energy that was more masculine, I guess, and, over time, I started hearing criticism from some women within the organization that we didn't have an environment that was conducive to listening to and hearing from them.

I hadn't seen it creeping up on us, but once I realized it, I couldn't miss it, and it bothered me to no end. The closer I looked, the more I saw that our environment was not inclusive, especially for women. That period, when I discovered the extent of the problem, made me feel ashamed that I had allowed it to happen.

So, at G Stock 2011 I made a public and personal apology to the women in our company for letting this happen under my watch. I took responsibility for it and promised I would make it right, that I would do everything in my power to try to change it.

The first major corrective step we took was to create Women's Leadership Camp. As I spent more time visiting our global offices, I realized that I was dealing with some cultural issues as well. In many countries women are conditioned to not speak up, and as a result, especially in a business environment, some of them were drawn to playing more of a supporting role. I knew we had to do something to create an environment that would allow everyone in the company to be heard. I needed more leaders, and I had to find them everywhere around the world. The idea behind Women's Leadership Camp was that it would be women-only in order to address those specific concerns and to nurture some of our best leaders over time.

The camp was open globally to any woman who worked for us in any country. Like CEO Leadership Camp, you still had to apply, but the applications were done differently. And when we put out the call for applications, the floodgates just opened. The applications from these women were just extraordinary. Or so I'm told. I've been completely cut out of the process; they won't even let me see the applications. I have no say. Part of me feels like I should use my authority to bust in at some stage, but again, they say I'm disruptive. I'm starting to believe there's some truth in it!

We held the first Women's Leadership Camp in California, in Napa Valley, and it *was* different. The result has just been so exciting to see. Everyone from every level of the company, from senior management to the call centers, was represented. The whole focus was on learning how to be better people, better leaders, better citizens, and creating more happiness. And, again, these women have taken that positive energy and learning back with them.

I wanted to start Women's Leadership Camp in order to get a better understanding of what we needed to change and what we needed to do. But after I made my speech at G Stock, a funny thing happened: The whole company's tone started to change. As I started opening the door and questioning our recruiting processes, attitudes began to quickly adjust. We always made sure our opportunities were open to women, but now we created channels that were more suitable for everyone, no matter what their gender, to be able to communicate and contribute. I'd just never concentrated on that before. Soon enough, we began to see more females on the executive team.

After that year, we appointed four global general managers for the company on the operations side, and all four of them were women. Then our managing director of the US, our VP of talent, and our executive director of Planeterra joined the company as top leaders; all three sit on my global C.O.R.E. team and all three are women. Together, we're learning how to build an environment where everyone can contribute and where everyone has the same opportunities. Sometimes you just have to create the intention and it just naturally happens. Our C.O.R.E. now includes seven women out of fourteen members. As an outgrowth of Women's Leadership Camp a new group formed to encourage the voices of the women that make our company great on a global scale. G Voice was launched a year later, in 2012.

*Scan this QR code or visit Looptail.com
/GWomensLeadership to experience how G
Adventures nourishes its female leaders.*

What I've learned while pursuing a desire to redefine social enterprise is that any organization with such aspirations should have an inclusive voice. As I had when I turned down the offer of one million dollars in 1999, I always stress that to be successful you must know your audience. It was clear to me that we were headed down a destructive path if we continued to foster a noninclusive environment. I believe we would have stalled, if not failed, had we not created the ability as a global company to create equal opportunities for everyone regardless of cultural barriers. Everything we did, from defining our core values to developing our company's culture, was created to transcend the business, and our leadership development should not be any different, regardless of what cultural differences blocked our path. The dream of G Nation would only succeed if we could unite everyone to our common passion and purpose, and that transcends cultures. To my amazement at our Future of Tourism on September 25, 2012, Almas Jiwani, the president of UN Women National Commitee Canada, honored me with a seat on their advisory board for the work we do with women around the world. It's the Looptail!

As we started to engage our global voice and to listen to the rich feedback from the growing freedom within the company, the impact on our customer service rose to hit new levels. The passion that was unleashed throughout the company started to create social innovation the likes of which I could have only dreamed, if I was still alone, thinking in isolation about how we could do things better than anyone else. All of that energy and creativity manifested itself in projects and initiatives like Incite or the Holy Trinity of Customer Service. Many of the unique things we do are not only about leading with service, but also about implementing social change and helping make the world a better place.

For a brief example, take just one project that we launched in Delhi, India. Every year, we carry thousands of passengers to India, and the majority of them start their journey in Delhi, where we offer travelers the opportunity to take a tour of the city on their first day. Before the project I'm about to describe, these city tours were arranged through a local company and were either included on the trip or were available as an option. City tours are common practice for any tour company, everyone does it—and that very statement is generally an invitation to social innovation.

We started working with a local street kids' home in Delhi. Most of the children there had either been abandoned because their families were unable to care for them or had been forced out of their homes because of severe abuse or drug or alcohol problems in their family. It was disheartening to hear stories of kids who had it so bad that they had to leave their homes and live on garbage dumps around the city, at ages as young as four or five. To create a program aligned with our core value of Lead with Service, we partnered with a group of street kids' homes and also supported their education center. We began to supply guide training to the kids so that they could give our passengers a different type of Delhi tour, one that showed how these kids saw the city through their eyes.

We first offered these tours as an option, giving our customers the opportunity to have an impact on poverty and engage them beyond travel. When CEOs suggested it, a large number of travelers wanted to do it. The project was a huge success—our travelers loved it. The volume of positive comments we received was off the charts, and this was clearly a better experience for our customers. So, we started to include it on some of our tours.

As it grew, the program addressed many related issues, such as helping to increase the English skills of some of the kids who were studying the language as part of their program at the education center. We also work with some of the older kids, who love the opportunity not only to meet people from around the world but also to proudly share where they come from and explain how they are breaking the cycle of poverty and abuse in their lives. The Delhi street kids program illustrates how we can merge social innovation, social enterprise, customer service, and our core values in a way that creates sustainability, all while leading with service.

Scan this QR code or visit Looptail.com /DelhiStreetKids to meet some enthusiastic, young tour guides in Delhi, India.

Changing the culture of a company is incredibly difficult, but when it really starts working, it's easy to tell. And asking your employees to believe in your brand and to deliver customer service that differentiates it takes connectedness. Everyone has to feel they are part of something special and a key part of the solution. In 2010, Culture Club embarked on a brave project to unite all of our people around the world. Homemade videos of people lip-synching to their favorite songs had been making the rounds of the internet for a while, and Culture Club decided it would be fun to do one of them for G Adventures. Our people around the globe shot their parts in it using simple cameras and iPhones, and then we edited it all together. The song we decided to use was "Can You Feel It" by the Jacksons. It was the perfect anthem for everyone in the company to show what they were feeling, and around the world they wanted to be part of it. As the reality of our revolution started to pulse through the veins of the company the employees could now feel the change and the benefits were palpable.

"Can You Feel It" became a viral sensation, so not only did it bind us together as a company and create community, it also showed the world what happiness and freedom looked like.

Scan this QR code or visit Looptail.com
/CanYouFeelIt to see G Adventures' first lip dub
video. Can you feel it?

Our lip dub was so successful that we decided we would release one every year, to send a message to our staff and our customers that we were a different kind of company. In 2011 we got hold of some better equipment and performed a tribute to our message of Freedom, and in 2012 we upped the production level to say nobody loves travelers like G Adventures. I know this is a book, but if you're anywhere near an internet connection, I really urge you to check them out right now.

Scan this QR code or visit Looptail.com/Freedom
to watch G Adventures second lip dub video and
the sense of freedom worldwide that G Adventures
employees embrace.

*Scan this QR code or visit Looptail.com
/SomeBodyToLove to see the third lip dub video
and to get a sense of how much G Adventures
loves its travelers.*

Our videos have become more elaborate, but the message is still clear. They are centerpieces of our culture, and we showcase them whenever we present our business around the world. Each year they became more anticipated and, by the time our third one was released at our Future of Tourism in 2012, we finally felt we had made that transition; our culture really is our brand.

When you live by a change-or-die mentality, it's often exhausting for the people around you. I have been criticized and lampooned because of my constant need for change. I'm not sure if it's a chip on my shoulder from my experience growing up or a reflection of my genuine feeling that we live today, for tomorrow we die.

One of my greatest challenges is to remain nimble as we grow. Our business model is about change. This is another reason, and it's only natural, that we focus on happiness, because studies have shown that most unhappy people fear change. The greatest gift you can give any business is the ability to be nimble, and to be that, it takes a culture that embraces change, which, in turn, drives growth. Charles Darwin once wrote something that I always relate directly to my views on business. I think it should be branded on the walls of every great company: "It is not the strongest of the species that survives, nor the most intelligent, but the one most responsive to change."

But when you push any group of people too hard without seeing results, there's a point of diminishing returns. It's important to document those moments when your company reaches its goals and to communicate and celebrate them throughout the organization. It's also important to me to give real-life examples and tangible results to support some of my theories. Nothing is worse than reading a business book littered with inspirational quotes and stories but has no results or tangible things to take away and use in your own life and work.

The Great Place to Work Institute is a global research and consulting organization that examines and reports on the world's best workplaces. G Adventures is on almost every list of the best managed companies and best places to work, but the lists compiled by the Great Place to Work Institute are more than just another subjective contest. They actually confidentially poll your employees, and in order to qualify, a certain number of your people must take part. It's one thing for a company to apply for one of these awards, but it's another for your employees to be surveyed in order to obtain their real feelings about the organization.

We registered for the list in 2008, just before the year we fired our HR department. A few months later, someone called to say we should send someone to the ceremony because we had made the list. When the night came, a bunch of us poured into the swank party and waited anxiously to find out where we had been placed. Given that there are hundreds if not a thousand companies that qualify, our people exploded with cheers when our name was called out at number twenty-six. At such an auspicious occasion, they were thrilled to be named. The next day, the office was abuzz with the news that we were on the same list as great companies like Google, Microsoft, Apple, and Facebook. Everyone in the office seemed to be extra happy, except one person—me! I thought being number twenty-six sucked!

I was not happy, not one bit. A few people rolled their eyes at me, thinking I was being my usual difficult self. Later, representatives of the institute came to our office and explained how we did better than they have ever seen for a company entering for the first year. They stressed that they had never seen anything like it, but I didn't hide my displeasure. I joked that I demanded a recount.

Exactly one year later, we entered again. By now, we had the Talent Agency in place, Culture Club was rolling, and all of our new programs to connect our global cast were going full force. Change was afoot and you could feel it. After a few months we once again got the call that we were on the list and that we should attend the awards ceremony. To be honest, I was so dissatisfied with the earlier results that I didn't even attend. Still, we bought a table at the ceremony and employed a gamification process so that people in the office could win tickets to attend the prestigious final event. Well, as they started to announce the names of the winning companies in reverse order, with the top winners coming up on stage to receive their award, we were soon past twenty-six. We either did better, or we really screwed up. Then they went past twenty, fifteen, and then ten. Cheers and squeals of joy emanated from our table. You could imagine the suspense as they read nine and eight, then seven and six. *Finally, they announced G Adventures at number five.* Our table exploded and before anyone could catch their breath, the entire group grabbed their smartphones and lit up Twitter to announce our winning place to our entire company and the world. Out of the four big companies I mentioned earlier, only Google was ahead of us. It wasn't just a proud moment because we had won an award; these were the results that showed everyone we were on the right track and that maybe I wasn't crazy; maybe I was onto something.

Since then, the amazing results have just kept on coming. Our customer satisfaction numbers did the unthinkable, rising from an average of 94 percent to 96 percent, then 98 percent, then peaking and maintaining 99 percent. Very, very cool.

We have another number we track, measuring the scores of people who take trips with us and who love talking about our brand. We call them Ravers, because they rave about you. Ravers love to tell their friends about you, they love taking to the social media airwaves to talk about you. We have a saying we share with our travelers: "If you share our brand with your friends, it's not because you like our brand, it's because you love your friends."

For years, we had a Raver number of 69 percent, which was already off the charts in the industry. By 2011, it had jumped to an incredible 74 percent, and in 2012, I stood up at G Stock to thank everyone for their hard work because our Raver number had jumped again to 76 percent.

Yes, we're a travel company, but your company can do this, too, regardless of what your product or service is. If you want to achieve that fifth gear in your customer service, it's all about creating an environment where people can achieve happiness and freedom. Your people will drop their preconceived notions about the work they do being just a job or a lifestyle choice. Your work becomes a calling. That's when the Looptail kicks in. You will begin to transcend what you do and engage anyone who touches your brand to a higher purpose.

PART V

KARMA

CHAPTER 12

Defining the Looptail

I have never really worked in a normal office environment. In a way, it's one of the biggest holes in my game as a leader; I've never really experienced it, but I'm intrigued by it. In fact, when I meet someone who has worked at a bank or an insurance company, I often find myself grilling that person about their experiences. "Tell me more about how that works. Do you like who you work for? Do you hate your boss?" Usually after a few questions, they get a bit freaked out by my curiosity, make their excuses, and shuffle away.

A lot of our employees come from that sort of corporate background and we have to put them through a kind of detox when they get here. It takes a while to shake off the effect of coming from that dog-eat-dog office environment, in which you're only as good as your last deal or your last quarter's results. I have grown used to dealing with people who arrive with trust issues because they had a bad boss. To this day, I'm just amazed that anyone can function, never mind excel, in that kind of environment. You can do a good job working with people you are not connected with, but you will never achieve happiness. I think it's very unfortunate that so many people don't aim higher. Imagine how much better life would be if we could all make our time at work more focused on pursuing our passion.

Why keep working away at something that you hate doing? Lots of people turn their passions into careers. Why can't you?

For the majority of people, work doesn't have to be an exercise in clock-punching in order to put food on the table. There's a good reason why we used to see it that way; for most of human history, we worked simply to survive. We are children of the industrial revolution, and so many of our parents or grandparents ground out an existence because that is all they knew. But our standards of living are higher now, especially in the developed world. We have choices about the kind of work we want to do, choices our ancestors never had. They worked to live and seemed to be paying their dues. Their ultimate goal was to get to when the wheel stops and they could retire. And at retirement, people's philosophies change. Some people retire and just want to do nothing because they worked hard all of their lives, while others retire and blossom because they can finally do the things they always wanted to do.

When you ask people about their passion, they'll usually tell you about something they do in their spare time or deflect the question to talk about their family or their partner. They rarely associate the word *passion* with what they do from nine to five, never mind happiness or fulfillment. In fact, a lot of the discussion around happiness and work focuses on the concept of work-life balance, which is something I don't really understand. If it means not spending every waking hour at the office, I'm into it. But if it means treating work as something boring or even painful that you have to endure and keep totally separated in its own little box in order to enjoy the rest of your life, then I just can't get onboard with it.

Personally, I love what I do, and I have since the day I started this company. It took me a long time to realize, partly through observing other people, that my approach to work was unusual—

that by running a sustainable business driven by purpose and empowering the communities we work with, I was creating happiness and freedom, and not only for myself. Nothing is handed to you in this life; however, everything is earned. I overcame insurmountable odds that worked against me on many levels: my origins, where I was from, what I believed, and so on. I knew my approach was different, and I knew that I was happy, but I didn't really put two and two together, not for a long time. I often wish I had been smarter earlier, but it wasn't meant to be; that's why my path has been an unorthodox one. After going through the trials of 2007, it became clear that I had to take what I had learned and put it at the center of what I believed in, to really make my ideas the driving force behind the company. That was the beginning of our cultural revolution.

The purpose of this book is to share with people beyond the G Adventures community the way that they can create happiness and freedom for themselves and for their businesses, in their work and in their lives, and how, in fact, those things are all linked together by the Looptail. In the future, the brands that will survive are the ones that make life better. Why can't that be your brand or the one that you are part of?

The Dalai Lama, who has been a great inspiration to me, once said, "I believe that the purpose of life is to be happy." He wasn't only talking about the kind of momentary happiness I mentioned earlier—the feeling you experience when you eat a cookie, or when you get your paycheck, or receive an award. A life based only around just those things would be pretty shallow. To me, that quote means that your purpose is to find sustained happiness. And you can't only do that during your nonworking hours.

If you ask people why they work, and then ask them what they believe their purpose in life is, how many of them will give you the same answer? There's no reason why they shouldn't. Like I say, we have choices, and we can choose to integrate our purpose in life and our work. I run a travel company, which from a certain perspective doesn't sound like something to get passionate about. But that's not how I look at it. My job is about changing people's lives, creating happiness and freedom, and transcending our industry. If we were just a run-of-the-mill travel company, I wouldn't be able to motivate myself or my employees to get out of bed in the morning. My purpose, and the purpose behind G Adventures, is much more important to me and my company than a means of just collecting a paycheck.

As I looked back over some of the things we had done in the early years and asked myself why I was passionate about my work when my competitors and even some of my former staff just saw it as punching a clock—a way to enjoy a certain lifestyle, where you get to travel and you don't have to wear a suit to the office—I saw that what made us different was that we viewed our work as doing more than just delivering a product or a service. In travel, the product mostly boils down to accommodation and transportation. We didn't incorporate those Tour Operator Standards into our brochure in 1996 because they would get our customers from the airport to their accommodation quicker; we did it because we believed that we could do great things through our work.

It's the difference between creating momentary happiness—such as putting travelers in all-inclusive compounds with Western creature comforts and high walls—and creating sustained happiness by improving the relationship between our travelers and the people hosting them, like Jimmy in Belize or Delfin in Ecuador. One creates inequality, diverts resources away from the people in the community, and gives the traveler a superficial experience; the other empowers people in the community to pursue their own passion and purpose, while taking people out of their comfort zones and giving them a greater appreciation for their own lives and where they come from. The Looptail is inextricably linked with the same philosophies of sustainability and preserving the world for future generations while also just making good business sense.

We didn't set up our arrangements with Jimmy or Delfin, or put the Tour Operator Standards in the brochure for immediate, short-term profits or return on investment. We did these things because we believed they were the right things to do, that they were in line with our principles, and because I believe that if you pay it forward, good things will come to you.

Business continues to evolve parallel to society. We've been through the stage in which businesses provided what the customer needed and through the stage after that in which they provided what the customer wanted. Now, successful companies tell you why you should want to be part of something bigger than yourself. Satisfying an under-explored human need: the need to be good. Being good is starting to matter more. We want to have our cake and eat it—and not feel guilty about it.

Paying it forward (or karma) is a crucial aspect of the Looptail. When Mr. and Mrs. Franz agreed to print my brochures, they didn't do it because they planned to hire a collection agency and chase me for every dime if I failed. They took a leap of faith; even though there was a risk that they wouldn't get paid back, giving me a chance to pursue my dream was, to them, the right and good thing to do. I've tried to do the same in my career. I've lost count of all the people who couldn't see why I wanted to let our customers know what we stood for with our Tour Operator Standards, or why we developed our own nonprofit arm, Planeterra. They couldn't see the return on investment, the direct benefit to the business. To me, those things were about paying it forward. If it's the right thing to do, you can't focus only on the short-term benefit. You have to pay it forward. It's the only way to transcend being a travel company, or whatever product or service you provide.

At this point you're probably thinking, "That's great that it worked out for you, Bruce. But what if it doesn't work for me? Am I just supposed to put my faith in this hippie-dippy pay it forward idea, cross my fingers, and hope for the best?"

Before I answer that, think back to the beginning of every successful entrepreneur's story. Without exception, they all start with having a great idea and then deciding to defy the odds and start a business. In nearly every case, that person's family and friends tell them they're nuts, they can't get a bank loan, and people constantly remind them that 50 percent of businesses fail in the first five years. Wouldn't it be easier, and less risky, to go work in an insurance company? Of course it would, but what distinguishes entrepreneurs from everyone else is their desire to take a risk and to hope that their passion will be what separates them from all the other people who start companies.

When you follow the Looptail—finding your passion and purpose in your work and in your company, transcending your industry, and paying it forward—you are taking another risk. You are betting that following your passion and investing your work with purpose will lead you to success. How is that different from the risk an entrepreneur takes when starting a company? Neither is certain. But in order to be successful in the modern economy, you have to do what you believe in. Moreover, you have to do what other companies are scared to do—you have to stand for something. As companies get bigger, they start wanting to be all things to all people, and that notion of universal appeal takes hold and waters down the distinctive message. Freedom lies in being bold. The secret to happiness is freedom, and the secret to freedom is courage. And I believe that G Adventures has transcended our industry and created that incredible relationship we have with our customers, with our employees, and with the people who admire what we're doing. It's a risk, but business is all about risk. There is a bit of karma in there because you have to really believe that if you get your business model right, everything else will fall into place. If you give, you get. What goes around comes around. The Looptail. I'm not asking you to stop thinking like a businessperson. I'm simply asking to look at your business, and your life, differently.

G Adventures isn't the only company to find success by looking at our core business and trying to engage our customers beyond it.

Take Starbucks. Starbucks is a coffee shop. It sells coffee. You could fill a dump truck with the articles, books, and lectures that have tried to explain how Starbucks became one of the world's most respected, beloved brands, or how they manage to charge five bucks for a coffee and get away with it. For years Starbucks had a minuscule marketing budget. As late as 2003, they spent only 1 percent of their annual revenue on advertising, which is ridiculously small for a company of their magnitude; most spend more like 10 percent. To me, though, a big part of Starbucks's success is how they engaged their customers beyond coffee—how they transcended their industry by doing the right thing.

When they started, the coffee industry was shrouded by criticism about its perceived inequality. So Starbucks decided to create their own Looptail and transcend their industry. They introduced a line of fair trade coffee in 2000, long before doing that was popular, and hugely increased the visibility of the fair trade designation. They've led the way with programs to use recycled paper in their cups and sleeves and to give a discount if you bring in your own mug. Sure, there could have been smaller shops that might have been doing it sooner, but not on the scale that Starbucks did.

These things don't make the coffee taste better per se, but they make the person spending five bucks on a latte—as well as the baristas and the people in the offices—feel better about the company and the brand. If all things were equal, wouldn't you want to buy a coffee from—or for that matter, work for—a company that you believe is doing the right thing? They differentiate with their service because their baristas are part of something greater than themselves. And the happiness that creates is the fifth gear in their customer service.

You don't even have to be a retail company in order to put the Looptail into practice. One of the most sustainable companies in the world is a company out of Mexico, called Cemex. They make cement. How do you transcend cement? Can you engage your customers through a higher purpose that somehow connects to making cement? Yes, and Cemex has proved it. Five percent of global CO_2 emissions come from cement manufacturing; Cemex works rigorously to cut down on their carbon emissions while making their product and have recently introduced a seal of "Ecoperation" that they put on products with what they call outstanding sustainability performance. They were the first in their industry to measure and disclose the amount of greenhouse gases in their production, and they cut their CO_2 emissions by 21 percent per ton of cement since 1990. And they make money, too—in 2011, in the middle of a huge downturn in construction in the US (a key market for them), Cemex's net sales rose by 8 percent. As I write this, their third quarter 2012 earnings (EBITDA) numbers marked the fifth consecutive quarter of year-over-year increases. It's not a coincidence.

Social enterprise, to me, is about solving standard business problems with solutions that address social issues like environmental sustainability and economic inequality. That idea started in the nonprofit world, but more and more, you see it creeping into the for-profit world—because the consumer is demanding it.

The consumer doesn't want to purchase something randomly; they want to know where that product is coming from and to identify with that brand. They want to know why they should purchase it and why they should purchase it from you. They want to understand what that brand and the people behind it stand for. It's happening every day. At the same time, social media is making companies more transparent and accountable to their customers. (The word *social* is used differently here than it is in *social enterprise*, but you'd be surprised how closely social enterprise and social media go together.) In this new environment, companies like ours are carving out a new space. We want to be a social enterprise—a for-profit company that uses business skills to solve social issues. We look at business problems that we have and find sustainable solutions to them, and in fact, it's what we've been doing all along, and it's what has driven our success.

It's what makes our employees love their jobs and what makes our customers love our brand, even in the midst of crises like 9/11, and even in recessions or downturns.

That's the Looptail: finding your passion and purpose in your work and in your company, transcending your industry, and paying it forward.

CHAPTER 13

People, Planet, Profit,
Passion, and Purpose

The freedom we created in the workplace had now seemingly taken on a life of its own. All over the world, our staffers started to change. Even outside the programs we were running through Planeterra, everyone wanted to do something to give back. After a while, departments in regions that didn't get involved with some socially innovative project seemed out of place. Among the projects they created were everything from our accounting department adopting a school, to our tour groups' department converting one of our empty offices into a coffee shop, the G Bean, which raised funds to change lives in Africa, to tree planting groups. We even had a promotion that saw someone shave their head to raise money—they called it Planet-hair-a. We helped fill a plane with food and supplies to deliver to Haiti when the earthquake hit in 2010, and we sent a crew on our vegetable-oil-fueled company bus, the M/V Freedom, into the heart of Hurricane Sandy in 2012 to bring supplies and relief. All of these activities showed how we could use our business model not only to do good but also to promote our movement.

*Scan this QR code or visit Looptail.com
/MVFreedom to see the veggie-oil-fueled M/V
Freedom in action, bringing relief to New England
residents in the aftermath of Hurricane Sandy.*

Planeterra, the nonprofit arm that we created in order to work with the communities interacting with our travelers, had already been active in places like Peru. But as we defined and honed our core values, we began to realize that projects like our micro-financing projects weren't just part of our operations—they were a main cog of the central mission of this company and a big part of how we could change people's lives.

My story about Peru started back in 1998. Peru had become our most popular destination worldwide, but on a 1999 visit to our offices in Cuzco, just after I had assumed the company's debt and went all-in, I found the operations were simply a disaster. I had to make some tough decisions.

We were running trips on the Inca Trail, and at the time we had so many customers going there, we became the largest single Peru tour provider in the world. (We are now, and I'm sure we were then, too.) As a result, whenever we switched our services to employ a different local tour operator—which we did several times—those tour operators in turn became the biggest businesses in Cuzco. But there were problems. We started getting letters from dissatisfied customers; some operators weren't keeping up with the maintenance of their equipment; some weren't paying fair trade wages; others, we discovered, didn't pay taxes.

After changing operators one too many times, our last-ditch solution was to allocate our business among just five different local operators. We thought it was the perfect solution because it was distributing wealth—it wasn't just one company benefiting. But in spreading our business to five different firms, we had even more problems maintaining overall G Adventures consistency, which for a company like ours is a huge issue. The biggest challenge for us is something I refer to in our office as the "Big Mac" theory. McDonald's is a master of having the Big Mac taste the same in Mexico as it does in Singapore as it does in Moscow. To be a widely recognized, beloved brand, the G Adventures experience has to be consistent everywhere; even though the trips are different in style, the brand promise and relentless customer service has to have a very similar thread.

It was becoming increasingly important to us that we find sustainable solutions for traditional business problems—the definition of social enterprise—and this was an area where fresh thinking could really set us apart. It ended up being a defining moment for us: We showed how tourism could aid in both conservation and cultural preservation.

I ultimately closed our offices and pretty much felt compelled to start from scratch. After having unsuccessfully tried all the other options, we figured that the only way we could deliver the kind of Peruvian experience that would be consistent with what we wanted the company to stand for was to get our own Peruvian license and operate our Inca Trail tours ourselves, locally. It felt like trying to do the impossible because in many countries, this isn't really an option. Governments are naturally hesitant to allow foreign companies to operate tours in their major tourist attractions since much of the profit would theoretically then leave the country.

That's something we're against as well, which might explain why we managed to convince the Peruvian officials to give us a license. We went all the way to the minister of tourism to explain how, as a social enterprise, we would recruit from areas where people were in need of jobs, then supply training to our new employees so that they could run all of our operations in the field, benchmark wages and compensate our workers fairly based on industry fair trade standards, and employ only local people in our operations. It was a tough sell, but we were determined.

Fortunately, the Peruvian government liked our proposal, and so we became the first Western tour company to run our own operations on the Inca Trail. It was a monumental moment, and we started the process of delivering on our promise to the people of Peru.

We were able to recruit from regions that had low employment— in fact, some regions had *no* employment—and people came from miles around for our training programs. The business started to grow more rapidly along with the quality of our programs, and the next thing we knew, we had 500 employees in Peru. It was a sustainable solution, it made for a better experience for our customers, and it delivered the brand consistency we wanted.

I have made some aggressive decisions, but this was one of the biggest. Over the course of three years, I had removed all of our Western office staff and CEOs. It wasn't easy; I have never been threatened as I was while doing this. Some people around us had all kinds of commission setups and shady dealings, which they weren't about to give up without a fight. As a result, I had to blow up their entire system. But, when we created an innovative social solution to the employment situation, the local people we hired were grateful to be part of our revolution. It wasn't just that we were providing jobs; everyone knew they were part of something special.

Scan this QR code or visit Looptail.com/IncaTrail
to visit Peru's grand treasure and to meet some of
the people who lead the way for G Adventures.

It took some time but by 2003, we were bringing tens of thousands of customers to that region. As our business around

Peru started to grow, however, it came to our attention that we were taking all of our passengers through an area that had zero employment for women. A lot of Peru's history and storytelling is incorporated in the traditional weaving patterns that have been passed down by women in the villages to the younger generation. But now, this current generation wasn't really learning the craft. Rather than absorb the traditions that had been carried through the centuries, the younger generation was going where the work was. And that meant moving to the city center in order to serve the growing tourist traffic, of which our customers were one of the biggest portions. These women were finding work in bars and restaurants and retail, the places where our passengers were shopping and eating, while Peruvian traditions were slowly dying.

I realized that if I were to keep speaking to audiences around the world about our solid commitment to the communities where we run trips, we had to do something in this region. But what? After giving the question some considerable thought, we came up with a plan. We would recruit 60 women in one of the villages outside Cuzco—30 older and 30 younger—and have them weave all day in a co-op that we'd help build. The older women would teach the younger generation how to weave; meanwhile, we'd be creating employment for both age groups. But we wouldn't pay them wages; instead, every single one of our groups who were on their way to their Inca Trail trip would stop by the co-op, spend a day there, learn how to weave, spend time with the women and girls, and then buy the textiles—the authentic weaving. It was a brilliant idea.

The next question, however, was how would we get the community to buy in? There had to be a dialogue. The village we chose was extremely poor at the time. We started out by asking them about getting the basics together that they needed for a project like this to happen. Through our dialogue, we showed them that we were serious about making this project happen and that we were not just a big corporate travel company.

The Peruvians would build the co-op themselves. They showed us the scope of what they wanted to do, which was to build a gallery for the weaving. Through Planeterra, we paid for a lot of the rental equipment, like cement mixers to pour the foundation of the co-op. As for the labor, the men from the community pitched in, and together, they built it all.

Once the co-op opened, the women started weaving, and our travel groups came through. Before long, it was massively successful. We started to bring in other communities; in the beginning there were only 60 people, but that number grew quickly.

To me, the great thing about the weaving co-op is that its value goes beyond just doing a project to benefit the local community. This was a business solution. When I talk about there being a glass ceiling on a great tour, the Inca Trail is a classic example. There are probably thousands of companies that run Inca Trail tours, and many of them are fundamentally the same. But I wanted to differentiate our product from other companies' products, and the weaving co-op is a perfect example of how to do it.

Some people criticize us for building a community project because it serves the needs of our business. My answer to that is, "Uh...yeah—that's exactly why we did it." Yes, it raised the bar for Inca Trail tours. Suddenly we had something that other companies didn't. We took the long road, creating dialogue with the community and getting the community involved in the creation of the project. We didn't just say to a community, "We're doing well over here with our tours, so here's a kickback donation to buy food." Just the opposite. They were actively involved in the process of building and running the co-op. The people there control their own destiny—they have jobs, and their success depends on their own hard work. It's about empowering people and giving the communities in which we operate long-term support instead of short-term relief. This project ran totally parallel to our happiness business model and focused on our pillar of creating sustained happiness.

And, for our customers and our employees, this showed we could change people's lives. Everyone who touched our brand saw that they could be part of something greater than themselves.

Scan this QR code or visit Looptail.com
/WomensWeavingCoOp to see the social
impact that G Adventures and its travelers
have made in Peru.

Another aspect that was becoming very close to my heart was fighting the injustice suffered by women in the developing world. As we were growing, I saw the disparity between men and women in many different areas. Yet women drive the tourism economy today. That's one of the reasons why the women's weaving co-op, for example, is all about women.

When I started to research the ways of alleviating poverty, I found that eye care could be a powerful tool. An estimated 65 percent more women than men are likely to need cataract surgery to prevent blindness, but they're much less likely to be treated than men. In most countries, I found that the priority in treatment was given to men so that they could go back to work. Remarkably, however, I couldn't find any studies being done about blind women raising their children. There are huge long-term cultural implications of kids being raised by vision-impaired mothers or blind grandmothers, who are often responsible for child care if the mother works. When blindness strikes the women in these families, their resources become stretched and everyone suffers. For one thing, most of these kids are homeschooled, and if your teacher is blind and has no resources to compensate for that, the kids learn less and end up being less able to function later in life. It perpetuates poverty because over the long term, it fragments the family's ability to focus on raising their children.

The really astonishing part, to me, is how simple and inexpensive cataract surgery is. It's a basic outpatient procedure; patients have their vision restored days later, sometimes even hours later. It takes only a few minutes, but the impact it can have is huge.

This was what we were looking for in terms of a broad issue that fit with our mission as a company and would help break the cycle of poverty. People always ask me why blindness is one of our causes. Our eye camp projects aren't about blindness. The issue for us is having a cultural impact in the developing world. You have not seen immediate meaningful impact until you witness a mother who's just had her eyesight restored, clearly seeing her children for the first time in years.

Tibet had given me so much and had metaphorically given me the vision I needed at a time of uncertainty. To go back and pay it forward was important as I started to think why karma mattered in business. As an example of engaging our customers to a higher purpose, we started to run eye camps in Tibet. These eye camps would allow us to fly sixty doctors and nurses into Tibet, and in ten days, we'd be able to restore the vision of three hundred Tibetans. The first eye camp, in 2008, was a huge success, and we've done many since then; we've restored just over 1,000 Tibetan people's vision, all funded by our travelers. Our goal was actually to do more eye restoration surgeries, but because the Chinese government has made it difficult for us to get the required permits, we have started running eyesight camps in Tanzania, Africa—another area we take a lot of travelers to.

In 2009, we realized we faced another corporate challenge, though it was a much more benign one: how to celebrate our approaching twentieth anniversary, which was approaching in 2010.

I'm not generally enthusiastic about anniversaries. I don't even celebrate my birthday; in fact, years ago, annoyed by the distraction caused by birthday celebrations in the office, I made the whimsical declaration that people should just stay home on their birthday. To this day, every employee of G Adventures still gets their birthday off work. I was also put off by how other companies use their anniversaries to offer discounts in order to boost their own business. Who's meant to be celebrating what, exactly? But other people in the company were excited. So, with our twentieth anniversary coming in 2010, I felt more and more pressure. As it came closer to the date, I thought, why don't we use the opportunity to do something innovative?

With two months to go, someone came to me and explained that they were trying to build a permanent eye hospital in a rural area of Cambodia that had over 26,000 people who needed simple cataract surgeries to restore their vision. After examining the proposal, I said, I'd love to do this but it's a $75,000 project. Then a thought popped into my head; with hindsight being 20/20 and this being our twentieth anniversary, we had the perfect opportunity to take on a really big, ambitious project. Everyone could contribute, and I realized that we could create a movement around it. We would call it the G Adventures 20/20 Eyesight Centre.

We decided to hold a circus fundraiser in Toronto. We rented a big hall called the Berkeley Church and booked a number of circus and street performers. The event and the fundraising drive around it would be a way to engage all of our partners and customers, and because of that, it felt right to me. It was aligned with our values as well as with our business model. The other thing that I realized as we were planning it was that people appreciate an opportunity to say thank you. I admit that I'm very antisocial that way; often I just want people in the company to do their jobs and I don't want to solicit any kind of self-congratulatory stuff. Like I say, I'm always looking forward. But I recognize that a lot of people want an opportunity to say thanks, an opportunity to say, "You guys are amazing!" And this seemed like the perfect time to give everyone a chance to bask in that a little and to do some good.

We called it Ignite the Night, printed up posters, and put the word out to our community. The tickets sold out in a matter of days. That night was magical in many ways. So many people said to me that they'd never seen a fundraiser like it. A lot of our corporate partners were so used to the Four Seasons banquet hall and the silent auctions and whatnot, while ours was all about what we stood for as a company and as people. And every cent was going toward changing people's lives.

Ignite the Night raised a stunning amount: $160,000. Not only were we able to build the hospital in Cambodia, we were able to start those eye camps in Tanzania as well. In Cambodia we'd be able to do thousands of eye surgeries every year and make a dent in this rural area. That money had massive impact, and it was all made possible by our community of supporters contributing to our growing global community.

And what could be better? It cost us nothing but delivered on my desire to engage our customers and our travelers to a higher purpose. It's about transcending what you do.

Scan this QR code or visit Looptail.com /IgniteTheNight to see how the G Adventures global community came together to make a massive impact in Tanzania and Cambodia.

We now have more than forty projects around the world. As I write this, we've just launched a women's sewing project in Egypt, which is similar to the women's weaving co-op, but it's not directly related to our business just yet. We're going to work with them to make some of our G Adventures gear, such as our t-shirts or laundry bags for our hotels.

One of the most successful programs we started is a relatively simple one: our New Hope project in Cambodia. It's a restaurant and training center that's completely run by local street kids and women previously involved in the sex trade. In addition to being a functioning restaurant, it's used as a training center to introduce new skills to marginalized men and women, reintroducing them to the workforce through the food and beverage industry. There's a school attached at which the women receive training and their kids can get their education right next door to where their mothers are working in the restaurant. We carry more than 10,000 travelers in the region and all of our groups stop there for lunch. It has been a huge success on many levels. It has been one of our most successful projects; our clients love to write me long letters of how a short visit to this wonderful program changed their lives. It's all about creating community through projects that give people control of their destiny, returning to them their dignity through employment and building a sustainable solution.

Scan this QR code or visit Looptail.com/NewHope to see how G Adventures built a sustainable employment solution for marginalized women in Cambodia.

The important thing is, even if they're not part of the tours, these projects aren't separate from our business—they *are* our business.

These have been examples of finding sustainable business solutions, paying it forward, and engaging through purpose, but how about a current example of what a movement looks like? As I said, it's easy to talk about these kinds of things in theory, but it's really important to me that, if I was going to write a book, I have real-life examples to back my ideas up. What is a movement, anyway? In the summer of 2011, I read a magazine article about a terrible drought in the Horn of Africa that was forcing Somalis from their home and into Kenya in search of safety in refugee camps. The stories about people becoming dehydrated on their way to get to these overflowing refugee camps were just awful. Somalis were arriving there and finding that the camps were already full to bursting. Families of eight or nine people who had left their homes would show up having lost children along the way, not because of hunger but because of dehydration.

The story struck me hard. These people were dealing with horrifying conditions during their journey. They had no food, unforgiving weather conditions, and many were reporting being robbed or even raped while in transit. The idea that they were also dying of dehydration was more than I could bear to think about, and I knew I had to try and do something.

I had already asked our Planeterra group to research water-related projects because the next thing I wanted to concentrate on was getting safe drinking water to communities in the places we run trips. We were already doing programs in Africa with these gigantic rain-catching water tanks, and we'd received a humanitarian award for our work in Tanzania from the government. I wanted us to start putting more energy toward that cause because, like blindness, the social and cultural impacts on families of not having access to clean water are huge. In some communities, kids have to walk long distances to get water and end up not going to school on certain days, or missing school because they're sick from drinking unclean water. In other areas, families are forced to decide which of their female members will make the long trek to retrieve the day's water, knowing they will be sexually assaulted along the way. The cultural impact is immeasurable.

I spoke to our Planeterra group and asked if we could find a way to put water tanks halfway along the route from Somalia to Kenya. They called around to find out who could install the water tanks for us, because this wasn't something we could do ourselves. CARE, a humanitarian organization fighting global poverty, was stationed there and said they could do it with assistance from the UN, but that it would cost $25,000 for a tank. Also, one tank would only cover one area, and you would need three or four to cover the route completely. Our goal was to put at least one tank out there. It seemed insurmountable but my heart was telling me I had to try.

So, once again, I sent out a tweet about the crisis: "We have to do something in Kenya. Can we mobilize, please. Kenya has opened their hearts to our travelers for years. We can't just watch."

We set up a donation page through Planeterra's website, and soon everyone in the company sent out messages on their Twitter accounts and we crossed our fingers.

Just like our appeal about the earthquake in Peru, the response was so massive that it nearly took down our servers. Everybody in the company was refreshing our website to watch the thermometer that we had built to track donations, and it just grew and grew. Within 24 hours, we had raised $50,000. It was an unbelievable outpouring of humanity! And there were very few donors over $100, it was all $5, $10, $15, and $25 at a time. Within a week, we had to shut it down, but not before we surpassed $100,000.

It was one of those moments when you're just blown away by people being united by a common purpose. You could feel the trust and the energy of our community. Donating to our projects isn't like giving to other NGOs, where it feels a bit like dropping money in a well. At Planeterra, 100 percent of your donation goes to a very specific, tangible cause, for the simple reason that G Adventures pays all of Planeterra's operating costs. So when you donate, you know you'll have an immediate impact on what you are donating to remedy.

This wasn't about being a travel company anymore—this was a movement and it was global. Donations came from every corner of the world. It didn't matter whether we ran the best trips on the planet at that point; it was about the human condition, relating to a human story and using our brand as nothing more than a vehicle to collectively create something that gave people the gift of life. I knew those people had many greater battles ahead of them, but I felt that if we could do anything to give them a fighting chance, we had to do it. And we did.

Scan this QR code or visit Looptail.com /AfricaWaterTanks to watch the outcome of an immediate appeal to G Adventures customers and the power of a global social enterprise in action.

According to the UNWTO (United Nations World Tourism Organization), in 2012 the world surpassed 1 billion tourists for the first time. That's up from 866 million in 2008. Tourism is growing faster than anyone could have anticipated, and the question remains: Is this a good thing? The issue that I've always focused on is how much money actually stays in the country. This statistic from the United Nations Environment Program (UNEP) stated that, of every $100 spent by a tourist from a developed country, only $5 stays in the country that they visit. It's not the fact that people aren't traveling to these places, it's that when you do travel, people have to be a bit more conscious and make decisions with a bit more purpose.

One of the biggest problems we face today is the distribution of wealth. There's a huge gap between the rich and the poor, and it's getting wider. People are angry about the disparity they see. When we're successful we're made to feel guilty, and yet, despite being in a terrible economy, people are giving more than ever before because we want to do something. We're searching; there's something inside of us that wants to give more. Poverty is one of the greatest global challenges that we face today. In the next ten years tourism will generate $10 trillion.

Here's what I propose: Couldn't tourism be the greatest form of wealth redistribution that the world has ever seen?

Here's an encouraging finding from the World Bank "Voice of the Poor" report: Next to illness and injury, they say, entrepreneurial activity and the ability to have jobs is the most important factor in determining the fate of the poor. Tourism could provide the vehicle for those jobs and have more of an impact on poverty than any single force ever has.

What would actually have to happen for you to go on vacation to give back instead of donating to the most marketed charity? The main thing that would have to happen is that business models would have to change. If the company you travel with changed its philosophy and the way it does business, and improved the way the money was distributed from your vacation, you could fight inequality just by going on vacation. I am also a firm believer that there is no faster path to peace than people getting to know one another. So much violence and destruction today is caused by ignorance and fear of the unknown; we are crippled by the fear of what we don't understand. I believe that travel done the right way can be a vehicle to create peace through understanding and appreciation of our other cultures while making the world a little more perfect.

Travel also gives us an appreciation or awareness of ourselves, which goes hand in hand with being able to appreciate others. How can we ever understand what we are and where we belong in the universe if we haven't experienced anything outside of our own nation, culture, or history? Travel opens us up to accepting the ways other people live, as well as creating compassion and tolerance—which is what the world needs now.

As early as 1995, we started to question the then-emerging trend toward ecotourism. When I look back, I sometimes wonder what inspired me to continue pushing for a different model, for what I thought of as responsible tourism. I was always more concerned with our relationship with local communities and cultural preservation, while our industry and our partners really weren't concerned about these ideas. Our first initiatives with Conservation International in 1995 and, later, our publishing Tour Operating Standards in our brochure fell on deaf ears in the travel industry.

But the original triangle vision of bringing NGOs, government, and G Adventures together had never left my mind. Over time, I became more determined to realize my dream that would bring the three elements together. The concept was simple and addressed a glaring problem: When institutions hired consultants to create tourism projects that depended on being successful in the market, they often failed to connect the projects with their intended audience. I thought that, if the project was driven by the operational needs of the for-profit businesses, the chances of success were greater—we already had a critical mass that would drive the immediate flow of customers. If we could ever make it happen on a large scale, I was sure it would change the way institutions looked at international development through tourism. The impact would be far greater than anything we had ever done. But this theory was hard to prove.

Then one day, we caught a break. My then executive director of our Planeterra Foundation told me he had met and had a conversation with someone from the Inter-American Development Bank (IDB), which provides development funding to Latin America and the Caribbean. He told me that one of their directors wanted to meet with me, so I flew to Washington and met Yves. Yves is a Belgian man with a strong energy and a passion for change. Yves was impressed with the work we were doing on the ground in other parts of the world and what others had apparently told him about us. He wanted to know more. I launched into an explanation of our business model and our core values. I told him about Planeterra and the projects we've initiated over the years. His eyes lit up, and he seemed impressed with what he heard. Not only did I tell him about all of the projects we had done over the years, I also talked up the different connections I had developed through my speaking about sustainable development at conferences around the world.

Yves said that he had never seen a company like ours before. We reviewed the graveyard of tourism projects that have failed around the world because of poor planning, and I promised that, given the chance, we could start projects that would have twice the impact and cost a quarter of the amount to complete. All of my passion poured out of me because I knew this was our next big thing.

By the end of our conversation, Yves and I were roughly speaking about proposing an incredibly innovative and brave partnership. It would take a lot of courage on his part to propose such a setup to the board of the IDB and also to leverage his relationship with the Multilateral Investment Fund (MIF). He would have to build a case around more than just the projects; he also had to show how different we were from other private sector companies. They would be evaluating how we'd evolved via our company culture.

Everything we had been working on was coming to a head.

Then the bureaucratic process took over, and I was reminded why we started Planeterra in the first place. Apparently it would be two years of planning and reporting before we even made it in front of the IDB's board. But during those two years, we developed a proposal for our first five projects in Latin America.

1. San Juan La Laguna (Lake Atitlan, Guatemala)—We would develop a homestay program with the local community that would take the place of the hotel we had been using in the area. We have more than 1,000 passengers traveling through this area every year, and spending a night in a local village would be a life-changing, once-in-a-lifetime experience.

2. Ometepe, Nicaragua—This would also be a community homestay. Again, we take about 1,000 passengers through this area, and a homestay project on this island composed of two volcanoes would provide a better experience for our customers.

3.   Sarapiqui, Costa Rica—Along a road where we carry more than 7,000 passengers a year, we would work with a local co-op coffee community to create a restaurant and training facility. The project would provide a day-trip stopover for our groups and local employment.

4.   Lares Trek, Peru—Years ago we helped spearhead the development of a new trek in Peru. It has grown incredibly popular; today we guide more than 9,000 passengers a year on this trek, but the communities along the way are not benefiting from tourists who camp in or near them. Some tour operators pay to camp on local farms, while others just squat anywhere they want. We would build community campgrounds along the trail, which would be open to anyone but mandatory to use, and the money would flow back to the community.

5.   Sacred Valley, Peru—This area surrounds one of the world's most iconic heritage sites, Machu Picchu. We would build a community restaurant and training center. It would not only supply jobs and training for locals to use in the restaurant, but it would also teach them transferable skills within the food and beverage industry. We carry a whopping 19,000 passengers a year through this region; they would all stop for lunches or dinners and all the money would go back into the local community.

These proposed projects represent everything we stand for. They envelop all of our core values and redefine the boundaries of both social innovation and social enterprise.

There were many complications and a lot of information we needed to supply, but we were steadfast in pursuit of our goal. I know it was difficult for the IDB to understand the scope of the project. I spoke to Yves on the phone a couple of times to find out what more we could do, and while he remained positive over the two years, the truth is, we had our ups and downs getting everything together.

I realized it was a situation I couldn't control. This is when karma counts in business. I just had to keep our intention pure and let the universe provide, and if it was meant to be, it was meant to be. I had come so far since Tibet that I actually said that last statement out loud!

Then, on the eve of our Future of Tourism event in September 2012, we got the call! The budget had ballooned and it was now a $1.3-million partnership between G Adventures and the IDB. After two years of dreaming and twenty-two years in the making, our proposal was approved!

It was a milestone. The lessons we learned would influence future development around the world, opening the door to a different business model. Our structure would affect government institutions and how they look at partnering with private sector companies to find sustainable solutions through tourism, and how we could help alleviate poverty. In fact, I believe that once the gates of cooperation between NGO and commercial organizations have been opened, it will transform the way the developing world is treated by the West. That tourism can aid in conservation, create sustainability, and most importantly be a fantastic vehicle for wealth distribution by people just going on holiday.

It was a very proud moment for us and it lifted our entire organization to a new level. The linkages between the IDB and G Adventures would live in the memory of the institution and would influence relationships and sustainable development in other parts of the world. Everything we had worked for was coming together, and finally, we would prove that we could change the world by reinventing business. Our desire to redefine social enterprise was on display, and now the concept of the Looptail was very real. Everything about this partnership united the company and our philosophies to think different. It was disruptive, innovative, social, and it connected all of our core values and represented everything we stood for.

The travel company I had started by maxing out my credits cards had now grown to transcend its industry, and we had grown more profitable than we had ever been before. Since the early days, we had changed the lives of more than one million passengers, running more than one hundred thousand tours and bringing in more than one billion dollars in sales. With travelers from more than 160 countries booking with us every year, we had become a global brand that had outpaced our industry in customer retention, customer satisfaction, and company culture.

Scan this QR code or visit Looptail.com/IDB
to see an announcement from Yves Lesenfants,
Senior Technical Advisor, MIF/IDB, regarding
that company's important partnership with
G Adventures.

PART VI
THE LOOPTAIL

CHAPTER 14

The End of the World as We Know It

My life is a loop that runs in five-year patterns. As much as I dislike the idea of being predictable, I have grown to accept this. If we all looked at our lives, we would find that, to a certain extent, we all have different patterns we run every day to make our world work. In 2012 it had been five years since the challenges of 2007, and we continued our meteoric rise. Fifteen years had passed since my trip to Tibet, where I had spent most of my time contemplating our bankruptcy. The company seemed to double in size every five years. By 2013 we rocketed past $200 million in annual sales, and it has been five years since I turned down those incredible offers to sell the business.

It was also five years after the summer of despair and, right on target, I started to face new leadership challenges. It wasn't summer-of-despair level angst, but I was sensing some of my own personal limitations. I wanted to push us into new territory again, and I was wrestling with my own motivation.

Then, one of the greatest honors of all took me by surprise.

251

I was informed that the Social Venture Network was celebrating their twenty-fifth anniversary by creating a Hall of Fame, and that they wanted to induct me into it, along with such sustainable pioneers as Richard Branson of the Virgin Group; Ben Cohen and Jerry Greenfield, the creators of Ben and Jerry's ice cream; Birkenstock USA's founder Margot Fraser; and Anita Roddick of the Body Shop (who was inducted posthumously). The formal ceremony at Gotham Hall in New York was humbling for me, not only to be recognized in the company of such great pioneers in sustainability, but also to be characterized as a workplace champion. Still, I felt like I wasn't ready for the Hall of Fame, at least in one sense: I didn't want to be put out to pasture just quite yet.

Around that time, I traveled to Hong Kong to speak to the members of the Royal Geographic Society. Afterward, I was chatting with a group of people who had attended my talk, and after a short time, they revealed that they actually worked for me. I had never met them before. We exchanged compliments and I thanked them for the great work they do. In fact, it was the second time in as many weeks that this had happened to me. I was in Nepal the week before, doing a keynote at a conference, and the same thing occurred—people who worked for G Adventures attended and I didn't realize it.

This sort of thing started happening more and more. These employees were people who worked hard every day, loved our brand, and yet, as I was standing there with them after the conference, I had to admit that I didn't really know them. The feeling took me right back to Las Vegas, when I had brought those randomly selected groups from around the world for the discussions that helped reshape the company. I came to the sobering realization that I had lost touch with many parts of my own business. I started thinking that I didn't only want to identify my best people, I wanted to know them and make time to share my views with them and hear their thoughts about everything we were doing.

For years, we had a shorthand term for an idea we used within the company called the Burning Building theory. It's kind of a morbid approach, but we used it anyway. To identify the top talent in someone's department, we would ask, "If the building was on fire and you had to jump out the window with one or two people in order to restart your department, who would they be?" The question wasn't about identifying the best performers per se, but more about identifying the most unique talent. That's an extremely important distinction.

You need to recognize people who are not just the best, but people who are unique and would be difficult, if not impossible, to replace. If you've ever had a chance to manage people, you know the kind of talent I mean. I'm talking about the people with a unique skill set or attitude that you don't find every day. Like an accountant who has a degree in computer programming, who can write code and do reports, or a person who works in sales but who has a degree in literature and is an outstanding writer who can contribute that skill to other parts of the business. They might even be people who are just insanely positive and happy and are quick to do anything to propel a team forward. Those are about as rare as the snowy owl! I'm talking about people who are motivated to do what is best for the brand and the company every time, not just pursuing their own personal gain or agenda. People who let their work speak for their commitment to excellence— nothing else. It isn't necessarily about being a superstar or being outstanding at your job; it's about much more than that. And it's a quality that's much rarer than you might think.

Before our cultural revolution, we used several different ways to identify who our top people were. For my own personal happiness, I needed more connectedness, and I knew the systems we had introduced wouldn't fully satisfy that. Besides, my five-year alarm clock was going off. Inspired by our Burning Building theory, and the great feelings I had when we brought those people from around the world to Las Vegas, I decided to start what I call the Zombie Apocalypse.

The theory was pretty simple but gross. The inevitable Zombie

Apocalypse is the collapse of society that would result if our movie heroes failed to keep the zombies from spreading and eating our brains. If the Zombie Apocalypse descended upon us and your zombie-proof bunker could only hold twenty-five people, who would you choose to restart the company in a post-apocalyptic landscape? You'd want the best, brightest, and, more importantly, the most unique people in your organization around you.

So, in my Zombie Apocalypse exercise for our employees, the chosen "survivors" are notified by an anonymous e-mail explaining that there's a Zombie Apocalypse upon us and stressing that they're not to say anything to anyone. They have to arrange with their immediate manager to get two days off work and to make up an excuse. They need a passport and are told to meet at the airport on a certain day, at a certain time. They're advised that they will be away from Thursday to Sunday and given a few tips on what to pack. At the airport they're met by someone from Black Ops (yes, I have a Black Ops department) who leads them through a check-in where they will eventually find out they're heading to Vegas. To everyone's surprise, I'll be waiting for them upon their arrival. The last one we held had twenty-nine Slayers, but you can never predict how many you're going to need. Zombies can be so unpredictable.

That kicked off a few days of sharing and running think tanks, as well as just bringing everyone together. It allowed me to have some face time with our young leaders and the opportunity to share my ideas on leadership and the vision of the business. It also kept me in touch with what was happening around the company. We had quite a wild time in Vegas, celebrating just being together and with other people who also hold themselves to high levels of excellence and who believe their work is their calling, no matter what specific role they have with the company. On Sunday we returned home together, and everyone went back to work Monday as if nothing had happened and it was all just a bad zombie dream.

I do the Zombie Apocalypse every year, and while some of the chosen survivors will rotate in and out, others will return again and again. As much as we try to keep it confidential, word always leaks out and people find out about it—mostly water cooler talk, though. I'm sure some people must feel left out, and there's no avoiding that. It's a bit of the Aspirational Culture I brought up earlier—you must recognize and celebrate your top people, and as a leader, you must get to know them.

In the end, the Zombie Apocalypse is all about my own focus and balance, enabling me to lead the company better and to continue to improve our culture for everyone. For my own motivation, I need to reach out to my most unique talent and really get to know them. What many don't understand is that it is all about me, nothing else. I also need to make meaningful connections, and it is important for me to stay on course. I need to get to know some of the people who give so much, but whom I may not be close to.

My door is always open, and so is the Talent Agency's, if people want to know more about the decision-making process or better understand what success looks like in our world and what the path is to achieving it.

A lot of terrific ideas came out of that first Zombie Apocalypse, but none of them were as valuable to me as realizing that I really had to reignite my passion for what I do and continue to remind myself why I do what I do. To stay sharp, I needed to be very aware of my own personal purpose.

What I was questioning during this particular period was my own motivation. It certainly wasn't the company, which was flying. People became more and more enthralled with our business, over and above the interest in our actual trips. I was asked to come and speak about our business model at major companies, including Google and Apple. Apple actually sent a crew to film a short movie about how we were changing the world with their products; it's featured on their website for anyone to stream.

*Scan this QR code or visit Looptail.com/Apple
to watch the video that Apple produced that
highlights G Adventures as a global leader in using
their technology for business.*

With all the work we were doing around the world, I decided we needed also to have an impact locally. I had heard that the city of Toronto ran a popular Christmas party program for kids living below the poverty line. It bothered me that the cut-off for the party limited admission to kids age five and under. I decided that we would cancel our company Christmas party. Instead, we would arrange with the city and a local inner-city community group to run our own version of a Christmas party for all kids ages *six and over*. We called it Christmas in the Community.

The night before, everyone in the office was given a raw turkey, along with instructions on how to cook it. The next day, everyone was to take part in entertaining 300 children and their families, which, for some of them, was the only Christmas dinner they would have. As a kid I was once in the audience of a community Christmas party, and I remember how it made me feel. In short, we wanted to make sure that every child was counted at Christmas, not just the ones who were five and under. Every department had to come together to create a station for the kids.

If ever there was a test of whether our people really lived our culture and our brand, it was canceling our office Christmas party and doing this instead. Well, we passed the challenge with flying colors. Our operations group became human Christmas trees and let the kids splatter them with glitter, snow, paint, and paste-on decorations. Another group gave break-dancing lessons. At the height of all the frenetic energy, our mayor of G Adventures, who was dressed up as Santa Claus, gave out age-appropriate toys to all the kids. The screams and cheers that we heard made all the hard work and effort of the day worth it. Like everything we do, it soon took on a life of its own, a movement, and everyone in all of our offices around the world in every region started taking part. It showed me how much our people loved and lived our brand, for them to be willing to take away something as sacred as our epic Christmas party and instead to create social good.

Scan this QR code or visit Looptail.com /ChristmasInTheCommunity to learn why G Nation thought this initiative was better than a Christmas party.

I decided that it was time for me to challenge myself and to reconnect with my own sense of purpose. I had spent so much of my energy rallying people around our collective purpose, I had lost myself in the shuffle.

I decided I was going to take on my greatest challenge as an explorer to date. I wasn't getting any younger, and I thought this might be my last big adventure. It's not that I would ever stop traveling, but the days of my going on epic, physically demanding trips—like climbing Kilimanjaro, going to base camp at Everest, or being one of the first people to scale the side of an uncharted mountain or see a newly discovered Inca tomb—were coming to an end. Still, I thought I had at least one more kick at the can left in me. I wanted to rekindle my desire for adventure to get back in touch with not just what I do, but also why I do it.

* * *

I've been infatuated with the notion of being an explorer for years because I've always admired travelers who see the world through new eyes. It's inspiring to share the experience of discovering travel itself. In order to stay innovative and to stay on top of my game, I'm constantly struggling with trying to break out of the normal way of looking at my work. It's important to remember that innovation is not about what you've done but what you've yet to do. You have to know that distinction, because if you get too caught up in celebrating what you've already done, you will become extinct.

Over the past few years, I had started to become intrigued with the histories of the original explorers, who risked their lives to discover places that no one from their countries had ever seen. I was particularly attracted to the story of Roald Amundsen, the Norwegian who was the first to reach the South Pole. Amundsen was maligned for many years; he wasn't as good at presenting himself to the public or to the media of the time as Robert F. Scott, his rival in the race to the poles.

To me, Amundsen was a brilliant leader, but he just didn't know how to win favor from the public—he didn't do much in the way of interviews, he didn't go on the lecture circuit, and when he came back from the South Pole, Amundsen was in fact dead broke. But he was innovative in his approach to everything he did. In the late 1980s, people outside of Norway started to change their views about Amundsen.

Amundsen and his crew reached the South Pole on December 14, 1911. I decided I wanted to get to the South Pole, and I wanted to make my trip during the one hundreth anniversary of Amundsen's journey. It would be my quest to take me way out of my comfort zone and retrace the footsteps of great explorers I admired. Lots of people on our trips visit the coast of Antarctica or pass by on cruise ships, but I wanted to see *inside* Antarctica; that meant preparation and overcoming logistical hurdles, from arranging flights to dealing with whatever nature wanted to throw at me.

At least I was fully kitted out this time, certainly as compared to my Tibet trip in 1997. If anything, I was overprepared. I was born in the tropics, so the idea of intentionally putting myself in a situation where I would be camping, *on ice*, for an extended period, was pretty daunting. The weather in Antarctica is unpredictable and unforgiving; not only is it as cold as anything I've ever experienced, it can turn at any second.

After months of preparation, the first leg of the journey was a flight to Punta Arenas, the southernmost city in Chile. From there, a five-hour flight in an Aleutian, a windowless cargo plane, with an Antarctic logistics group who typically move doctors and scientists around. You land in a base camp just inside of Antarctica called Union Glacier, but you're still four or five hours of flying away from the South Pole itself.

Base camp is a bubble dome where they cook food, and outside that was a row of tents that would be home for the foreseeable future. During our winter, there's bright sunlight all the time in Antarctica, their summer. There's not even a period of dusk, it's just sunny—all day and all night. And, of course, it's freezing, but every day is different—it could be minus 30 or minus 50, or lower, and this was only summer.

Among the people I met at base camp was a guide who managed climbers who wanted to brave the elements and reach the top of the highest peak in Antarctica. It was a requirement to achieve the Seven Summits honor, which is given to people who have climbed the highest peaks on all seven continents. He told me that he had climbed all seven summits in a single year. I suddenly had the feeling that he was looking at me as one of those fat-cat CEO types who was paying someone to drag them up the side of Everest. I thought I still had game.

I've never really been good at sitting around, and I was looking for a way to get over my mental aversion to the cold. Then I met Adam. Adam was hired to live at the camp and take people for walks in and around the area, in order to keep them active and fight boredom while they waited for their weather window to go to the South Pole. With a bit of a chip on my shoulder about proving myself to be a true adventurer, I set out to climb some peaks. And I'm glad I did. What were supposed to be days spent waiting became some of the most amazing experiences of my life. The highlight of my adventure was reaching the summit of three local peaks: Charles Peak, Mount Rossman, and Peak 942. Each varied in degrees of difficulty but presented me with the challenge I needed and created my best memories of the interior of Antarctica. From the emergency crevasse training to the white blind climbs, it was totally exhilarating. It also gave me time to be alone with my thoughts, standing in unbelievable silence on the tops of these mighty peaks and looking out over incredibly harsh, stark landscapes. It was beautiful and perfect and gave me everything I needed to remember why I do what I do.

Mercifully, our weather window opened at the perfect time—we'd be staying over through New Year's Eve. Off we went. By the time we got into the US research station, the scientists there had been partying all night. They're on New Zealand time, so they were just waking up after their New Year's celebration. They let us in and gave us a tour of their entire station. I got to speak with a number of fascinating people about their motivation in terms of science and living at the South Pole and got an idea of what their lives were like. (They even gave us South Pole stamps for our passports.) We saw the historical writings of past explorers, including Scott and Amundsen. We were a few days from the actual 100-year anniversary of Amundsen's triumph, but regardless, my traveling buddy Dani Reiss (the CEO of Canada Goose) and I shared a great sense of accomplishment.

That's what creates happiness, I realized—when you have a goal for such a long time, it isn't about the actual achievement, it's the years of planning and the ride along the way. As they say, it's the journey, not the destination. Earlier, I mentioned the difference between momentary and sustained happiness. One of the lessons I read in Shawn Achor's book *The Happiness Advantage* was that when people looked forward to something, it creates a greater sustained happiness. Without even knowing it at the time, this adventure supplied me with a great deal of happiness along the way because I was returning to my true passion.

I remember thinking from atop Mount Rossman about how few people had seen what I was looking at and how fortunate I was to be there. On top of that mountain, I was in touch with everything that I had become, looking down on the unimaginable and thinking back to having done the impossible. I was reloaded and fired up for the next chapter of my life, and all it took was a little bit of remembering where I came from, taking my own advice, and becoming a better, stronger version of myself.

My lifelong fascination with and connection to the lost continent, Antarctica, as well as all the lessons I've learned there go beyond what I could put in my book.

CHAPTER 15

The Infinite Loop

It was a freezing evening on March 23, 2012, and I was shivering outside the Air Canada Centre, waiting for a friend of mine who was running late. We were about to check out Jeremy Lin, the Chinese-American sensation who was playing basketball for the New York Knicks. Normally I would just send the other ticket by e-mail and tell the person I would meet them inside, but for some reason that day I decided to meet them outside the arena.

As I was standing there, a fellow with a broad smile came up to me. He had a friendly face and seemed to have a warm, cheerful disposition. "You're Bruce, right?" he asked. I nodded warily.

"You don't remember me, do you?" he said. I didn't.

"Ten years ago," he explained, "I was in the audience when you spoke at the first Tibetan Film Festival, which I was involved in organizing. It wouldn't have happened without your sponsorship. And I remember your talk vividly."

That I did remember. I had heard they were trying to organize the first ever Tibetan Film Festival, but they needed someone to sponsor it in order to rent the movie theaters. This was after I had come back from my big trip to Tibet, and even though I couldn't really afford it back then, I agreed anyway, because it was more of a fundraiser than a festival.

The organizers had asked me to give a talk, before the movie to the opening gala audience at a local cinema, about my experience in Tibet and my thoughts on the Dalai Lama. It was the first time I had been asked to speak about that in public; in truth, I never used to mention it.

When I stepped on stage, it was very clear that everyone was there to see the movie; they didn't want some schmuck up there selling them trips. So I just went up and told my story. The audience seemed indifferent at the start. I told them about my experience crossing the border in 1997 and the group of monks saying, "Welcome home." I also explained about how I smuggled in pictures of the Dalai Lama to distribute and how, whenever I gave them to anyone, they dropped to their knees in tears—they were just so moved to find out that he was still alive and that he believed in them. Then I mentioned how, when I came home, I was on the cover of *Profit* magazine with my "Free Tibet" t-shirt, and that, somehow, Tibet had changed me.

But something happened by the time I had finished my story. The crowd, which had been a bit impatient with me when I started, had somehow warmed up. In fact, I was stunned when I finished: I was greeted by a most vigorous ovation. Apparently they had enjoyed my story. In any event, I quickly got off the stage and left for home; I couldn't stay for the movie. But I do remember walking down the street and feeling completely energized after getting such a receptive round of applause.

I didn't think anyone in that audience would remember what I had said, but this man in front of me, tonight, in the freezing cold in Toronto, remembered how I made him feel. I was finding out that I definitely wasn't the only one who felt great that night.

Since then, he told me, he had become a senior government official in the Canadian Parliament in Ottawa. Wow. "I am Tibetan and I will never forget that night," he continued. "That was a night when I was proud of where I came from, and it would not have happened without your support." He went on to explain that the Dalai Lama was coming for a visit to Canada the following month, that he was arranging all the details, and that he wanted me to come to Ottawa to watch His Holiness speak.

I was so touched, but at the same time, I had this sinking feeling because I knew I couldn't go. After all these years, that trademark infringement trial was about to begin on the Monday of his visit. I was gutted. It was one of those feelings of disappointment that was so intense, it made me want to scream. And the reason for my not being able to go made it worse. I would be in rooms full of lawyers—my personal hell—and the thought just made me sick.

"It would be great to have you there," he said. "I know that His Holiness wants friends of Tibet to be there, and you're definitely a friend of Tibet."

Listen, I told him, there's nothing more in this world that I would want to be doing, but I can't change the legal system—this court date has been set for almost a year. But if I'm meant to be in Ottawa, it will happen, I said, because my heart wants to be there. Standing in the cold, I told him how I had been inspired by *Great Ocean* and how our logo had been redesigned so that the looptail swung back around the "g" to create an "o" in tribute to the Great Ocean of Wisdom.

"I think you're going to be there," he replied calmly. "Just keep in touch," he added, and gave me his business card.

Afterward, I couldn't stop thinking about how I wanted to go to Ottawa so badly. I kept fantasizing in my head about calling in sick for the court date. I was desperate to get out of this pointless legal case and, as I stewed on it, it just created more anger and bad energy. If I skipped court and anyone saw me, I'd be in it deep. I guess I hadn't learned enough about destiny, because I spent most of my waking moments trying to figure out how I could game the system.

But in the end, I didn't have to decide. Sure enough, three

days before the trial, the lawsuit settled, and I was finally free. I pulled the Tibetan's worn business card from a pile on my desk and sent an e-mail to Tenzin, the chief of staff whom I had met on that frigid night in March.

> *Hey Tenzin.*
>
> *Bruce here. Well I think the Universe is providing for me. If you can remember I told you I had a legal case around the time HHDL would be in town and it would be tough for me to make it. It looks like it ended today! I have had you on my mind hoping this would happen for me. Is there any way I can still come? I would be forever grateful.*
>
> *Peace.*
> *Bruce*

He replied:

> *Karma! Of course. I will put you on the "VIP backstage" list. You will be my guest. And bring a copy of* Great Ocean *for a signature.*

Tenzin's mention of going "backstage" was what intrigued me and got me even more excited about going. In fact, it kind of made me giddy—and I don't think I have ever described myself in that way in my life.

I'm not the kind of person who gets really starstruck over famous people. I've had the chance to meet many of them over the years, but unless it's part of an actual, genuine conversation, I rarely feel compelled to say anything to them. I once found myself running on a treadmill beside Michael Jordan in a gym and managed to keep my cool. (Of course, I dialed up the speed and tried to outrun him, but I was cool about it.) This was different, though, because of what I had been through in the fifteen years since my visit to the Dalai Lama's homeland. I wasn't so much starstruck as full of admiration and appreciation for his influence on my thinking.

Tenzin said he knew that I would be coming all along and that he had made plans for me to be there. I scrambled to make arrangements to get to Ottawa.

In 2004 I had received a letter from the Office of the Dalai Lama inviting me to come to Vancouver where His Holiness would be appearing and attending a lunch. When I got to the event, I was disappointed because it wasn't very intimate. His Holiness was definitely in the room, but there were many other people there, so I never really got much of a chance to connect with him.

I did, however, get to speak to him during a question-and-answer session. As I waited for the microphone, I listened to the other questions, which were mostly very arcane historical or theological questions about Buddhism. When my turn came, I said, as someone who's an entrepreneur and in business, where many of the decisions you have to make are devoid of emotion, how do I justify that while at the same time staying true to the need for compassion?

At first, His Holiness said, "I have the benefit of studying scripture 24/7. That's all I do, all day. Very few people have the ability to do that. The expectations of life, and what I do, can be quite far apart, and you just have to always remember where you come from."

Then, His Holiness told a story that I will never forget. He described a woman from France who showed up one day in Dharamsala, India, where he lived in exile. She had been a Catholic nun for some years and became a female monk who, over time, became one of the Dalai Lama's closest confidantes. He spoke very affectionately about her, saying that she was an instrumental influence in his inner circle, that she was one of the most dedicated people he had ever known.

His face then turned serious as he detailed how she became sick one day, and after her illness continued to worsen, word eventually reached him that she was not going to live. So he rushed to see her. On her deathbed, however, she told him that she had returned to her Christian beliefs. She had accepted Christ back into her life and began praying to him to ask forgiveness for her sins.

The Dalai Lama then said emphatically, "You can never get away from where you come from. No matter what you do. As hard as you try, you never will. You can never forget where you come from, and you must never forget that."

I then began to realize that part of the Looptail is to understand where you come from because it is critical to understanding your purpose. You need to create a story or narrative about how your company came about, and why it exists, in order to engage anyone who touches your brand. Remember, you don't own your brand; your brand is what other people think of you. All we can ever be in this world is the best we can be. To do that, you must accumulate the knowledge you gain from compounding experience after experience in your life, which allows you to continually become a better version of yourself. Remembering your core purpose and staying true to your core values are an important part of your work and your life.

Even though I didn't get much in the way of face time with His Holiness, I was still really appreciative and just blown away at being in his presence, however distant.

When I arrived in Ottawa, I called Tenzin right away. He started to tell me that I should come across the street to an event they were doing right now and that there was a fundraising dinner in the evening as well as other events. As he went on, I couldn't believe I had considered missing this; yet in the moment, I was actually intimidated. I said, "No, you're busy, how am I going to go? I don't have a ticket." Next thing I knew, Tenzin had sent someone to come to the hotel to pick me up and walk me into the House of Commons.

We entered a very small private room with a few people waiting, seated in chairs, and they announced that the Dalai Lama was going to arrive in about ten minutes. I was startled and kind of freaked out. Not long after, the double doors blew open and His Holiness seemed to float in, accompanied by Richard Gere, who is a dedicated Buddhist and fantastic supporter of the Tibetan movement. When His Holiness walked through the door, the entire room jumped to their feet. It all happened so fast. I'm not sure about anyone else, but I was breathless—something I had never experienced before. His Holiness sat in a chair a few feet in front of me and looked at me with knowing eyes. Of course, like a dork, I pulled out my iPhone and took some photos.

I sat in amazement at how close I was and hung on his every word. Someone in our group welcomed him to Canada, and he stood up and said a few words about his cause. I became kind of self-conscious because he seemed to know the people who were in the room, but he would look over to me occasionally. I would stare back and smile—then pull out my iPhone and snap another shot! I was just excited and so grateful to be in his presence. As fast as he swooped in, he swept out, shaking everyone's hands in between clasping his hands together in a symbol of prayer atop his forehead. As he passed me, he grabbed my arm and gave me a knowing smile.

That was the beginning of two days of being spiritual and close: I became part of the entourage following the Dalai Lama wherever they went. I was in and out of cars, traveling to receptions, just hanging in the entourage of His Holiness the Dalai Lama. The first thing I noticed was how busy he was and how much he does every day. He is totally committed to people in a manner I have never seen in my entire life—and I don't say this lightly. I have never seen someone from the depths of their soul be so committed to being available and present for every sentient being on our planet. His day was mapped out down to the second; people lined the streets to get a glimpse of this friendly, slightly hunched-over spiritual leader who has captured the imagination of the world.

There were times I was so close to him, he would ask me to pass him a cup of water and just look up at me with the warmest smile—a smile that lights up crowds of people who just want to be in his presence to experience what he represents: peace, happiness, and freedom. This was the beginning and end of my Looptail. Everything I had been through and believed was on display, and my purpose had never been clearer.

After a day of going in and out of various meetings and government buildings, I was exhausted and asked to be dropped back at my hotel to get some rest. The next day, His Holiness was set to address a sold-out crowd at the local stadium, which, actually, was the event I had thought I had come to see. No sooner did I get back to my room than my phone rang. It was Tenzin saying that Richard Gere had to make a round of appearances around town and asking whether I was ready to go out. I grabbed my jacket and was out the door, and when I got downstairs I was rushed into a waiting van. From the backseat, I tweeted this (along with a photo of the back of Richard's head): "My life just got weird...er. I'm in a van with Richard Gere!"

We went to a private party that people had paid an extraordinary amount of money to attend, on the grounds that Richard Gere would show up. It was a fundraiser for Tibet and everyone was joyous for a good cause. Whether they understand the cause is another story, but even if only a few people's thinking is changed by events like these, they're still worth it.

The next morning my phone rang in my hotel room. "Where are you?" Tenzin exclaimed. "Where have you been? We've been trying to text you. The Dalai Lama is upstairs having breakfast and wants to sign your book for you." I had turned off my phone to get some sleep. How did these guys do it? Were they on some kind of karmic jet fuel?

I jumped in the shower, grabbed my copies of *Great Ocean*, and flew up in the elevator. When the door opened, I was stopped by a gang of big, burly dudes with earpieces whom I was about to get to know really well on a more personal level. Their body search made the airport pat-downs I have grown accustomed to seem like a friendly how-do-you-do. As the last guard pulled his hand out of my pants, I saw Tenzin, who walked me into an open room in which His Holiness was meeting elderly Tibetans.

It was touching to see these older people just burst into tears as they entered the room. It brought me back to the flood of emotion from the stableman in Tibet who dropped to his knees when I gave him a picture of the Dalai Lama whose return he awaited. I could hardly contain my own emotions again as the elder Tibetans would drop to their knees and tell His Holiness of the hardships and losses they had suffered. He would caress them and tell them to be strong, as well as to reaffirm their purpose and importance in the universe. I have never seen a more powerful exchange of human emotion and energy. His Holiness would kiss and bless white scarves and drape them over their heads. Then he would pull his forehead to theirs while they would be uncontrollably shaking, and he would assure them that everything would be all right, that they were part of the movement. One by one, he made each person feel like the most important one in his universe for that moment in time.

Scan this QR code or visit Looptail.com/DalaiLama to see more pictures from Bruce's collection of his experiences with the Dalai Lama.

His Holiness glanced at my copies of *Great Ocean*, then held and looked at one of them for a while. He didn't remember where the book came from and was fascinated by it, as well as amused at the picture on the cover of himself as a much younger man. He thumbed through the pages and was even more amused by the collection of black-and-white photos in the middle of the book that had pictures of him as a child and a teenager. He laughed aloud.

Eventually, security came and told us the cars were ready to take us to the stadium where the Dalai Lama was scheduled to speak to a sold-out crowd. I followed along, and before I knew it, I was backstage once again with His Holiness, holding my freshly signed *Great Ocean* books. It was now starting to play with my head, and I began to feel as though I were in a dream state. His tireless giving never stops, though. There were camera crews backstage that had come from around the world, and the Dalai Lama graciously sat for interviews.

Then it was showtime. His Holiness took to the stage amid chants and cheers from rabid fans, who treated him to a rock star's welcome. Tenzin had saved me a seat at the side of the stage, a short distance from His Holiness. The blinding lights rendered the crowd into faceless shadows that rose up, row by row, to the rafters.

It was quiet in my mind, but the words from His Holiness rang out loud like a thunderstorm. Everything came crashing in on me, and I was overwhelmed. *This was my Looptail.* This was the full circle I had completed, and after everything I had been through, I was now free. And yet, deep in the pit of my gut, I thought to myself that I was not doing enough. I needed to work harder, I needed to work faster. At the same time, I was awash in a blanket of joy. Everything he said reaffirmed my belief in what we were doing and our movement to engage our customers to a higher purpose, to transcend our industry, and to foster a culture of freedom and happiness. It seemed like he was talking directly to me and nobody else was in the room.

My life was flashing before my eyes and it took me right back to March 14, 1997, when the same thing had happened as I stood before the most beautiful blanket of stars on the roof of my hotel in Tatopani. My mouth was dry and my eyes watered. It all hit me. This was one of those moments when you know you've found your place in the universe, that you're doing what you were meant to do.

It was dark, I was in a stadium, and I was in a reflective state of mind. I felt a hand on my knee and a soft voice tell me, "Keep up the great work, you must keep doing what you're doing. Don't stop believing and keep moving forward." I looked over—it was Richard Gere telling me that I had to keep fighting for what I believed in. It was surreal. Everything seemed to be moving in slow motion.

For more than a decade, people had asked me to write a book, and I would respond that I didn't have anything to say that was relevant. As I sat there watching His Holiness and absorbing his words, the energy, the intention, and the goodwill among the men and women who were there that day, I said to myself, "I have something to say now."

As I was finishing the first draft of this book, I looked up the definition of *looptail*: "A loop at the end of a tail." In that moment, I knew this was the loop at the end of my tale.

It was just like my teacher Mr. Mason told me, all those years ago; "Bruce, you need to speak up. You can't help yourself or others if you don't use your voice."

G.A.P Adventures
Ecotourism Tour Operator
Standards, 1996

Company-Wide Policies

1. Permanent Standards committee established, meets twice a year and all results published—membership to include a representative from CI, operations, sales & marketing, reservations, and tour leaders
2. Use of locally owned transportation encouraged
3. All G.A.P Adventures staff and partners aware and knowledgeable of Standards program on an ongoing basis
4. Reduce, Reuse (and Recycle when available)
5. Minimum contribution of $10,000 to conservation NGOs

Marketing

1. Promote Standards in all marketing campaigns
2. Marketing materials: brochure and newsletter use more than 10 percent post-consumer recycled paper

Tour Operation

1. Visit to at least one officially established Protected Area included on every tour
2. Provide employment and/or business opportunities to local people
3. Suppliers encouraged to improve environmental standards of their own: yearly form completed that includes questions on what is currently done and next steps to improve these practices
4. Maximum group size of 12 passengers (except for Galápagos tours)
5. No suppliers that sell endangered species products

Tour Leaders

1. Tour leaders fluent in English and national language of country in which they lead tours
2. Tour leaders receive special training in low environmental and social impact behavior, regional conservation issues and/or projects, G.A.P Adventures interpretation, and safety/emergency/rescue techniques
3. Tour leaders encourage local partners to adopt similar environmental standards; G.A.P Adventures Standards distributed to all local partners

Accommodations

1. All hotels have less than 40 rooms, except joining and departure points, which have less than 100 rooms (Best Feasible Option)
2. Majority of accommodations are locally owned

N.B. Best Feasible Option means that if there is an alternative that can be shown to be a more responsible option in terms of the social and natural environment, then this can be taken.

Future Targets

1. Pre-trip info packages contain water/waste and energy management tips, environmental issues at site, and information on low social and environmental impact activities at destination
2. Information on local conservation issues and projects available for tourists when possible
3. All G.A.P Adventures tour leaders qualified through certification program
4. Encourage the use of responsible waste and rescue management at all accommodations that G.A.P Adventures uses

Acknowledgments

This section has been the most difficult part of this entire process. It's overwhelming to try and thank everyone who has had a hand in shaping my story and helping me become the man I am today, or who have been part of my success.

After spending a long time thinking about whom I should thank, it occurred to me that it wouldn't have to be only people who had a positive effect on my life. So many people have impacted me, be it positively or negatively, but they are all still housed in halls of my mind and memory, and they ultimately have made me who I am today.

I will start by thanking my family, who have allowed me to do what I do every day with the fullest support and unconditional love. They have given me every reason to wake up and to give everything I have every day, and they make me want to continuously strive to be a better person.

My parents gave me the gift of what it means to go all-in when you believe strongly in something. They fought to give their children the not-so-simple gift of opportunity, which I never take for granted, and I pay tribute to their sacrifices by working hard every day.

I had been asked to write a book for more than a decade and never thought I had anything to say, so when the time came, and I had to get this book out of me or I was going to explode, there needed to be a team of people who believed in the project. I'd like to thank HarperCollins and Brad Wilson in Canada, Rick Wolff at Business Plus/Grand Central Publishing in New York, and my agent, Rick Broadhead. It just takes one person to believe in what you're doing before you go from being a lone nut to a movement. I was very lucky to find three people who believed in this book.

I would also thank Dave Morris, who has been a bit of everything for me on this project. Besides being a smart dude who can edit, write, and serve up words with the best of them, he was a great sounding board and a patient listener who waded through my frenetic ideas and tolerated my constant changes.

In many ways my strongest skill has been knowing about people, and there has been a cast of characters at G Adventures who would all have a starring role in the after-school special of my life. So, to everyone who has in past, present, or future been a part of this unstoppable G train, I wholeheartedly thank you for being you-er than you. Individually we are all misfits, rebels, and revolutionaries, but collectively we are capable of changing the world. I get to stand on the shoulders of giants every day and take credit for the hard work of a great group of people who simply believe...and make me look good. Thanks to everyone out there in "G Nation" who help turn my vision and sometimes crazy ideas into the magic we create every day, changing people's lives, and being the greatest adventure company on earth.

The rest will have to fall into the category of "all the rest." A heartfelt thanks to everyone who has been part of my life at any stage because ultimately you had an impact on me. You have made me who I am and given me the tenacity and confidence to do what I do. There are so many people and the list would get ridiculously long if I tried. You all know who you are, and the ones who matter understand how I feel about thank-yous.

Index

Accenture, 138
Achor, Shawn, 260
Adam (camp guide), 259–260
adventure travel. *See* travel/tourism
    industry
advertising. *See* brochures and sales
    materials
Africa
    drinking water projects, 239–241
    G Adventures Leadership Camp, 206
    health and vision programs, 236–237
all-inclusive resorts/travel experiences.
    See travel/tourism industry
altitude sickness, 4, 7
Amanda (HR candidate), 168–170
Amnesty International, 88
Amundsen, Roald, 258, 260
Antarctic Diaries, 258–261
Antarctica, 114–126
Apple Computers, 14, 190, 214, 255–256
Asia trips (1989 & 1990)
    awareness of tourism potential, 39–41
    travels in Thailand, 41–42
    visit and imprisonment in Burma,
    42–45
aspirational culture, 157
Australia, 51, 116, 150, 201

backpacking, as a travel option, 39–40
Belize, 67–68, 75–76, 222
below-the-line values, 175–176. *See also*
    core values and culture
Best Adventure Travel Companies on
    Earth, 178
Bhutan, 176–179

Blue Ocean Strategy (Kim and
    Mauborgne), 145
Bolivia, 80–82
bookmark business, 28–30
brand/brand development
    adventure travel, 64–65
    arriving at higher purpose, 92–93
    changing the company name, 127–129
    creating culture of excellence, 152–153
    culture is the brand, 15, 110, 131, 213,
    256–257
    early efforts at G Adventures, 55
    G Adventures transparency, 79
    G logo, meaning behind, 129–131
    importance of people in representing,
    189–192
    reaching beyond core business, 93–95
    using social media, 137–140
Branson, Richard, 252
brilliant jerks, 171–172
bring-your-kids-to-work (Little G Day),
    185
brochures and sales materials, 52–54,
    77, 88, 153, 202–203. *See also* core
    values and culture; Tour Operator
    Standards
Buffett, Warren, 94–95
Burma, author imprisonment in, 42–45
Burning Building theory, 253
business model
    alignment with company values, 101
    change-or-die mentality, 213–214
    disruptive innovation, 46, 141–142,
    148, 200, 246
    early maverick style, 113, 160

business model (*cont.*)
  G Adventures, 14–18, 46–47
  G Adventures non-profit initiative,
    87–89
  incorporating customer service,
    192–193
  incorporating happiness and freedom,
    94, 107, 180–184
  incorporating social media, 137
  triple bottom line philosophy, 148–149

Cambodia
  health and vision programs, 235–236
  women's employment project, 237–238
Can You Feel It lip-dub video, 211–212
Canada
  adjustment of family to immigration,
    19–23
  author relocation to Toronto, 45–47
  beginning tour operations, 48–51
  Dalai Lama visit to Ottawa (2012),
    264–266, 267–272
  Dalai Lama visit to Vancouver (2004),
    266–267
  G Nation Christmas in the
    Community, 256–257
  National Committee for UN Women,
    209
"Canada's 100 Fastest Growing
  Companies" (*Profit*, 1997), 56–58
celebrations. *See also* motivation
  achieving goals, 213–214
  building winning culture, 174–176,
    185–186
  company growth, 113
  creating an environment for, 155
  of differentiation, 157
  of freedom and happiness, 183
  redefining the company, 145
  of self-awareness, 106–107
  20th Anniversary, 235–237
  of uniqueness, 34
  Zombie Apocalypse, 253–256
Cemex, 192, 225–226
chain-of-command/management
  structure, 160–162
change-or-die mentality, 213–214
changing the world. *See also* core
  values and culture; Looptail; social
  innovation and enterprise
  about vision of this book, 18
  embarking on plan for, 23, 45

engaging the G Adventures
  community, 93
  harnessing social innovation for, 140
  reinventing G Adventures, 150–151,
    183, 246–247
Chief Experience Officer (CEO), 152–153
China, 9, 85–86
Christmas in the Community, 256–257
Churchill, Winston, 104
Cirque du Soleil, 145
"CNN factor," 46–47
"coaching leadership," 112, 137
Cohen, Ben, 252
communications. *See* Culture Club;
  social media
community tourism, 77–78
company culture. *See* brand/brand
  development; changing the world;
  core values and culture; social
  innovation and enterprise
complacency and entitlement, 102–105,
  111, 196
connections. *See* meaningful
  connections
Conservation International (CI), 76–81,
  243
C.O.R.E. (Chief Operating and Reporting
  Executive) group
  creation as leadership body, 161–164
  formulating "Holy Trinity," 197–202
  hiring new employees, 166–169, 173
  learning Disney experience, 193–194
  team visit to Silicon Valley, 190–191
  women's leadership role, 206–209
core values and culture. *See also* brand/
  brand development; brochures and
  sales materials; changing the world;
  Culture Club; social innovation and
  enterprise
  achieving happiness through, 179–183
  bonding activities, 186
  brochures (QR code), 202–203
  creating culture of excellence, 152–153
  customer service as part of, 192–193
  defining G Adventures, 209, 229
  differentiation, 156–157, 163–164, 171,
    174
  driving business with, 175–176
  importance of customer service,
    193–198
  Lead with Service program, 205,
    210–212

Looptail movement and, 267
phase 1, reinventing G Adventures, 135–145
phase 2, reinventing G Adventures, 145–151
Planeterra projects reflecting, 243–247
role of leadership, 99–101
videos (QR code), 147
Costa Rica, 245
courage, secret to freedom, 30, 130, 163, 224. *See also* freedom
create-your-own-adventure program, 185
Crown and Anchor wheel, 172–173
cultural heritage preservation, 85–86
cultural immersion, 80
cultural revolution, 49, 136, 153, 174, 221–222, 253–255. *See also* social innovation and enterprise; social revolution
Culture Club, 215. *See also* core values and culture
about creation and goals, 170–171
company communications and gamification, 184–185
GNN news broadcasts, 186–187
Karma Chameleons and the mayor, 183–184
lip-dub videos, 211–213
sports activities, 185–196
culture killers, 172
Culture Vultures, 155, 157
customer service
about importance of, 192–193
Disney experience as model of, 193–194
empowering employees to deliver, 152–153, 195–197
measuring customer satisfaction, 206–207, 215–216
remaining customer-centered, 197–198
strategy behind "Holy Trinity," 198–202

Dalai Lama XIV (Tenzin Gyatso)
author experiences with, 270
escape into exile, 10–11
Great Ocean (English translation), 129
teachings of, 16, 102, 221
visit to Ottawa (2012), 264–266, 267–272
visit to Vancouver (2004), 266–267
Darwin, Charles, 213

death threats, 13, 60
Delfin and the Pimpilala tribe, 71–75, 82, 85, 222
Delhi Street Kids, 211
Denny's Restaurants, 30–32
Despair (Munch painting), 111
Diego and the Guachala monastery, 69–70, 73, 82
differentiation, value of, 153, 156–157, 163–164, 171, 174
Disney, Walt, 187–188, 202
Disneyland, 193–194, 198
disruptive innovation, 46, 141–142, 148, 200, 246
dot.com boom era, 35, 57
Dove, 138–139

Eco Escuela Spanish School, 80
ecotourism. *See also* sustainable tourism; travel/tourism industry
about beginnings of, 50
beginning of NGO role, 76–78
early G Adventures efforts, 242–243
"greenwashing" with charitable donations, 88–89
Tour Operator Standards, 77–79, 84, 195, 222–223, 273–275
Ecuador. *See also* Galapagos Islands
Amazon River and the Pimpilala tribe, 71–75, 82, 85, 222
early G Adventures planning, 67–69
Guachala monastery, 69–70
Egypt, 237
Elizabeth II (queen of England), 30
Elkington, John, 148
England. *See* United Kingdom
Enron Corporation, 146
entitlement. *See* complacency and entitlement
entrepreneurial motivation, 8
entrepreneurship
alleviation of world poverty, 242
company-building process of, 99–101
importance of storytelling, 27, 29–30, 91
leadership models, 112–113
passion and desire to succeed, 65
"paying it forward" is crucial to, 223
recruiting employees, 165
tolerance for risk, 144, 223–224
environmental pollution/threats
Amazon River and the Pimpilala tribe, 71–75

environmental pollution (*cont.*)
 "greenwashing," 88–89
 sustainability in the face of, 225–226
 wildlife habitat destruction, 82–83
Environmental Program, United Nations
  (UNEP), 241
ESPN Turning, pinpointing the, 108
eye and vision programs, 235–237

Facebook. *See also* social media
 author profile, 27–28
 G Adventures employee policy,
  154–155
 G Adventures presence, 130–131, 193,
  214
Fair Trade designation/prices, 77, 225
Falling Stars, 173–174
fear
 change-or-die mentality, 213–214
 decision-making from point of, 122
 is not an option, 52
 as obstacle to peace and
  understanding, 242
firing people
 author's early experience with, 24
 experiences at G Adventures, 13–14
 getting fired from Denny's, 30–32
 getting fired from McDonald's, 32–33
 not always a negative thing, 105–107
 offering an option to leave, 142–143,
  150–151
 Star Mapping System, 173–174
 20/70/10 rule, 155–159
 $5000 challenge, 105–106, 204
Forbes (magazine), 102
Ford, Henry, 141
Ford Foundation, 87
"The Founder's Dilemma" (*Forbes*,
  2009), 102
Franz (Mr. and Mrs.), 53–55
Fraser, Margo, 252
"Free Tibet" movement, 57, 58, 263
freedom. *See also* courage; happiness
 appreciating meaning of, 44–45
 basing business model on, 94,
  106–107, 140
 as company goal, 131
 creating an environment of, 66, 82,
  87–88, 154–155, 160–163, 216, 228
 decision-making, 195–197
 expression of ideas and feedback,
  205, 209

Looptail and achieving, 211–213,
  271–272
 placing limits on, 166–167, 170
 as secret to happiness, 182–183,
  220–224
 social media and creation of, 181
Freedom to Watch lip-dub video, 212
Future of Tourism (2011), 128, 131, 202
Future of Tourism (2012), 209, 213, 246

G Bean, 228
G Factor Interview, 171–173, 183
G Force, 161
G logo. *See also* Looptail
 about meaning behind, 129–131
 creation of, 264
 understanding meaning of, 145
G Nation, 209, 256–257
G Stock, 149–151, 185, 203–204,
  207–208, 213
G Voice, 208
G.A.P. Adventures (Great Adventure
  People), 45–47, 126–129
Galapagos Islands, 68, 130, 205, 274.
  See also Ecuador
gamification, 184–185
The Gap Inc., trademark infringement
  lawsuit, 126–128, 264–265
G Adventures (annual revenues)
 $6 million (1997), 57, 111
 $7 million (1998), 59
 $16 million (2000), 65
 $50 million (2005), 100
 $80 million (2007), 108
 $100 million (2008), 135–136
 $150 million (2010), 193
 $200 million (2013), 251
G Adventures (business operations and
  principles). *See also* core values and
  culture; firing people
 adapting to traveler types and styles,
  85
 brand development, 55, 79
 buyout offers, 14, 63–65, 108–111, 125,
  136, 149, 251
 changing company name, 127–131
 the culture is the brand, 15, 110, 131,
  213, 256–257
 dollar-per-day program, 95
 $5000 challenge, 105–106, 204
 human resources and, 102–103,
  154–155, 164–169

impact of September 11 attacks on,
83–85
launch of Planeterra, 87–89
managing to lowest common
denominator, 154–155
pinpointing ESPN Turning point, 108
recognizing creativity and flexibility,
81–82
trademark infringement lawsuit,
126–128, 264–265
transparency, 79, 115, 122, 124, 181
G Adventures (early years)
about start-up and growth, 13–14
business model, 14–18, 46–47
dealing with debt crisis, 59–63
financing start up, 47–49, 58
first tour offerings, 49–50
international marketing, 51–53
learning lesson of "paying it forward,"
53–55
nomination as "100 Fastest Growing
Companies," 56–58
G Adventures (transformation process)
phase 1, reinventing the company,
135–145
phase 2, reinventing the company,
145–148
phase 3, reinventing the company,
154–155
creating an environment for
happiness, 180–184
creating management structure,
160–162
hiring new Human Resources VP,
165–170
hiring process for new employees,
162–165, 172–173
implementing 20/70/10 rule, 155–159,
173–174
rebuilding brand and winning culture,
160, 174–176
redefining human resources, 170–172
women and gender diversity, 206–209
Zombie Apocalypse, 253–256
G Adventures (travel and tours). See
also brand/brand development;
brochures and sales materials
Antarctica, 114–126, 258–261
Australia, 51, 116, 150, 201
Belize, 67–68, 75–76, 222
Bhutan, 176–178
Bolivia, 80–82

cooperation with NGOs, 76–82
Costa Rica, 245
Ecuador, 67–75, 222
Egypt, 237
Galapagos Islands, 68, 130, 205, 274
Guatemala, 80, 244
Guyana, 82–83
India, 210–212
Kenya, 239–241
Nepal, 252
Nicaragua, 244
Peru, 89–95, 245
Tanzania, 235, 237
Venezuela, 67, 75
Vietnam, 197
G Adventures 20/20 Eye Center, 236
General Electric, 101, 155–156
generic tours/travel experiences. See
travel/tourism industry
Gere, Richard, 268, 269, 272
G-lympics, 185–186
GNN news broadcasts, 186–187
GO Adventures, 129–130
Goodall, Jane, 83
Google, 14, 190, 214, 215, 255
Great Ocean (Dali Lama), 7–10,
129–130, 264–265, 269–271
Great Ocean of Wisdom, 129, 264
Great Place to Work Institute, 214–215
Great Recession of 2008, 14, 135–136
Greece Leadership Camp, 205
Greenfield, Jerry, 252
"greenwashing," charitable donations,
88–89
Gretzky, Wayne, 142
Gross National Happiness, 176–179
group travel, limitations of. See travel/
tourism industry
Guac-off Golden Avacado
Championship, 185
"Guaranteed Departures," 200–202
Guatemala, 80, 244
Guyana, 82–83
Gyatso, Tenzin. See Dalai Lama XIV

Haircuts and Hot Dogs, 175–176, 185
Haiti, earthquake of 2010, 228
Hanks, Tom, 71
happiness. See also freedom; motivation
about secret of finding, 93
achieving life-long goal, 260–261
Bhutan as role model, 176–179

happiness (*cont.*)
  creating an environment for, 180–184,
    220–222
  Dalai Lama teachings, 16, 102
  freedom as secret to, v
  incorporation into business model, 94
  incorporation into core values, 146–147
  leadership role in creating, 112–113
  Looptail movement and, 16–18
  overcoming an office environment,
    219–220
  using social media to find, 181–182
  Walt Disney as visionary for, 187–188
The Happiness Advantage (Achor),
    260–261
health and vision programs, 235–237
Heller, Rich, 114
"HIRE PEOPLE YOU HATE" (magazine
    story), 164–168
"Holy Trinity of Customer Service,"
    199–202
Hong Kong, 252
Hurricane Sandy relief, 228–229

Ignite the Night (fundraiser), 236–237
ignorance. *See* fear
Inca Trail adventures in Peru, 229–231
India, 210–212
indigenous tourism, 86
innovation. *See* disruptive innovation;
    social innovation and enterprise;
    value innovation
"inspire leadership," 112–113, 137, 196,
    242–243
Inter-American Development Bank
    (IDB), 243–247
International Ecotourism Society,
    178–179
intolerance. *See* racism and prejudice

Jack: Straight from the Gut (Welch), 156
Jackson, Phil, 62
Jackson Five (singing group), 211
Jamaica, Poon Tip family origins, 9, 19,
    21, 23, 34
Jiwani, Almas, 209
Jordan, Michael, 62
Junior Achievement Companies
    Program, 28–30

karma. *See also* "paying it forward"
  author meeting Dalai Lama, 264–265

as business matter, 235
  if you give, you get, 224
  Walt Disney beliefs and, 187–188
Karma (Bhutan guide), 177, 178–179
Karma (Tibetan monk), 12
Karma Chameleons (Culture Club),
    183–184, 185
Kenya, 239–241
Kim, W. Chan, 145
"Know your audience," 65

Las Vegas conference (2008), 141–144
Lead with Service program, 193, 205,
    210–212
"lead-by-example" leadership, 112
leadership
  characteristics to look for, 162–163
  creating change vs. popularity,
    103–105
  implementing 20/70/10 rule, 155–159
  "Michael Jordan effect," 62–63
  redefining company values, 99–101
  self-evaluation, 113–114
  there's no crying in business, 71
  in times of crisis, 121–122
  types of roles, 112–113
  value of differentiation, 153, 156–157,
    163–164, 171, 174
  women's role at G Adventures,
    206–209
Leadership Camps
  about need/creation of, 204
  Africa (2012), 205–206
  Greece (2011), 204–205
  Women's, 206–209
A League of Their Own (movie), 71
learning from mistakes, 66–67, 112,
    196–197
learning from the wisdom of others
  Charles Darwin, 213
  Dalai Lama, 16, 102, 221
  Henry Ford, 141
  Jack Welch, 101, 155–156, 166
  Walt Disney, 188, 202
  Warren Buffett, 94–95
  Wayne Gretzky, 142
Lesenfants, Yves, 243–247
"Lifetime Deposits," 147–148, 199–200
Lin, Jeremy, 262
lip-dub videos, 211–213
Little G Day (bring-your-kids-to-work),
    185

London School of Economics, 102
Looptail. *See also* changing the world;
   G logo; meaningful connections;
   social innovation and enterprise
   about origins, 66–67
   applying theories, 113
   arriving at an understanding of, 269,
      271–272
   bringing happiness and freedom to
      workplace, 188–189
   bringing together ideas of, 92–93
   defined/described, 16–18
   defining company purpose, 192–193
   demanding excellence and celebrating
      achievement, 155
   meaning behind company logo,
      129–131, 145
   "paying it forward" is crucial to, 223
   redefining G Adventures into, 140
   requires risk-taking, 224
   Starbucks as model of, 224–225
Looptail.com (website). *See* QR codes
"Lord of the Flies law of nature," 156
Luis Maria, 90–91

Madonna (performer), 103
management structure/chain-of-
   command, 160–162
Mandel, Saul, 114
"Mary Kay style of management," 157
Mason, Mr. (teacher), 21, 23, 272
Massachusetts Institute of Technology
   (MIT), 102
Mauborgne, Renée, 145
*Maverick!: The Success Story Behind the
   World's Most Unusual Workplace*
   (Semler), 160
McDonald's Corporation, 32–33
McTurk, Diane, 82–83
Me, We, and G days, 181
meaningful connections
   achieving happiness through, 180–184
   casual contact vs., 112
   Delfin and the Pimpilala tribe, 72–75
   keeping life on course with, 255
   life as string of, 189
   street children of Cuzco, 90
mediocrity. *See* complacency and
   entitlement
"Michael Jordan effect," 62–63
microfinancing programs, 76, 229
Microsoft, 214

motivation. *See also* celebrations;
   happiness
   commitment to excellence, 188–189,
      253–255
   creating positive impact in the world,
      192–193, 221–222
   entrepreneurial, 8
   G Adventures core values, 150–151
   happiness as, 176, 182
   "inspire leadership" inspires, 18, 63
   money as, 156–159
   work detail and accuracy, 165
M/S *Expedition*, 125–126
M/S *Explorer*, sinking of, 114–126
M/S *Nordnorge*, 118
Multilateral Investment Fund (MIF),
   244–247
Munch, Edvard, 111
M/V Freedom, 228

National Committee for UN Women-
   Canada, 209
National Geographic Adventure, 178
Nepal, 3–8, 129, 252, 271
New Hope project (Cambodia), 237–238
New York Times, 151–152
NGOs (non-governmental organizations)
   beginning role in ecotourism, 76–77
   endorsement of Tour Operator
      Standards, 77–78
   G Adventures cooperation with, 78–82
   "greenwashing," charitable donations,
      88–89
Nicaragua, 244
9/11 terrorist attacks, 83–85, 227

Olympic Games of 2012, 185
"Open 24/7," 199
"open innovation" concept, business
   model, 113
organizational chart, 160–162

paper route, 23–25
"paying it forward." *See also* karma
   about first lesson of, 53–55
   creating an environment for, 155, 227
   evidence that it works, 84
   finding happiness in act of, 17–18
   G Adventures examples, 228–238
   Looptail movement and, 183, 195,
      223–224
   origins of Looptail, 66–67

"Pennies for Peru," 91
People of the Sun project, 92
Peru
   earthquake of 2007, 93–95, 240
   Inca Trail adventures, 229–231
   Lares Trek (tour), 245
   People of the Sun, 89–92
   Sacred Valley (tour), 245
   Women's Weaving Co-Op, 232–234
The Peter Principle (Peter), 159
Pimpilala tribe of Ecuador, 71–75
Planeterra Foundation. See also
      social innovation and enterprise;
      sustainable tourism
   creation of non-profit initiative, 87–89
   donations from customers, 95
   drinking water projects, 239–241
   health and vision programs, 234–237
   MIF/IDB partnership, 243–247
   non-profit/for-profit cooperation,
      79–82
   People of the Sun project, 90–91
   Peru earthquake of 2007, 93–95, 240
   relief efforts, 228–229
Planet-hair-a, 228
pollution. See environmental pollution/
      threats
Poon Tip, Bruce (education and
      entrepreneurial beginnings)
   awareness of tourism potential, 39–41
   beginning paper route, 23–25
   being fired from Denny's, 30–32
   being fired from McDonald's, 32–33
   bookmark business, 28–30
   breeding dwarf rabbits, 25–28
   college and tourism education, 34–35,
      39
   origins of G.A.P. Adventures, 47–55
   racism in Canadian society, 19–23,
      31, 33
   relocation to Toronto, 45–47
   travel to Jamaica, 34
   travel to Thailand and Burma, 41–45
poverty
   author's beginning awareness of, 41
   breaking cycle, 210–211, 234–235
   distribution of wealth, 241–242
   G Adventures and alleviation of, 102,
      140, 153, 256
   tourism and sustainable solutions,
      245–246
Product Weekend, 149

Profit (magazine), 56–58, 263
Profit, People and Planet, 148–149
prostitution, 41

QR codes (Looptail.com)
   African Water Tanks appeal, 241
   celebrating winning, 176
   Christmas in the Community, 257
   core values and culture brochures,
      202–203
   core values videos, 147
   C.O.R.E. visit to Silicon Valley, 191
   culinary competition, 185
   death of traditional HR, 171
   dedication to late M/S Explorer, 126
   Delhi Street Kids, 211
   dodgeball tournament, 186
   election of Culture Club mayor, 184
   experiences with Dalai Lama, 270
   G-lympic celebration, 186
   GNN newscast, 187
   Haircuts and Hot Dogs celebration,
      175
   House of the People of the Sun, 92
   Hurricane Sandy relief, 229
   Ignite the Night, 237
   Inca Trail adventures in Peru, 231
   Leadership Camps, 205, 206
   lip-dub video Can You Feel It, 212
   lip-dub video Freedom to Watch, 212
   lip-dub video Somebody to Love, 213
   meeting in Las Vegas, 144
   partnership with MIF/IDB, 247
   power of meaningful connections, 75
   use of technology in business, 256
   women's employment in Cambodia,
      238
   Women's Leadership Camp, 209
   Women's Weaving Co-Op in Peru, 234
quintuple bottom line, 148–149

rabbit breeding business, 25–28
racism and prejudice, 19–23, 31–34
Ravers, 140, 215–216
Reiss, Dani, 260
return on investment, 223
revolution. See cultural revolution; social
      revolution
risk-taking, 7, 76, 143–144, 223–224
Roddick, Anita, 252
Royal Geographic Society, 252
Russell, Jeff, 114

Schuran, Frank, 114
Scott, Robert F., 258
The Scream (Munch painting), 111
Semco SA, 160
Semler, Ricardo, 160
September 11 terrorist attacks, 83–85, 227
Seven C's (leadership traits), 162–163
Shooting Stars, 173–174
Sloan School of Business, 102
social innovation and enterprise.
    See also changing the world;
    core values and culture; cultural
    revolution; Looptail; Planeterra
    Foundation
  addressing gender diversity, 206–209
  creating an environment for, 188–191
  defining issues, 226–227, 230
  enveloping core values around, 245
  harnessing energy of, 204, 209–212
  Looptail movement and, 187, 192–193
  redefining G Adventures for, 73–74, 139–141
social media. *See also* Facebook; Twitter
  applying Looptail ideas through, 187
  brand development, 137–139
  creating connectedness, 181
  creating social innovation through, 139–140
  creating transparency and accountability, 226–227
  dealing with Facebook factor, 123
  searching for happiness through, 181–182
social revolution, 15, 18, 191. *See also* cultural revolution
Social Venture Network, 252
solution-based thinking, overcoming obstacles, 52
Somebody to Love lip-dub video, 213
Spence, Rick, 58
Star Mapping System (SMS), 163, 173–174
Starbucks Coffee Company, 224–225
storytelling
  connection to higher purpose, 91
  creating marketing pitch, 29–30
  role in entrepreneurship, 27
  role in history and traditions, 232
Summer Olympic Games of 2012, 185
sustainable companies, 148–149, 225–226

sustainable tourism. *See also*
    ecotourism; Planeterra Foundation
  about beginnings of, 50
  creating business solutions, 237–238
  Ecuador example of, 71–75
  employment opportunities for women, 231–234
  G Adventures operations as, 66–67
  health and vision programs, 234–237
  Looptail movement and, 14–18
  Peru Inca Trail adventures, 229–231
  United Nations conferences, 85–86
Sweeting, Jamie, 76–77

Talent Agency, 170–171, 173–174, 215, 255
Tanzania, 235, 237
Tatopani, Nepal (1997 trip), 3–8, 129, 271
Tenzin (Canadian government official), 263–266
Thailand, 41–42
"Think Tank Pizza Parties" (TTPPs), 102–103
Tibet
  Dalai Lama escape into exile, 10–11
  "Free Tibet" movement, 57, 58, 263
  health and vision program, 235
Tibet trip (1997)
  a soul-searching journey, 56, 263
  arrival at Tatopani, 3–8
  Chinese border crossing, 8–9
  travels across Tibetan plateau, 10–11
  "Welcome back" by Tibetan monk, 9–10
Tibetan Film Festival, 262–264
Tour Operator Standards. *See also*
    brochures and sales materials
  development by G Adventures, 77–79
  G Adventures goals for, 222–223
  "paying it forward" with, 84, 195
  statement and principles, 273–275
trademark
  The Gap Inc. infringement lawsuit, 126–128, 264–265
  lifetime customer deposits, 147–148, 199–200
transcendent leadership, 162–163
transparency
  about importance of, 115
  G Adventures model of, 122, 124, 181
  social media and, 137, 139, 226

travel brochures. *See* brochures and
    sales materials
travel/tourism industry. *See also*
    adventure travel; ecotourism
    about early travel options, 39–41
    all-inclusive resorts/travel experiences,
        15, 40, 85, 222
    backpacking and group travel, 45–47
    Best Adventure Travel Companies on
        Earth, 178
    community tourism, 77–78
    consolidation and buyout offers,
        108–111, 142, 153, 193
    cultural heritage preservation and,
        85–86
    customer deposits on trips, 147–148
    G Adventures as employer of choice,
        152–153
    G Adventures impact on, 59
    generic tours/travel experiences, 40,
        78, 202
    "greenwashing" with charitable
        donations, 88–89
    indigenous tourism, 86
    September 11 terrorist attacks impact
        on, 83–85
    traveler types and styles, 85
    World Travel Market, 51–52, 202–203
    worldwide growth and economic
        impact, 241–243
Trinidad. *See* Jamaica, Poon Tip family
    origins
triple bottom line philosophy, 148–149
20/70/10 rule, 155–159
Twitter, 131, 185, 215, 240. *See also*
    social media

United Kingdom
    Elizabeth II's Diamond Jubilee, 30
    World Travel Market, 51–52, 202–203
United Nations
    China conference on cultural heritage
        preservation (2000), 85–86

Environmental Program (UNEP), 241
    New York conference on sustainable
        tourism (2002), 85–86
    Quebec conference on sustainable
        tourism (2003), 86
    World Tourism Day (2011), 128
    World Tourism Organization
        (UNWTO), 241

value innovation, 145
Venezuela, 67, 75
Vietnam, 197
"Voice of the Poor" (World Bank report),
    242

weather worms, 28–30
Welch, Jack, 101, 155–156, 166
Westby, Jimmy, 76, 82, 222
wisdom. *See* learning from the wisdom
    of others
women
    achieving gender diversity at G
        Adventures, 206–209
    employment in Cambodia, 237–238
    health and vision program, 234–235
    marriage in Bhutan, 177
    United Nations efforts, 209
    Weaving Co-Op in Peru, 232–234
Women's Leadership Camp, 207–209
work-exchange program, 185
World Bank, 76, 80, 82, 242
World Tourism Day (2011), 128
World Tourism Organization, United
    Nations (UNWTO), 241
World Travel Market, 51–52, 202–203
World Wildlife Fund, 88

Year of Sustainable Tourism (UN, 2002),
    85–86

Zombie Apocalypse, 253–256

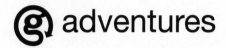 adventures

Almost **2,000** employees
in more than **100** countries
and **30** offices around the world.

In the last year, travelers from **160** different
countries booked trips with us.

We service more than **30,000** travel
agencies globally.

We've run more than **100,000** tours,
hosted more than **1,000,000** passengers,
and brought in more than **$1,000,000,000**
in revenue.

For more information, please visit
www.looptail.com.